SPIRITUAL
AUDACITY

Six Disciplines of
Human Flourishing

A MEMOIR

REV. DR. JIM SHERBLOM

WISE Ink
CREATIVE ★ PUBLISHING

TESTIMONIALS FOR SPIRITUAL AUDACITY

"This is a rags-to-riches Horatio Alger story, first of finding the streets of the American Dream paved with gold, and then of finding the spiritual path paved with extinction of ego."

—**Rev. Scotty McLennan,** ethics educator and author of
Christ for Unitarian Universalists

"This book is both a fascinating memoir and a guidebook for discovering your own spiritual path. Jim Sherblom offers inspiration and wisdom for the journey."

—**Rev. Amy Freedman,**
Unitarian Universalist Minister of Religious Education

"Jim Sherblom's spiritual journey takes him to the farthest reaches of the earth—and to the inner sanctum of his heart. In this compelling memoir, Jim shares his victories and wounds with generosity and insight."

—**Sheila Heen and Douglas Stone,** coauthors of *Difficult Conversations*

"Jim manages something quite remarkable with this book: he throws himself headlong into life's complexities and navigates his way through with grace, integrity, and compelling good humor."

—**Sandro Galea, MD, DrPH, dean,**
Boston University School of Public Health

ISBN 13: 978-1-63489-076-2

Library of Congress Catalog Number: 2017942855
Printed in the United States of America
First Printing: 2018
22   21   20   19   18   5   4   3   2   1

Cover design by Nupoor Gordon
Interior design by Dan Pitts

Wise Ink Creative Publishing
837 Glenwood Avenue
Minneapolis, MN 55405
wiseinkpub.com

To order, visit ItascaBooks.com. Reseller discounts available.

With deep unconditional love for my wife, Loretta, who saved me, and for our audacious children.

CONTENTS

INTRODUCTION

I am fascinated by human flourishing. Why does one human being, reacting to life's trials and tribulations, emerge stronger with greater health and well-being, while another human being facing very similar trials and tribulations gets crushed with a broken spirit? What is the ultimate source of human flourishing? This goes beyond nature or nurture, though genetics and environment do seem to play an important role.

A key difference appears to lie in the practice of six spiritual disciplines that greatly enhance human flourishing: resilience, surrender, gratitude, generosity, mystery, and spiritual awakening. They are called disciplines because they require sustained effort, though every person can learn and practice them. And they greatly enhance human flourishing.

My life story has included an active pursuit of these six disciplines that lead to joy, accomplishment, and a sense of well-being. Different religious traditions have called the resulting states of bliss by such names as awakening, enlightenment, nirvana, heaven, or paradise. I will sometimes call this state of being by all these names and others.

This is my story—a spiritual memoir—of practicing these six spiritual disciplines to achieve human flourishing. Along with these disciplines, my sense of spiritual audacity helped guide me on my path. Spiritual audacity assumes we were born into this life with a purpose and seeks human flourishing through the practice of spiritual disciplines for spiritual well-being.

Let me begin by acknowledging the extraordinary amount of privilege inherent in my story. I grew up white, male, heterosexual, baby boomer, and Christian. I have been fortunate and blessed. That said, I also grew up in a large family in the impoverished seaside town of Tiverton, Rhode Island. My life's journey took me to Yale and Harvard, and as such, I had incredible access to wealth and power. I have been an international strategy consultant, biotechnology executive, venture capitalist, ordained clergy, and finally, creative nonfiction writer. I think I did well given my situation.

True, I worked extraordinarily hard for my success. But I was very lucky at key moments, and I took advantage of opportunities most people could only dream about. I now live as a nature mystic—an intuitive—in transcendentalist Concord, Massachusetts. It's a far cry from the Tiverton, Rhode Island of my youth and childhood.

Spiritually, we each live out of a different reality given our social locations. My lived reality is unique, as is yours. Yet there is also something universal about my story of being and becoming. Picture life as a crowded tour bus driving through Concord. An elderly man and woman who grew up during the Great Depression marvel at the rich houses and fancy stores. An aging white man wonders whether the people who live in these houses have greater meaning in their lives than he has found. A middle-aged black woman is frustrated at the signs of racism still apparent here. A young professional couple looks with hope and aspiration to one day live in a place such as this. A young mother scouts for activities to keep her two children interested and occupied while the two children play a game of their own making.

We are all riders on the bus. Our lived realities are as different as spring, summer, fall, and winter in New England. Yet we experience the same tour, with each rider looking for human flourishing, happiness, and well-being—both spiritual and material. I regard spiritual well-being and material well-being as the yin and yang of a balanced life. Yin and yang are two sides of a circle to be kept in balance, or even more accurately, a Möbius strip, constantly folding back upon itself. They're ultimately not in conflict with each other. Rather, each contains the seed of the other. They dynamically flow into each other, with each appropriately dominant at different spheres and stages of a lifetime.

All human beings have a capacity for joy in the midst of suffering, resilience in the face of despair, love in the midst of strife, and peace in a time of turbulence. This is the peace beyond understanding. This is the well-being that can be achieved through the six disciplines. Yet developing these human disciplines is the story of a lifetime.

Humanity Awakening

Through the story of my own life, this book describes six ancient mystic wisdom disciplines drawn from many religious traditions. Roughly 2,600 years ago, religious philosophers in different parts of the world simultaneously began to organize systematic descriptions of how to achieve human enlightenment.

We know little about Zarathustra, Pythagoras, Gautama, Confucius, or any of those from this first wave of systematic philosophers. All we know is what their subsequent followers taught or wrote about them. They appear to have lived within nearly one human lifespan of one another. They may have been influenced by one another or even other earlier traditions.

Whatever happened during this one ancient century forever changed the human spiritual journey. What had always been a solitary pursuit, with each student receiving oral teachings from a living master, now became religious tradition. Unfortunately, the earliest records of their teachings were compiled many years later and filtered through their students' understandings and emerging religious traditions. But ever since, spiritual teachers have been divisible into mystics, who interpret through their own experiences, and traditionalists, who rely upon the orthodox teachings of ancient traditions. I am an intuitive mystic.

Growing up in 1950s Tiverton, none of this was even imaginable. There were a few Jews and a few atheists, but otherwise we were all

Christians. We were mostly divided between Roman Catholics, with various ethnic divisions, and Reformed Protestants of various denominational flavors. I was the fifth of ten children born to a poor American Baptist minister. But my spiritual audacity emerged in my later years as I engaged with mystics who were Jewish, Christian, Sufi, Hindu, Buddhist, Taoist, Confucian, and indigenous shaman. Along the way, I learned these six spiritual disciplines, which helped accelerate and magnify my spiritual journey to enlightenment.

In my sixtieth year, I became a mature spiritual being. Not a master, a guru, or a spiritual teacher in any orthodox tradition. Nor a buddha, prophet, or shaman. But simply a spiritually mature human being. Mystics have many names for aspects of this indescribable experience of awakening, including wisdom, gnosis, oneness, enlightenment, ecstasy, bliss, liberation, dancing with the divine, insight, truth, transcendence, divine mystery, heaven, self-realization, illumination, inner clarity, transformation, emptying, selflessness, and pure consciousness. With deep humility, I offer these stories of my awakening with the hope that they may assist you in becoming what you were born to be.

Some orthodox religious traditions describe the spiritual journey as a straight path to heaven. Perhaps for some people it is. But I found the journey to spiritual maturity reflected in the elliptical path of a seven-story labyrinth. In a classically designed labyrinth, commonly called a meander labyrinth, you begin by walking directly inward on the path, only to discover the path twists and curves, making it impossible to see beyond the next turn in the journey. You do not head inward any longer but rather explore the outer reaches. You gradually return toward the center, until centered in divine mystery you awaken, only to discover the way leads on.

For mystics, the spiritual journey is ever thus. The mystic walks a meandering labyrinth, seldom heading directly toward a clear destination, but instead, spiraling away into outer regions, then returning elliptically at a higher level, closer to the goal. Mystics accept that the path is nonlinear and unpredictable, yet requires spiritual discipline.

Human life is unpredictable. Growing up in the 1960s, we thought the world would end in nuclear holocaust. Or a meteor would strike the earth and wipe out humanity, as it did the dinosaurs. Or a dramatically expanding human population would lead to mass starvation. Or we'd run out of fossil fuels and hurtle humanity back to a much smaller Stone Age population.

We were an apocalyptic generation. In elementary school, we practiced Duck and Cover, going under our desks in case of nuclear missile attack. Even to a six-year-old, it was clear grown-ups were paranoid warmongers. I never expected to live into my thirties and certainly knew better than to trust anyone over thirty. I journeyed outward to career success and inward to spirituality.

Growing old was not on my agenda. I never imagined living to be sixty. I didn't expect to attain wisdom either. Life has been infinitely surprising!

Six Spiritual Disciplines

I have structured this book around the six spiritual disciplines. The first spiritual discipline is resiliency. I have been extraordinarily fortunate in my life. Attending Yale and Harvard enabled me to rise above the economic circumstances of my birth. I became a founder of the Massachusetts biotechnology industry and a wealthy investor, helping create new biopharmaceuticals to improve human welfare. At the same time, I built my spiritual life and a family of my own.

I had my share of misfortunes as well. I was overwhelmed and nearly defeated, competing with kids so much better prepared than I was at Yale. I faced challenges living among the urban poor. I experienced the life-changing impact of tearing my writing hand open on a riot gate and the soul-crushing devastation of being betrayed by the first woman I ever loved.

With many successes and failures to recount, my story could be compared to a Horatio Alger type of story. But it's more than that.

Through the ups and downs, I learned the spiritual discipline of resilience, which is foundational to my sense of being.

The spiritual lesson of ego surrender saved my life but was perhaps the hardest lesson of all. Surrender provided me with the courage to live my life boldly, to take audacious risks, and to live to see another day. The redemptive power of winning the love of my wife, Loretta, transformed my life.

We met in college during the darkest period of my life. She is two years younger and the third of four sisters born to Chinese parents. Loretta saved my life and set us on a path to a wonderful and audacious life. She emboldens me in times of joy and comforts me during my darkest hours. Loretta created the circumstances for us to become our best selves as we built our family and communities and intertwined our lives like flowering vines on a trellis. All that I am and all that I do, I owe to Loretta's love. Surrender means decentering your ego-self.

Spiritual gratitude is a powerful practice. I am grateful for my life with Loretta, our children, our travels, our incredible business successes—even our hobbies, such as volleyball. I am also grateful for my dad's remission from lymphoma, for how he healed the breach with his many children on his deathbed, and for how my gay brother David's long, losing battle with AIDS transformed my father's Baptist congregation. There's also gratitude for Loretta's benign ovarian cyst, which we survived when our kids were so little.

These challenges transformed the nature of our family and our lives together. Our joys and sorrows are woven finely together in our lives, for which we are grateful. Life is a blessing, even when it hurts, and we are better for engaging life in all its joys and pain.

Generosity of spirit gives life vibrancy. Generosity shapes the material dimensions of our lives and thereby liberates us. Loretta and I built, then nearly lost, our financial security on more than one occasion. Our generosity helped us maintain an even keel through those tumultuous seas. My success as an entrepreneur and venture capitalist helped make possible my deepening understanding of the spiritual lessons discerned through retreats, vision quests, and journeys with mystics. Generosity of spirit is the fuel that powers our awakening.

I learned a deeper mystery—what it is to live in divine mystery—when I became ordained as a Unitarian Universalist minister and was called to serve a congregation. Increasingly, I spent my sabbaticals and study leaves with spiritual mystics. I have whirled with Sufis in the rural mountains of Turkey, practiced Taoist meditation techniques for shifting perceived reality in China, and visited ancient tribes in the foothills of the Himalayas—all were pilgrimages of the spirit. I have experienced ayahuasca visions with indigenous people in the rainforest, sat in sweat lodges and completed vision quests in an Ecuadorian mountainous desert, and sought visions and transformation along tributaries of the Amazon River in southeastern Peru—all led to spiritual deepening. These spiritual journeys wove together experiences of family, of living and dying, and of successes and failures to contribute to a deepening spiritual life.

Finally, my call to awakening as a more fully realized human being would culminate in the pilgrimage of a lifetime. With a prominent Harvard Divinity School comparative religion scholar, I traveled by boat up the Ganges River and passed through some of the most desperately poor parts of India, following in the footsteps of the Buddha. I walked in areas where the Buddha taught most of his life. The Hindu concept of the stages of a mystic's life—from student and scholar, to married and employed householder with children, to spiritual seeker and searcher, and finally to awakening to reality—deeply influenced my spiritual journey. This pilgrimage ultimately led to this book.

Mastering the spiritual disciplines of resilience, surrender, gratitude, generosity, mystery, and spiritual awakening helped me make sense of the arc of my life and my enormous joy in living. Now I encounter the world with amazement and awe. I am living the life that I was born to live.

Emergent Reality

I acknowledge that many people have intimately shared parts of this life journey with me, including my parents, my nine brothers and sisters, my childhood friends, and my fellow travelers along the way. I love these people and owe much to their love of me—especially Loretta and our two now-grown children. I cannot tell their stories but can tell only my own.

And I can tell my stories only from my own perspective while recognizing that others might very well have different memories of the same occurrences. Again, we are all riders on the same bus, experiencing different realities. I have sometimes changed the names of fellow travelers to protect their privacy, but each is a real person I have described from my perspective. I have not used any composites or narrative shortcuts. These are my recollections. For anyone who experienced these events differently than portrayed, my apologies in advance—your reality is as real as mine. This book represents my lived reality as I recall it.

It's the kind of book I wish someone had handed me in high school or college to help guide me on my journey. It is the spiritual memoir of one soul's thoroughly improbable and audacious journey to awakening. Awakening is as life giving as water, as purifying as fire, as transitory as the wind, and grounded in heaven and earth; so we rise with the rays of the sun and wonder as we descend upon moonbeams. This is its source of joy! I hope you enjoy it!

DISCIPLINE ONE:

RESILIENCE

Resilient people use a well-developed set of skills that help them to control their emotions, attention, and behavior. Self-regulation is important for forming intimate relationships, succeeding at work, and maintaining physical health.

—The Resilience Factor
by Karen Reivich and Andrew Shatté

Small-Town Boy

I was a skinny, boisterous, energetic boy with a buzz cut and a pronounced Rhode Island accent, struggling to make my way in a turbulent world. In order to survive and thrive, I became a storyteller.

My story begins in Newport, Rhode Island, on a sunny Saturday in 1961. I was five years old. Nature was green and alive. The sea breeze gave a certain wistfulness to the day. My heart pounded as I raced six of my eight siblings, mostly older, across the lawn of the Baptist minister's retirement home. I was intent on beating them to the used-book tables at the home's annual bazaar. I loved books. Every June, my family would go to this giant yard sale to help support the retired ministers.

In my small fist, I clutched a single quarter, the spending money my mother had given me for the day. I wanted to spend it all on books.

Adult books were a quarter, children's hardcover books a dime, and children's paperbacks a nickel each. I was goal oriented and very focused. I carefully picked up and perused each book, wondering how to maximize my money's worth, until I caught the sales lady's attention.

> Sales Lady: Little boy, how old are you, and how much do you have to spend?
> Me: I'm five, and I only have a quarter, but I need to buy some books to read.
> Sales Lady: We have a new rule, not posted yet, that any five-year-old can fill a brown grocery bag with as many books as he can read for only twenty-five cents.

I was in heaven! In those days, kids learned to read in first grade, which I wouldn't begin for another few months. However, I had listened to and carefully copied my brother David who had just finished second grade, as he had learned to read. I already read at a first-grade level. I proudly demonstrated my prowess at reading. I went home that afternoon with two dozen books stuffed into a shopping bag and the biggest grin on my face. Heaven is when the world conspires for your happiness and well-being. I would engage in a lifelong endeavor to spend as much of my life as possible in such a heaven—and usually with plenty of books.

My life was bound and buffered by my siblings. At my birth, my mother already had four children under the age of eight. She became pregnant again two months after my birth with my sister Pat. She was pregnant again four months after Pat's birth with my brother Steve. The three of us were born within twenty-four months of one another. In total, my mother gave birth to five more children after me, for a total of ten kids by the time I turned eight.

David, two years older than me, and Pat and Steve, born so soon after me, might have been even more greatly affected by their birth order in such a large family, but we mostly got along. Pat and Steve were my most frequent companions growing up. We had very different experiences than our older and younger siblings.

After Pat was born, older siblings would often look after me while my mother focused on the new babies. I am told my mother did not breastfeed me (possibly because formula companies were claiming that formula was better than breast milk), did not hold me or cuddle me, and did not spend any time with me unless I made a big fuss. There was little opportunity for human attachment in suckling, breastfeeding, or snuggling close.

This is not to say I had it worse than my siblings. Just how it was for me. But those first years, without sufficient parental comfort and attachment, seemed to have greatly influenced how my life would unfold. My parents loved us deeply but were overwhelmed by parenting for most of my childhood. They were good people. They did the best they could, given the circumstances, but they had perhaps too many children.

I was a willful child. That summer of 1961, I was trying to play baseball with my older brothers but wasn't very good at hitting. I wanted to hit a home run or at least get on base, even if only through sheer desire and power of will.

My oldest brother, Johnny, was pitching. My turn finally came at bat. I swung with all my might and landed in the dust. Strike one. I stood up, brushed the dirt from my clothes, and prepared to do better. I connected with the second pitch with a firm smack of the ball. I ran with all my might to first base. They told me to go back. It was a foul ball. I desperately wanted to stay on first—I had hit the ball. But they made me go back. I was so furious that I could not see straight. I missed the next pitch. Strike three. I threw the bat at Johnny. My mother immediately appeared and made me take a time-out in my room. She set her egg timer at thirty minutes and left me to fume.

It was hot in the room. I could hear my brothers continuing to play baseball. The tick-tick-ticking of the egg timer taunted me. I hurled it to the floor, smashing it. But now I had no way of knowing when my time-out would ever be over. Finally, my mother came to see why I hadn't reappeared. She told me how disappointed she was in my behavior. She picked up the pieces of the broken egg timer, then told me that any money I received for birthdays or Christmases would go to the cost of replacing the broken egg timer. I was sent back out to play, but my day was ruined. Baseball no longer held any appeal. My ego-self was thoroughly frustrated and dissatisfied. I slunk off to be by myself and cry. I never cried in front of my siblings.

Our family was incredibly and increasingly poor. In 1961, my father Ed was a forty-year-old American Baptist minister with nine children, earning $3,000 a year (equivalent to $23,000 today), serving a small white working-class church he founded in Portsmouth, Rhode Island. The birth of my parents' final son was still two years away.

This was poverty. But in a small-town way, it had its own sense of belonging. New England small-town poverty seems to me more dignified and humane than urban poverty or Southern poverty. We didn't know how poor we were.

We learned to do without nevertheless. Late twentieth-century American middle-class consumerism has never held any appeal for me. We didn't need all that stuff. But we did hunger for more than we had— to be someone special, to have enough food. Ministers' families were looked up to as somehow special. Poor kids from large families were not. We had both circumstances. Being highly educated poor is a rather complex socioeconomic location.

Needless to say, my parents struggled to feed so many on so little. With so many children to care for, including three under five and another on the way, my mother Rae was a somewhat indifferent housekeeper and a utilitarian cook. With so many mouths to feed, I was always hungry, even though each spring we plowed and planted the lower portion of our property for a vegetable garden with potatoes, corn, squash, carrots, and beets. But the garden never produced enough to feed us all. We children were responsible for weeding and tending it. I loved carrots but hated beets. When I weeded the garden, we grew bumper crops of carrots, but somehow, few beets survived.

Tending this garden, we learned transience. To paraphrase Ecclesiastes, for everything there is a season and a time for every matter under heaven: a time to plant and a time to harvest, a time to seek and a time to lose. Everything had its place and time. This growing understanding would greatly influence my spiritual journey and my life path.

The garden vegetables were a major part of our diet. Rae made do with what she could buy cheaply to supplement our vegetables. She bought loaves of three-day-old bread and #10 cans that were cheaper if they were dented or had lost their labels. Imagine the game of roulette in opening poorly labeled #10 cans for dinner. No one knew for sure what we would be eating from it. Our freezer was stocked with various indeterminate, inexpensive cuts of meat. Most of the meat was discolored with freezer burn, ruining its taste.

Ed was a big man and violent when angry. I loved him, respected him, but also feared him. Sometimes his spirit seemed broken. His most prominently expressed emotion was anger. He had deep emotional scars from the Great Depression, in which his father had lost their home and livelihood.

Ed feared losing everything, so he frequently buried himself in his work, even though he didn't earn an adequate living at it. He often returned home angry and frustrated. He had grown up in the Swedish immigrant community that had developed around the precision machine tool industry in Worcester, Massachusetts. Many immigrants had gone directly from Sweden or Norway to Worcester to work in machine tools. They were prized for the exacting standards of their work ethic, but this often gave them a certain misplaced perfectionism.

These Swedish Baptists were mostly Calvinists, viewing everyone as a wretched sinner and believing that only through strict adherence to the teachings of the church could anyone find salvation. This meant, among other things, no drinking, no dancing, no lying, no gambling, no swearing, no inappropriate sex, and generally a deep suspicion of anything that smacked of idleness or fun.

This religion of rules never did hold any appeal to me. Jesus, it seemed to me, taught a religion of love. "They will know we are Christians by our love." I would eventually break all the rules, though I never did learn to swear. And I knew better than to openly challenge my father's religious beliefs. My father's faith did not fit me well, so I eventually found my own.

My mother, two years younger than Ed, and called Rae since college, grew up in a religiously relaxed middle-class White Anglo-Saxon Protestant (WASP) Congregational family in Washington, DC. She recalled going to church on Sundays, visiting various Smithsonian museums, taking long, lazy bike rides, playing tennis, and enjoying interesting visits with friends. She enjoyed the best of early twentieth-century American WASP culture.

She wasn't very expressive—seldom hugging us and never saying, "I love you"—but that was common for New England WASP culture at the time. We children were the center of her existence for decades. We loved her dearly in a formal and distant way. In later years, she would regret how formal and distant she had been with her own children when we were small.

My parents met at Bates College in Maine, where Ed worked forty hours a week as a scholarship student on top of his regular course load. Rae fell in love with this energetic, charismatic upperclassman. They married when Rae graduated with a degree in sociology in June 1945. By then, Ed was studying at Andover Newton Theological School to become an ordained minister.

In marrying Ed, my mom adopted a whole new way of life. Initially, she worked helping immigrants at the East Boston Settlement House, but with marriage, she was expected to provide unpaid help for Ed's ministry. Marrying outside her class and culture meant a remarkably different life path, yet she never openly complained or despaired of her choices.

Marbles Mogul

Ranger Elementary School was a small, aging brick building that served kids from the poorer side of Tiverton. It faced Stafford Road, the main street on that side of town, with a parking lot on one side and a large, grassy playground on the other side and behind the school. Written in stone over the main entrance door, the school motto said: "We do things because they are right, not because we are being watched." And that was the spirit of the place, with a proud claim to righteousness and relatively little monitoring of each child's behavior.

The teachers were not particularly well educated, and most had similarly low expectations for their students. However, it played a major role in our socialization process. Behaving appropriately was generally held in higher esteem than displays of intelligence. Being respectable was far more important than being good.

Beginning in first grade, I discovered the boys played marbles at recess. I didn't know how to play. Marbles cost money. No one was allowed to play unless you played for keepsies, where the loser must give his marbles to the winner. This felt like a form of gambling. And even if you won, you could still lose your marbles. If they spilled onto the floor, the teacher would confiscate them and give them to the janitor.

Accumulating marbles was a risk, but having no marbles was a disaster. Many boys bought bags of fifty shiny marbles for one dollar per bag at the local variety store. For those who didn't have that kind of money or couldn't get it from their allowance or their parents, it was possible to buy three shiny new marbles for a dime. As a last resort for the truly destitute six-year-old, the janitor was willing to resell any used marbles gathered from the classroom floor for a penny apiece.

So everybody could afford to play, except me. I was still in debt due to that broken egg timer, so no marbles for me. I had no money, not even a penny, and knew better than to ask my mom or dad for gambling money. I couldn't afford to play marbles. Yet I had to play! I knew I could be good at it. If only I could find a way to escape my poverty long enough to accumulate some marbles!

I didn't want poverty to define me. At Ranger Elementary, everyone looked down on the Sherblom kids as poor. Our house was always dirty, overcrowded, and in a state of disrepair, with six-inch nails protruding from unfinished interior walls. As the fifth child in this large family, my clothes were mostly hand-me-downs. Many of these were cheap clothes when they were new, and all of them showed signs of wear and tear. Marbles felt like my destiny. My older brothers were too focused on other things to play marbles. This would be my proving ground and would become my domain. I became absurdly focused on this quest.

One day coming out to recess, I found a marble lying at the edge of the grass. Someone had forgotten it or dropped it running for the bell. Now I had my chance. I chose to play one of the smaller boys, Paul. Paul shot his marble and won. Again I felt doomed to no money and no marbles. But Paul lent me a marble to keep playing. This time, I won. By the end of recess, I had played dozens of games and miraculously had won more than I lost. I went triumphantly back to class with two warm marbles nestled in my pocket.

Every recess thereafter, I played, and every recess, I got better. I brought an intensity and focus few could bring to marbles. By spring, I was the best marble player on the playground. This is my earliest remembered experience of being in the zone, concentrating completely, and everything feeling right. I loved it! This sense of mastering the universe is highly addictive.

My marble collection grew to several hundred marbles. I began to sell them back to the other boys at two marbles for a penny, undercutting the janitor by half and virtually eliminating any competition from the variety store. Because my prices were the best in town, everybody bought marbles from me. Most days after school, my pockets bulged with marbles and increasingly with money. Now I had some spending money, so I began to buy my own used books at a nickel or dime each. I no longer thought of myself as poor. I had resources.

By the end of third grade, it was no longer cool to play marbles at recess. But by then, I'd spent some of my newfound wealth buying social status, tithed 10 percent to the church, opened a bank account with $18 from marble sales, plus given over three thousand marbles to my younger brothers. My sense of the possible skyrocketed! I was an entrepreneur. I had a facility for money making, understanding how money works, and making my way in the world. In short, I had a facility for success. Much I would later accomplish in life took root in those playground victories. I would never underestimate the power of focused intent and awareness.

There is no way to adequately express how this experience of being in the zone changed me—for better and for worse. I experienced the joy of being the best at something. I didn't need to settle for being poor. I learned the value of taking risks, persistence in the face of failure, and intense focus above all else. I developed a spiritual resilience. Anything is possible! I even developed a sociable and pleasant personality to get people to support and encourage my success as their own. I developed a taste for the sweet fruits of success—and wealth—as I went forth to take on the world.

Focus, persistence, risk taking, and resilience have been key elements in my story throughout my life, but the very first element I learned was audacious resilience. All my subsequent spiritual disciplines were built upon this foundation of resilience—the kind of resilience that comes only from being put to the test and rising to great challenges. In later years, when people would ask where and how I developed my unsinkable confidence, audacious resilience, and sense that anything was possible and that many risks really are worth taking, I'd say I learned it all playing marbles.

Father's Faith

Life directions unfold anew in every generation. My father's faith grew out of his life choices and would deeply influence my own. In 1945, twenty-six-year-old Ed faced an ordination council, as required by the Northern Baptist Convention, in order to be ordained to work as a minister to support himself and his twenty-four-year-old pregnant wife.

The ordination council perhaps found Ed too religiously liberal, too focused on God's love rather than God's judgment, without a sufficiently developed Calvinist sense of most people's damnation. Through his reasoning and reading, Ed knew God was primarily love. He said that being kind to others was the surest sign you were in God's graces. His ordination council proposed he either preached what was expected of him or be blocked from ordination. To save his livelihood, Ed relented. They agreed to ordain him only when he agreed to conform his preaching to what congregants expected to hear from the pulpit.

This would have enormous implications for my childhood faith. As part of the body of Christ, I knew one should love God and do what is righteous. However, as part of 1960s American Baptist culture, one also needed an outward appearance of conforming to law and culture whether you actually felt they were righteous or not.

Respectability was essentially our childhood faith, though no one ever spoke of it in such terms. We could follow our hearts' calling only if we kept up appearances of being acceptable in the eyes of the church. An intimate relationship with the divine mystery didn't really fit comfortably within late twentieth-century American Christian cultural expectations. Being too spiritual was actually a little suspicious. Yet a minister, and even his children, were expected to square this circle—to be the most upright, obedient, and beloved by God in the community and to always live righteously.

By 1950, Ed was scraping together a living by serving simultaneously as part-time minister at two poor working-class Baptist churches in North Taunton and Dighton, Massachusetts. Rae cared for their three small children at home.

Tiverton's Central Baptist church had been for generations the WASP congregation in a town with an increasingly Roman Catholic and Portuguese immigrant population. Central Baptist was the church for *Mayflower* descendants and WASP middle classes as they existed in post–World War II small New England towns. Yet as demographic changes accelerated, they were increasingly concerned about their future. They wanted to attract younger families and youthful vitality.

The church's deacons took a risk and called twenty-nine-year-old Ed— from a non-Anglo-Saxon white working-class background—to be their youthful, charismatic minister.

With their three children, Ed and Rae moved into the lovely parsonage across from the church. Five years later, I would be born there, as were my older brother David before me and my younger sister Patricia after me. With a full-time minister's salary and not having to pay for housing, Ed and Rae suddenly became middle class along with their growing family. Both my parents would later say it was perhaps the happiest time of their married life together. A time before I was born. Such is the impact of birth order.

Over the next seven years, Ed worked diligently to attract new families and build the congregation. Sunday morning attendance nearly doubled during that time. The programs for high school youth nearly quadrupled. He gave it his heart.

This should have been celebrated as a very successful ministry. But there was a problem. The new families joining the church mostly weren't *Mayflower* descendants. They certainly weren't WASPs. And they didn't fit in with 1950s small-town New England culture in the way congregants always had. The church's deacons decided they had made a mistake. They needed to make a change. Ed lost this respected ministerial position and its middle-class status. He would always resent it. This largely led to the anxious and angry father I would grow up with.

But he quickly became excited about founding a new white working-class Baptist church in the next town over, Portsmouth, near where Roger Williams had baptized his first followers. Ed invited the rest of the Tiverton congregational misfits to join his family in this new endeavor. We would be a Baptist congregation built on love and kindness, as is the nature of God.

In 1638, twenty-three Baptist exiles from the colony of Massachusetts signed the Portsmouth Compact. They baptized one another in Founder's Brook to create America's first Baptist church, locating it in Providence, Rhode Island. So in 1957, Ed at thirty-six became the founding pastor of Founder's Memorial Baptist Church in Portsmouth, with three dozen members in this newly covenanted congregation.

That Sunday's *Providence Journal* includes a wonderful picture of Ed holding two-year-old me, James Peter—named after James, the first head of the church in Jerusalem, and Peter, the first head of the church in Rome—and explaining the Portsmouth Compact to me. Growing up in a minister's family as a preacher's kid often has an incredible impact on a child—usually positive but always significant.

After meeting in a rented hall for three years, the congregation borrowed $14,000—all they could afford to borrow—to purchase a small farm on a Portsmouth hill overlooking the Sakonnet River. Over the next year, through $3,000 of goodwill offerings, we converted the barn into a sanctuary and used the farmhouse as an educational wing. Money was always tight. The congregation did nearly all the renovations by hand.

Our family lived in poverty for the ten years that Ed served as the pastor of this struggling working-class Baptist church. Yet it seemed with God, anything was possible. My family celebrated my ninth birthday by attending the Billy Graham Crusade in Boston. Billy Graham spoke of the power of God's love and the community of saints. He was talking about us. At ten years old, I had helped dig the foundation for and then helped construct our new fellowship hall. The church grounds became a second home.

The converted barn sanctuary could seat only about one hundred people, but we filled it with song. It stood on the highest point of our land, so the steep church driveway brought you directly to its backdoor before turning left for the church parking lot. My father adapted the old Baptist hymn celebrating "The Church in the Wildwood" to "The Little White Church on the Hill." We had the sense of being religious founders of a Baptist tradition centered on love of all.

Every Sunday, my siblings and I would file into the church, often roughly by height or birth order, though some of the older ones would sit next to the younger ones to manage our boisterousness. Jackets and ties for the boys, and dresses for the girls. We were to look attentive whenever my father was speaking, sing the hymns loudly, bow our heads in prayer, and generally model perfect church behavior.

Every summer, I worked in our Baptist youth summer camp to complete our church buildings. I learned to drink my coffee black because my older brothers would make fun of me at our coffee breaks if I needed to add lots of milk and sugar. I learned to measure twice and cut once. I knew which slopes of the lawn were finest for rolling down and which spots were best for sitting in the shade with a good book. I learned how to frolic and play out of the sight of grown-ups.

There was a large pear tree on the property. We learned how to time it so the pears were ripe and juicy but hadn't yet fallen to the ground, and we'd reach up with a homemade pear picker for a free treat: juicy, ripe pears soft and sweet.

We knew which closets were locked, which pews creaked, and where you could safely hide when you didn't want to be found. We knew our church buildings and grounds by heart. This was our community. This was God's love manifest in creation.

I studied my Bible, reading it cover to cover several times and memorizing key passages. Divine mystery is about being in a relationship. A loving God generally forgives and overlooks our shortcomings. King David had wildly misbehaved: getting drunk, having sex outside marriage, and killing people. Yet God continued to love and cherish him.

Job behaved perfectly, following all God's rules. He was a righteous man but didn't seem to connect or commune with the divine. God and the devil took away all Job had. Living into divine mystery obviously had little to do with following rules and everything to do with who we become in pursuit of God. Seek God with all your heart and all your mind, and he'll love you as he has always promised to.

I was awarded my own Bible after being baptized. I wore the cover off that Bible through reading it so much. I routinely won church Bible contests, and in high school would sometimes preach from the pulpit on Youth Sundays. I preached parental responsibility and Calvinist faith.

I was in high school when Ed and then Rae returned to school to earn MAs in education so they could teach in the Tiverton public schools and return our family to a middle-class existence. I therefore mostly grew up Free Baptist working-class poor. Yet we were among the most highly educated families in town. It was in many respects a delightful life, but it shaped my spiritual journey in unexpected ways—many but not all of them good.

In the Baptist tradition, a minister is expected to look for signs of the Holy Spirit in at least one child in every generation and then groom that child for the Baptist ministry. Years later, I discovered my father had seen the gifts of ministry in me in my earliest years. He carefully cultivated my spirit in order that God could call me when the time was right.

My understanding of God, however, was a problem. Many Christians worship some form of ancient anthropomorphic male deity, which can cause much confusion about the nature of God. Like many small children, I sometimes confused my father by birth with my Father who art in heaven. Both fathers would end up having enormous impacts on how my story unfolds. As I got older, I struggled with my father, struggled with my image and understanding of God, struggled with my faith, and struggled ultimately with my sense of divine mystery.

I resisted the strictness of my upbringing and what it meant to be a "good" Christian. I often did things beyond comprehension in order to establish my own independence as a human being. Preachers' kids often rebel, sometimes in surprisingly dysfunctional ways, yet often have more intimate relationships with the divine mystery.

Our community believed many things I would eventually reject, but it also gave me a deep love of divine mystery. When thinking about belonging to any religious community—really belonging—and the incredible transformative difference it can make in one's life, it is this emergent Baptist church that holds my heart. A loving community dependent upon the will of God. But in such communities, there is seldom discussion about the existence or even nature of God. When I had doubts, I learned to keep my own counsel and keep my private esoteric and mystical experiences to myself.

I knew there was something more. I have early memories of lying in bed in a quasi-dream state, feeling my consciousness leave my body and ascend toward the ceiling, from where I could look back down at my sleeping self. On later hearing stories of astral projection, or one's spirit leaving the body, such things made perfect sense to me and were consistent with my spontaneous experiences. I wondered how much more a well-trained Sufi, Taoist, Hindu, or Buddhist monk might be able to accomplish compared to my accidental and infantile spiritual journeys.

But such things did not fit into the worldview of my rational home environment in which I was only one of many children, the ultimate middle child. Such things also were not allowed in our Baptist belief system. In the early 1960s small-town, working-class environment of my youth, sin and redemption made a world of sense, but any form of cosmic consciousness was suspect.

Big-Family Dynamics

Big families have their own peculiar dynamics. In the sixteen years between 1947 and 1963, my mother was pregnant nearly half the time, the primary caregiver to revolving sets of babies and toddlers. So it is perhaps understandable that our house was a shambles and food preparation was strictly utilitarian.

Our food was generally overcooked, occasionally undercooked, and often burned. With oatmeal, my mom somehow managed to achieve all three conditions in a single pot on the stove. We would have a big Sunday lunch after church, but it might be followed by crumbled saltine crackers with milk and sugar for supper. My father couldn't cook, wouldn't clean, and seemed not to notice the squalor we lived in. He was generally working, and if he saw us, he would put us to work too.

When she wasn't busy taking care of children or the house, my mother always seemed to have a book in her hand. Rae was a voracious reader and imbued her children with a love of reading. My love of books and my rich interior life owe much to my mother's passionate love of reading.

My father preached every Sunday, and the whole family was always there. We filled two pews in that small congregation. However, one particularly rare Sunday in 1964, my youngest brother, the baby of the family, was quite sick, so my mother stayed home to care for him. Following worship, my father would shake the hand of each of the church members as they left the church.

We children would sit in his large wood-paneled station wagon waiting as he did so. However, I was eight years old, and as we waited in the car, I felt a sudden need to go to the bathroom. So I got out and ran into the outhouse in the parking lot. When I came out a few minutes later, the parking lot was empty. My father had seen the last congregant off, jumped into his car, seen behind him what looked to be approximately the right number of children, and headed home for lunch.

I watched clouds drift across the sun and a squirrel dance in a tree seeking nuts. I noticed birds singing their songs. Finally realizing I had been left behind, and they weren't returning anytime soon, I walked down the driveway and headed along East Main Street, Portsmouth, on my way home to Tiverton. A number of cars passed by as I walked. This was an era long before cell phones.

A few minutes later, a Portsmouth police officer stopped to ask if I was running away from home. I told him my father had left without me, so I was walking home. The officer happily gave me a ride the five miles home, if only to confirm what I had said and to keep me safe.

Meanwhile, my mother counted noses as each child entered the house. She pointed out to my father he was one short. He desperately raced back to church to find me. When the officer subsequently brought me home, my mother informed him that my father was still off looking for me. The officer radioed the police station to have someone find my father at church and let him know I was safely home.

I suspect much of my attention-seeking behavior as an adult has something to do with being lost in the middle of this very big family. I have always desperately wanted to be seen and appreciated. Being ignored or taken for granted too often plays into my childhood insecurities.

We siblings encompassed an entire generation. Between the oldest born in 1947 and the youngest born in 1963, we pretty much spanned the post–World War II baby boom generation. The oldest three have warm childhood memories of living in the parsonage at Central Baptist in Tiverton, growing up in the center of town. They were only between six and ten years old in 1957, when Ed lost his job and we moved economically downward.

Those of us whose earliest memories are of a rapidly expanding family in a ramshackle house constantly under repair experienced a different childhood. The youngest kids, who came of age after my parents were earning good incomes as elementary school teachers, had yet an entirely different experience of childhood. This was life in this large family. It had joys, passion, and problems entirely its own, plus its own peculiar behavioral dynamics, which I would take with me into the world.

We called my dad's large wood-paneled wagon "the woody." It was built to seat up to nine people in three rows of seats. When our family became too large to all fit in his woody, my dad simply tore out the back two rows and let us sit on the floor. No seat belts. Just leaning onto one another for support. Sometimes if he took a corner too fast, we would all topple over onto one another.

There were screw holes in the floor where the seats had been anchored.

My younger siblings sometimes used to drop sticks and dust through the holes, then dash to the back of the wagon to look for them on the road. With so many kids to get ready, we always seemed to be running late for church. So Ed routinely speeded on the winding back roads of Tiverton with his kids flopping about in the back. As far as I remember, we never got injured, and he never received a speeding ticket.

Of course, being such a large family, we couldn't really afford to go anywhere on summer vacation. Summers thus became a time for physical labor and reading. Though on really hot summer days, my mom often would take us swimming in the afternoons after we finished working in the garden.

My mom's older cousin Esther owned a lakefront cottage ninety minutes from us on Lake Boon in Stow, Massachusetts. The happiest summers of my childhood were the couple of summers when Esther loaned us her lake cottage for two weeks. We would set up tents in the yard—one for all the boys, another for all the girls—and take turns waiting to use the only outhouse on the property. My parents would sleep in the one-bedroom cabin.

We converted the combined living and dining rooms into one long table for eating, card playing, and whiling away rainy afternoons. The rest of the time, we were on the lake, fishing, boating, swimming, and just hanging out, or we were going for long walks in the surrounding woods. Summer sunrises were as glorious as the late evening panoramic sunsets. We woke and went to bed with the rhythms of the earth. Life was sweeter at the lake. We were at peace in nature. This was living in heaven.

I would take a small canoe and traverse the length and breadth of the lake, visiting the dam at one end or the marshes at the other—long, languid summer afternoons, paddling my way to peace of mind. I could spend the entire afternoon fishing or just sitting on the dock, watching the world go by. Free just to read.

None of dad's rules about always working applied. There was no work to be done, except for setting the table, cooking, cleaning, or the general tasks of living. We had a sense of idleness on Lake Boon. Later, discovering Henry David Thoreau's description of such a life in *Walden*, I knew exactly how he felt. I was at peace in nature and everything was good.

Free-Range Children

Our unfinished, dilapidated house—with a second story added on, a garage, and a large greenhouse—was on about two acres of sloping land ending in a swamp. Our entire property had a downward slant. I could hide in a small unmowed grassland at the top of the property, next to the sloping basketball court and a narrow baseball diamond in the side yard. The backyard had a swing set and picnic tables. The bottom of the property included our large vegetable garden and a small section left in woods. There was a shed for bicycles, a cold cellar, a car-repair pit, a workshop, and a two-story storage facility we called dad's carriage shed.

The Great Depression had scarred my father so deeply that he wouldn't throw anything away that could ever be useful. In his carriage shed he kept excess lumber, old car tires, batteries, and assorted used materials. For the first fifteen years of my life, the first and only new car my dad had owned—a 1947 coupe—sat on our side lawn, rusting and falling apart with a cracked engine block. Finally my mother put her foot down, saying she never wanted to see that rusting pile of junk again. So my father built a shed over it, hiding it from sight. That was our property. Junk gathered everywhere without any order or cleaning. I learned not to invite friends over.

Our house was the center of the larger territory. Our yard backed onto a cow-feed cornfield, which in late summer, provided great opportunities for complex mazes and secluded hiding places. The other side of that field faced Hurst Lane, the dividing line between the worst part of Tiverton and the financially depressed immigrant city of Fall River. Along Hurst Lane were a few rundown farms and houses, some cow pastures, and wet, swampy woods, which appeared as if terraformed by beavers. This swampland at the edge of the city gave the poor rural whites of these parts their pejorative nickname of Swamp Yankees.

As we grew, especially after we began getting on the school bus from a stop six blocks from our house, we discovered more places to explore. My school friend Ray lived in a trailer while his house was under construction, though his father never seemed to have the money to finish building it. We haunted that house. Most afternoons in good weather there was a pickup touch football or baseball game in the empty lot next to Henry's house five blocks away. There was a good-sized pond with seasonal polliwogs in the woods behind the dairy just across from the top of our street and a house with four girls around our ages always open for a visit just about eight blocks away.

We spent many hours roaming and hiding in this child-scale wilderness. In such a place, you could roam or simply get lost. Growing up in the middle of this large family, with overwhelmed parents and constant financial worries, we were more or less free-range children. With a home where there was always work to be done, and with so many interesting places beyond my father's scope of discovery, I began to stretch beyond the world of my parents and siblings. Always on foot, I came to know this geography intimately. Some days I would be gone for hours, returning only for meals.

I also spent much of my time with Pat and Steve, eleven and twenty-four months younger than me, respectively. We usually worked on one project or another for our father. But we sometimes played baseball, football, or basketball or went for long runs on the country lanes. Pat, Steve, and I ran for miles undisturbed down Hurst Lane. Legs thrusting, hearts pumping, free to experience the joys of unrestricted movement. We reveled in this quiet and secluded nature and in being alone. We found our way through muck and mire, discovering rural walks in the woods and the quagmires no one would suspect this close to the city's edge. We had nature and anonymity just beyond the boundaries of our own yard, and we were allowed to run free.

Pat was a naturally gifted athlete and beat me at just about any athletic contest. She would go on to captain almost every woman's sports team in high school. Steve was quiet and intense, with a more poetic and artistic nature. He would go on to study in many settings from the Berklee College of Music to the Harvard Graduate School of Education.

From our older siblings, we learned how to build an argument, display intellectual arrogance, and win a discussion. Sunday lunch following worship was often a time for heated discussions, in which my father freely engaged with us. To hold my own as a middle child, I needed rhetorical audacity to be able to survive.

David was perhaps the one who suffered the most in the middle of this family, with three siblings three or more years older, and six siblings two or more years younger. David was too young to keep up with the three older children and felt too old to play with Pat, Steve, and me. David always seemed to be odd man out, keeping a safe distance from our parents and the rest of our siblings. He would go on to become a perceptive artist, a sensitive poet, and a truly gentle soul. He saved me on a couple of occasions. When I couldn't learn to drive under the direction of our volatile father, David taught me. When kids made fun of me as a geek, David defended me.

With no doors on any of the bedrooms and just a curtain on the main bathroom, we lived together with very little privacy. I shared a bedroom with Davey and Stevie for most of my childhood. We learned to play together, to ignore one another while working side by side, and to accommodate each person having his own space when he needed it most. We learned to read one another's body language to judge when someone wanted to be left alone and when he might want to join an activity. We learned not to touch one another's stuff—or at least to put it back the way we found it, then refuse to admit we had ever touched it. It was an odd sort of communal existence, stretching across a generation's worth of differences. It left us with our own peculiarities.

From my dad, I learned to be always working. He firmly believed idle hands were the devil's plaything. In this sense, I am my father's son. At six, I was weeding the garden daily in the summer. At eight, I was working on his construction projects. At ten, I was mowing our lawn. At twelve, I was mowing multiple lawns each week for money, some miles away from our house, always walking to these jobs.

By thirteen, I had a paper route to deliver on foot each afternoon. Some days, as the afternoon turned to dusk and then dark, I would deliver papers in the damp and in the cold. No matter what the weather, I would always make my evening paper rounds. This was the working-class culture I grew up in. We took pride in being responsible, for doing what was difficult, for working right through our pain and our suffering. This is a big part of how I learned the work ethic that has served me well the rest of my life.

One cold, dark winter night, I was collecting for my paper route. One of my customers answering the door took one look at me and said, "It's really cold out—where's your winter coat?" I said, "This is my winter coat." She asked me to step inside. She came back with the money for her newspaper and a thick, blue, warm woolen coat. She said, "This was my son's coat, and he's outgrown it."

I was surprised and touched by her kindness and generosity and also overjoyed to replace my worn, thin jacket with a true winter coat. I returned home in ecstasy with my new coat, and so was shocked when my mother was angry that some stranger had judged me to be in need of charity—and that I had accepted such charity from a stranger. My mother's reaction made me pause, but that coat was so warm that I never regretted having it.

Yet I was very much my mother's son. My favorite pastime was to find a good book, escape somewhere no one would find me, and read it cover to cover. I often had two or three books going at any one time and would borrow books from the library four at a time, only to return two or three weeks later for more.

My appetite for reading was insatiable. Most of my siblings did their homework around what had once been a big dining room table, talking to one another as they worked. My mother found me a large used desk so I could work on my school projects undisturbed for days at a time.

I hungered to master games, moving from marbles to checkers, Monopoly, Parcheesi, ping pong, chess, and pool. I never played just for fun. I played to win, preferably to win big and in as short a time as possible. Eventually, it got so my siblings would no longer play competitive games with me.

Over time, I became skilled at games of all sorts, something my father could never understand, having grown up in a culture that never played games. He could neither learn to play such games nor understand why we would waste hours of our lives happily doing so.

Small-Town Life

In elementary school, I was the clever but academically unmotivated student teachers often hate. I loved to learn for the sake of learning but was not particularly motivated to try meeting parents' or teachers' expectations of me.

I mastered reading before even starting school but bored quickly in first-grade reading classes. I read at home but seldom participated in class. My first-grade teacher Mrs. Almy got so frustrated with my constant talking and playing with my friends in class that she lifted me out of my chair by pulling me up by my hair. After that, I kept my hair in a shorter buzz cut.

My second-grade teacher was an older woman, nearing retirement, who didn't have the energy anymore to keep up with the class. She used to tell us not to eat food that had fallen on the floor because the devil had taken a bite out of it, and if we then ate it, we would be forever condemned to hell.

In second grade, they introduced us to what was called the New Math. It was carefully explained in some handouts our second-grade teacher distributed but that she failed to understand. So I read the handouts and solved the math problems. When my answers matched the teacher's guide, she had me teach the rest of the class this New Math. I loved teaching the class but was generally bored with school and was known as a wisecracker and class joker.

I played with the other boys in class, focusing on friendships and what was going on in our neighborhood. School seemed like a distraction from what was true and meaningful in life. For my first three years of school, what happened at recess was far more interesting and exciting than whatever happened before and after recess. Being successful at marbles and becoming a marble mogul centered me and gave meaning to my life, much more than schoolwork.

This began to change in fourth grade, when a conscientious teacher guessed I had the capacity for doing additional homework. She frequently gave me extra assignments. I happily wrote reports on books she recommended and ones I found on my own, and I researched answers to questions I had asked her. It opened up a world of independent study opportunities.

Then I moved to the Pocasset Middle School (named after the local Indian tribe that had previously lived here) for fifth grade. It served kids from every part of town. For sixth grade, I went to Fort Barton Middle School (named after the fort used in the Indian wars), in the wealthier part of town. My world was expanding.

In fifth and sixth grades, they began to track us educationally. There were five levels of fifth grade based on academic potential. Like all students from Ranger School, I started out at the bottom. Ranger was known in town as serving the poorest neighborhoods. Every three months or so, I was moved up to the next higher group, leaving behind my childhood friends and playmates. By the end of fifth grade, I was in the highest academic group. By sixth grade, I was consistently a leader in that group. My sense of self was changing and taking on new forms as well.

I had really enjoyed my time at Ranger School, but now at Fort Barton, I became a serious student. My self-identity was of someone focused, smart, sociable, capable of anything, and happy to help everyone. I became a leader in my class and really enjoyed hanging out with smart kids. This was my first social-class crossing, and I learned its importance for having new opportunities.

Smart kids often faced problems on the playground, where there was always someone bigger and stronger, often annoyed at your knowing what he didn't. In middle school, I was literally a ninety-eight-pound weakling. A skinny kid with a buzz cut. About as gentle a soul as you could find, with no real interest in fighting. This easily made me a target, and I took my share of kicks and punches. But here was where having three older brothers helped. Bullies learned if you picked on one Sherblom, you might well meet more. I did fine with bullies thereafter. I also made sure I was around to help my younger brothers whenever necessary.

I still did school on my terms. On nice days, a well-chosen friend or two might skip an afternoon class with me. We'd climb the hill behind the school, where there was a reconstructed façade of the colonial-era Fort Barton. From this vantage point, we could see the entire town, the river traffic on the Sakonnet River, and the world beyond. Being in nature was transcendent for me. This is still one of my favorite viewing points, though foliage has grown up around it over time.

Sakonnet River

We are often shaped by the geography of our childhood. Mine was shaped by swampy woods and Rhode Island's rocky shores along the Narragansett Bay. The Sakonnet River, a large navigable waterway separating Aquidneck Island from Tiverton and Little Compton on the mainland, features in my story. Little Compton was Tiverton's wealthier and more rural neighbor to the south. Just south of Tiverton Four Corners is the wildness of the ocean, possibilities beyond boundaries, especially at its furthest reach, called Sakonnet Point.

My brother David and I loved to walk that beach, to feel the sea breezes pulling at our clothes, to listen to the squawking of the gulls, and to watch the fishing boats do their work. The fishermen and boaters often seek the deeper water of the navigable channel offshore, while swimmers seek the sandy beaches closer to Tiverton, leaving Sakonnet Point for contemplatives, artists, intellectuals, mystics, and lovers. Our house was on the poorer side of town, but parking near the point was then free and open to anyone who wished to feel the mist thrown up by the waves crashing against the shore or watch the moon rise on a summer night.

A classmate's father ran the Fo'c'sle restaurant on Sakonnet Point, where fishermen mingled with wealthy tourists, and the town's locals could find food and warmth. I experienced deep peace walking on that rocky shore, listening to the waves—and still do so today. In some ways, it is the place I picture when I picture heaven. I dreamed big dreams on that beach. Dreams of who I was and could be. Walking along the deserted beach, with the sea breeze blowing in my face and all my responsibilities somewhere further inland, I wished only to become one with the rhythms of the sea.

Even though we couldn't afford it, my father bought an old wooden-cabin fishing boat that was no longer seaworthy. My siblings and I spent many hours sanding, caulking, painting, and bilge-pumping that leaky old vessel just so we could be on the water. We renamed the boat *Seaflower* and moored it in a small cove, locally called the Gut, on a borrowed mooring just below the town's best neighborhood.

This was not a fast boat, but whether we motored on the Sakonnet or just moored, it was like heaven. Hours of painstaking work were rewarded by quiet afternoons hanging out and sometimes nights sleeping to the rhythmic motions that even this old fishing boat made rocking on the waves. Keeping the *Seaflower* afloat took constant work and vigilance, but it was worth it.

When Hurricane Camille raced up the Atlantic coast in August 1969, we pulled *Seaflower* from the Sakonnet to protect it from nature's destruction. We stored it for the storm's duration in my father's carriage shed. Next, we secured the outdoor furniture and windows of our house. Then, much to my mother's dismay, my brothers and I went out on Sakonnet Point to watch the hurricane make its way ashore. (When observing a hurricane, people certainly should be safely onshore.) We watched the water turn wild, churning in the wind, crashing brutally against the shore. Hurricanes viscerally connect us to the incredible wildness of nature. The ocean waves crashed with ever-greater violence, reaching far higher than we had ever seen before.

I love the wildness of the ocean. The salty dampness of a spring gust of wind. The unmistakable perfume of a summer tempest. The deep, rich colors of a crisp autumn afternoon at the beach. The wet, cold fingers of icy chill along the shore. Oceans remain nature untamed. Ever since witnessing that hurricane, wherever I live, I carry a bit of the wildness of the ocean in my soul. My deep feelings about resiliency, risk taking, and being alive to nature are viscerally connected to the Sakonnet River of my youth.

Diverse Baptisms

Baptist youth achieve young adulthood around the age of thirteen. They become Christians by studying their Bible, faithfully attending worship services, participating in Christian youth activities, and then being plunged below moving water in what Baptists call full immersion baptism. Approaching my thirteenth birthday, I was ambivalent about being baptized. I didn't know if God thought I was ready yet. But Pat, David, and Stevie declared they felt ready. So ready or not, I prepared to take the plunge!

I knew what to expect from reading about Jesus's baptism in Mark 1:10: "Just as he was coming up out of the water, he saw the heavens torn apart and the Spirit descending like a dove upon him." Now, I was pretty sure the affirmation Jesus received from God—"You are my Son, the Beloved, with whom I am well pleased"—was unique to his situation. But I was still counting on the heavens opening and descent of the Spirit. Or at least some kind of warm feeling of welcome to salvation, along with the sense of "well done, good and faithful servant."

So I was more than a little disappointed when after being prayed over and then plunged under the cold water, I emerged merely breathless, wet, and cold. The earth did not quake, there was no descending

Spirit, and I felt no different than I had before. This disappointing lack of transcendence shook my confidence and made me wonder what else wasn't true.

It is often said that our adult worldview is deeply shaped by what the world was like when we came of age. I was quite circumscribed in my emerging worldview, growing up in white, twentieth-century, small-town America, but our country was about to experience a revolution.

The year 1968 began with the Tet Offensive, which justified an escalation of the American war in Vietnam as well as sparked anti-war protests around the country. Then Martin Luther King Jr. was assassinated in April, apparently by the Memphis police working with the FBI. The fight for black civil rights turned increasingly violent with riots in urban centers.

By May, youth protests to overturn corrupt governments seemed to be spreading worldwide. Then someone assassinated Robert F. Kennedy as he ran for president of the United States. That was the turbulent year I was baptized and came of age. It deeply affected my sense of being American. I wanted to be part of Kennedy's vision of America, not the corrupt and violent government I saw on television.

Then came my thirteenth birthday in October 1968 and the dawning of the Age of Aquarius. Of course, we weren't allowed to attend a rock 'n' roll musical, such as *Hair*, featuring nudity. But we couldn't entirely avoid its musical and existential angst either. Like many others that year, I started growing my hair longer as a means of self-expression.

America no longer appeared to be a true democracy. The war in Vietnam changed everything. Anti-war Democratic voters entered that August's Democratic convention with an overwhelming majority of votes. Yet brutal police tactics suppressed violent demonstrators, and a pro-war Democratic candidate was selected as the nominee. The world had gone askew.

Thanks to extensive television coverage, I emerged forever radicalized, not trusting big governments or big business. I was open to new experiences, yet not willing to accept the status quo unquestioned.

I now understood that the police often treated minorities and radicals differently. Protest songs and rock 'n' roll helped me make sense of what had happened in Chicago, at Kent State, and in Vietnam. My family's Christian faith seemed as ill placed as my father's support of Richard Nixon. It appeared we had been lied to all along.

I experienced my first radically transformative spiritual phenomena the next year. We were in the woods at a Baptist youth retreat. We had spent most of the morning sitting in a dark, stuffy room watching what can best be described as some form of cheap teenage indoctrination videos. When we finally took a break in the late morning, I shot out of the room into the bright daylight of the surrounding forest, making my way quickly up the path before anyone else could engage me in conversation. I just wanted to be alone with my thoughts.

Suddenly, I noticed the path was shining before me. The leaves on the trees were emitting light, and the very trunks of the trees were luminous. The surrounding forest burst into song, almost as if to the sound of the music of the spheres. I saw more shades and nuances of color than I had ever seen before. My eyes were dazzled. My ears could perceive and distinguish sounds at greater distances. I felt my hands and arms as waves of pure energy. I was pure energy. One with all being. At peace with all that could be perceived. This was my first truly spiritual awakening! I felt both joy and awe.

This feeling of unity with everything was pure bliss. I was one with all sentient beings, merging with the surrounding environment, exploding into the universe. Each bird was beautiful and brought a message from beyond. The passing clouds protected us from the ultraviolet rays of the sun while holding the water the earth needed to feed its cycle of life.

After momentarily living in Technicolor, it seemed my entire previous existence had been sepia colored. My life was so much bigger and more meaningful than I imagined. It was all so much to take in, to notice, and to care about. Being permeated all. I participated in all being.

Having discovered transcendence, I didn't want to go back to mundane reality. I didn't want to live my life in black and white. I wanted to live in the vivid palette of colors experienced in my first transcendent states in nature. It reminded me of how astounded I was as a child when television went from being black and white to Technicolor. That transformation was magical!

You can still capture a little sense of how seeing the world in vivid colors changed our perspective on life by watching the *Wizard of Oz*. In the late 1960s, everyone we knew used to gather around the TV the one evening each year when it was shown. It's the story of a small-town girl growing up in sepia-colored Kansas until a tornado carries her over the rainbow to a Technicolor Oz.

I always assumed growing up there must be a transcendent existence just beyond our recognition, far more colorful than our everyday existence, if only we could access it. My transcendent experiences suggested any spiritual path with heart might bring us there—to awakening, to experiencing life in Technicolor.

Transformed and knowing what is important to know, I still experience joy and awe whenever I remember that deeply spiritual experience. For a moment, I occupied a transcendent dimension. This created a spiritual hunger for such experiences that would help shape my life's path and eventually lead me to awakening.

Working-Class Ethics

My opportunities for making real money took off when I turned fourteen and could be hired by the local McDonald's two miles away. They started me on the prep table, but within months, I was one of their fastest grill masters at $1.15 per hour. Eventually, my rhythm and timing became so good I could keep sixty hamburger patties cooking at once. I'd flip them each when they were half done and plate them perfectly on their buns, while beginning another five dozen burgers on the grill.

One busy rush hour, McDonald's sent someone down from corporate headquarters to time us. They awarded me and my older coworker Owen prizes for being the fastest grill masters in southeastern Massachusetts. That award earned me a fifteen-cents-per-hour raise.

During my second summer working at McDonald's, Owen and I persuaded the assistant manager to always let us close the store on Saturday nights. So after cleanup was done, we could drink beer and play poker into the wee hours. This was an adolescent's working-class dream. Drinking and gambling felt particularly sweet on Saturday night. I'd win enough at poker at least to cover the cost of my beer, then I'd head home for a few hours' sleep before getting up for church with my family. This was heaven.

Over the next four years, I would work many hours at McDonald's, eventually earning thousands of dollars before finally leaving for college.

On turning sixteen and earning my driver's license, I also landed a job as the weekend dishwasher at the fanciest restaurant in Tiverton. They had previously needed to pay two people to handle the Friday and Saturday night rush. It was a stressful job, between clearing plates, running the dishwasher, and stacking and returning the hot dishes coming from the machine. The restaurant was perpetually short-staffed, so I reorganized the process such that I could keep the dishwasher running virtually nonstop for several hours. I handled the entire dishwashing process by myself, even on the busiest nights. The owners were so impressed, they increased my pay to $1.70 an hour.

More importantly, the cook took me under his wing. I ate my first filet mignon, first lobster, first chicken cordon bleu, and many other culinary firsts while working in that kitchen. Who knew eating food could be such a source of joy! I began to put on weight and fill out for the first time in my life. I no longer weighed less than one hundred pounds or looked like skin and bones. I also began to develop a larger group of friends of all kinds.

I loved the idea of eating in fancy restaurants—not only for the quality of the food and the ambience but also for the sense that this was how those who could afford it chose to live. In 1972, I determined I would never live as we had lived growing up in Tiverton. There must be a middle way between poverty and materialism. A way to serve God that included eating filet mignon and lobster from time to time. A way that was far less financially constrained than a small-town, working-class ethic.

Education would be my path to that wider world. Doing really well in school would become my path to success. I began to focus upon and take very seriously my academic standing and opportunities. I wanted a very different standard of living.

By the summer of 1972, I was working most weekends at this fancy restaurant until well after it closed. The cooking staff and some of the wait staff had become quite good friends of mine. So we initiated Saturday nights of beer and poker. By now, my beer consumption was a good bit higher, but so were my poker winnings. They became a substantial addition to my take-home pay.

One night, we were playing until almost 3:00 a.m. before I headed home to at least let the engine cool off before my father got up to begin getting ready for church. I was driving along our only state highway, Route 24, at too high a speed and somewhat intoxicated, when a Tiverton police officer pulled me over. Fortunately, he was not much older than I was and had some sympathy for my situation.

When asked for my license and registration, I promptly gave them to him. I was terrified. Sweat poured off me as I considered how my father might respond upon hearing of my arrest and incarceration. My father seemed oblivious to my nighttime pursuits but would not be pleased if he even suspected them.

The officer noticed my great discomfort and saw the car was registered in Reverend Edward Sherblom's name. He asked, "Are you one of Reverend Sherblom's boys?"

"Yes, sir," I said.

"Do you think he would approve of your behavior?"

"No, sir."

"Can you imagine what he would do to you?"

"Yes, sir," I said, "that is something I can clearly imagine."

My father could be violent when angry. The policeman paused, then said, "I think you have been punished enough. Go home, and never let me catch you like this again."

I headed home, relieved—and suddenly sober—with joy in my heart for New England small-town justice. Now, looking back, I realize not all Americans engaged with local power received such an outcome. If I had been black or Hispanic, this encounter might have ended quite differently, and not necessarily well.

This incident reinforced my sense of confidence and resilience in the face of troubles. I might make mistakes but could survive and learn from them. My lifelong sense of ease in the world draws heavily upon this small-town consciousness of being accepted and beloved for who I am and forgivable no matter what I do.

Because we were such a large family, coming of age between 1960 and the late 1970s, my siblings and I had a wide divergence of childhood experiences. But education was our family's core value. Being a highly educated family in a small Rhode Island town was a great way to grow up. Of my nine siblings, one would become a professor of nursing, one a professor of communications, one for a time a very leftist political science professor, another a public school teacher, one a professor of physiology, one a professor of moral development, another a marine biologist, and the youngest two a consultant and a general contractor. Six of my nine siblings earned PhDs and served as college professors.

I think you can say we grew up with a great sense of resilience in life, largely grounded in our educational attainments, though not entirely so. This small-town environment helped create the successful transcendentalist capitalist I would so enjoy becoming. Thank goodness for small towns.

Mr. Robinson

There was perhaps a 1970s innocence, since lost, which made our world seem a safer and kinder place in which anything really could happen. Mr. Bradford Robinson, the Harvard-educated WASP English department chairman at our high school, took me under his direction beginning my freshman year.

He introduced me to Shakespeare, Tolstoy, Albert Camus, and Friedrich Nietzsche. When he discovered I was particularly interested in the mystics, he led me to Lao Tzu's *Tao Te Ching* and the Taoist *I Ching*. Then we read and discussed Alan Watts's *The Wisdom of Insecurity* and *The Way of Zen*. Mr. Robinson also introduced me to the writings of Ayn Rand, Milton Friedman, and other libertarians. I would soon leave these authors behind for the subtler writings of Immanuel Kant's German idealism in the *Critique of Pure Reason* and Plato's *Republic* but would always hold a soft spot in my heart for anarchists and libertarians.

I discovered many mystics wrote about transcendence without any reference to God—rather, with just the experience and the transformative feel of divine mystery. Many described experiences remarkably similar to my own transcendent experiences in the woods, from the top of Fort Barton or alone on Sakonnet Point. Such experiences seemed to be what made life interesting and worth living.

As I probed ever-bigger questions, Mr. Robinson took to calling me "The Philosopher." He introduced me to the American transcendentalists, beginning with Henry David Thoreau, Ralph Waldo Emerson, and their natural reason and nature-based transcendentalism. Now I had found my kindred spirits. They were reading and discussing the Bhagavad Gita, Upanishads, Koran, and teachings of Confucius. These were bookish extroverts sucking all the marrow out of every bone in their experience of life. I would have loved to play marbles with Henry David or take long philosophical walks with Waldo. For them, living mattered! I started to pay attention to my spirit, my senses, and my setting more closely.

Throughout high school and Mr. Robinson's tutelage, I attended my father's church, memorized Bible passages, and even preached once or twice from his pulpit on Youth Sunday. At my mother's request one Sunday, I even sang a solo of her favorite hymn:

> *Let there be peace on earth,*
> *and let it begin with me.*
> *Let there be peace on earth,*
> *the peace that was meant to be.*
> *With God as our Father,*
> *brothers all are we.*
> *Let me walk with my brother,*
> *in perfect harmony.*

I still love those old hymns, but in those years, my private spirituality was increasingly non-Christian and more transcendent and able to take me places my father could not even dream about.

Perhaps Ed was as naïve as we teenagers thought. Or perhaps he recognized we were growing up in a world he could not fathom. Or perhaps he just wanted to give us our own space. But when George Harrison's ode to Krishna consciousness, "My Sweet Lord," started playing on the radio, my father let us turn it up loud as a song to God. Our Baptist youth group even went to see *Jesus Christ Superstar,* that blasphemous Christian rock opera telling the life of Jesus. Even Jesus Christ could rock 'n' roll in the Age of Aquarius!

When my reading list grew beyond the confines of the high school library and our two town libraries, Mr. Robinson took me and two other students from our school to a book depository in Providence, where we had a $500 budget to spend on non-textbooks for our classmates' reading pleasure. The four of us managed to spend that allowance in about an hour and a half. My choices included Theosophists, Sufis, Buddhists, Hindus, and Christian contemplatives. I was in a state of bliss both that afternoon and for months to come as I read all those new books. I had discovered the path of knowledge to enlightenment! Focused reading, along with vision quests, would be my path. I was now reading nearly one hundred books a year.

Big Fish, Small Pond

I really came into my own at Tiverton High School. There were 195 of us in my year, which felt enormous at the time, but each of us found our own place. I was a geek. President of the chess club all four years. I served on student council, on the prom committees for both junior and senior proms, and as newspaper editor. I participated in the variety show and created a football cheerleading club called the Big Mouth Club. This is the great advantage of a small town. Geek that I was, the homecoming queen was a good friend of mine, as were two of the four members of her court, the prom queen, and two of the four members of *her* court.

The top ten students by GPA were evenly split between boys and girls, but the girls tended to be more studious, and the boys more often into sports or other activities. We helped one another through our trials and tribulations—those we caused ourselves as well as those thrust upon us. We partied and we played.

I knew life could be in Technicolor and filled with transcendent experiences. But this was a simpler time. It was a time before drugs were so prevalent in small towns. We heard rumors of drugs but never saw any. Social norms still frowned upon premarital sex. We heard rumors of sex but never got any. Being a couple involved lots of handholding, some kissing, and perhaps arousal, but nothing more. In my late twentieth-century, white, small-town New England experience, people looked out for one another and were mostly kind to one another—at least to people within our own social groupings, for our society was still very homogeneous.

By the time we graduated, the top academic students mostly liked one another, had grown up together, were mostly in the same classes, and were members of the National Honor Society. I had the second-highest GPA, exceeded only by Lydia, whose father owned the Fo'c'sle. The National Honor Society included the captain of the football team, head of the cheer club, captain of the basketball team, class president, lead scorer on the basketball team, and a collection of just plain academic geeks and misfits.

This was small-town America. This was an environment in which I could be seen and recognized as the person I was becoming. This was an environment that fostered a strong sense of self, resilience, and being a worthwhile human being.

One of my best friends, John, a football player with his own car, often took it upon himself to free me from boring classes—calculus or whatever—by taking me bowling instead. He had an 8-track tape player in his car, a wicked curve shot when he bowled, and a laidback sense of humor. He taught me how to play tennis on spring afternoons.

We hung out with one of the prettiest girls in school, Sheila-Marie, who would tell us tales of skinny-dipping in the Sakonnet and call us her dirty uncles when we offered to join her. Yet her primary aspiration in life was simply to get married and have children. To be a good wife and mother was more than enough. Getting a job, starting a family, and having a life were typical life goals among my friends.

Beyond the top students, few others aspired for college. I wanted more and worked mightily to achieve more. Eventually, I was voted most likely to succeed, with a great passion to make my way in the world. My classmates would challenge me to solve complicated math problems in my head, devise limericks and poems to capture the essence of a moment, play three chess games at once, or engage in metaphysical conversations while helping a classmate with her math problems and completing my social studies homework at the same time. This was a time of great satisfaction as a big fish within a very small pond.

Rhode Island itself is a very small pond. I served as Tiverton High School's representative on the governor's advisory council, serving as chairman of the council my senior year. I also served in the Rhode Island Model Legislature, serving as majority leader of the House of Representatives. By senior year, at least once a week, I drove the half hour to the state capitol. They gave me a small office at the statehouse for our legislative materials.

My high school experiences confirmed my expectation that with enough passion and hard work, and with a certain kind of resilience, if God was willing, anything was possible. Bound for better things, I began to dream bigger dreams.

When it came time to apply to college, my father and my guidance counselor agreed I ought to apply to the University of Rhode Island, Boston University, and/or Providence College. Mr. Robinson suggested Harvard, Yale, and Dartmouth University. I decided to follow Mr. Robinson. I was accepted at two of these colleges and waitlisted and eventually accepted at the third.

My dad was not happy with me. Both my parents finally had well-paying teaching jobs, which meant the college-aid formulas expected substantial financial contributions from them as well as from me. Ed was now earning nearly $12,000 a year, and Rae nearly $10,000 (their combined income equal to $123,000 today), but they had already committed several thousands of dollars annually to send one sibling to Bates, another to the University of Rhode Island, and a third to Boston University. And Pat and Steve would presumably head off to college over the next two years as well.

My father pointed out that few working-class Baptist ministers were Yale or Harvard graduates. I didn't care. I trusted in God's grace and accepted Yale, moving myself out of state, beyond parental influence, and into a world of wealth and knowledge I had barely known existed. As a result, my father left me to my own devices as to how to pay for it.

I didn't fully appreciate at the time how different my white small-town Rhode Island working-class and public-school upbringing was from that of my future classmates at Yale. I wasn't sure if I had even met anyone from America's upper-class financial elite, much less people who traveled internationally for pleasure. But now they would mostly be peers and classmates. This would be my hero's journey. With small-town resilience and spiritual audacity, I felt prepared to take on the wider world.

My small-town upbringing, growing up within a very large and highly intellectual family and a working-class Baptist church, provided me with a sense of resiliency that would serve me well. I could head to college and embrace the wider world, testing myself in a more diverse and heterogeneous society. Yet I was in equal parts excited, scared, pleased beyond reason, and just plain anxious as I prepared to leave my small-town world behind. I carried some of my small-town limitations in my soul, yet the spiritual discipline of resiliency made all things possible.

AUDACIOUS RESILIENCE

Chalice-Lighting Words

Resilient people use a well-developed set of skills that help them to control their emotions, attention, and behavior. Self-regulation is important for forming intimate relationships, succeeding at work, and maintaining physical health.

—*The Resilience Factor* by Karen Reivich and Andrew Shatté

Check-in: How does spiritual resilience factor into your life today?

Reading

In 1638, twenty-three Baptist exiles from the colony of Massachusetts signed the Portsmouth Compact. They baptized one another in Founder's Brook to create America's first Baptist church, locating it in Providence, Rhode Island. So, in 1957, Ed at thirty-six became the founding pastor of Founder's Memorial Baptist Church in Portsmouth, with three dozen members in this newly covenanted congregation.

That Sunday's *Providence Journal* includes a wonderful picture of Ed holding two-year-old me, James Peter—named after James, the first head of the church in Jerusalem, and Peter, the first head of the church in Rome—and explaining the Portsmouth Compact to me. Growing up in a minister's family as a preacher's kid often has an incredible impact on a child—usually positive but always significant. . . .

Like many small children, I sometimes confused my father by birth with my Father who art in heaven. Both fathers would end up having enormous impacts on how my story unfolds. . . .

I resisted the strictness of my upbringing and what it meant to be a "good" Christian. I often did things beyond comprehension in order to establish my own independence as a human being. Preachers' kids often rebel, sometimes in surprisingly dysfunctional ways, yet they often have more intimate relationships with the divine mystery.

Questions to Ponder

1. What do we discover about the author at the Baptist minister's retirement home?

2. In what ways is playing marbles a spiritual practice?

3. How does the author's childhood faith compare to his father's faith?

4. How does the spiritual orientation of Founder's Memorial differ from Central Baptist?

5. How does the author's Christian baptism contrast with his baptism in nature at the youth retreat?

6. What does this story teach you about resilience in your own life?

Closing Words

I could head to college and embrace the wider world, testing myself in a more diverse and heterogeneous society. Yet I was equal parts excited, scared, pleased beyond reason, and just plain anxious as I prepared to leave my small-town world behind. I carried some of my small-town limitations in my soul, yet the spiritual discipline of resiliency made all things possible.

BOOK GROUP DISCUSSIONS

AUDACIOUS RESILIENCE

Author's Comment

This chapter employs the first seventeen years of my life as a white, small-town, working-class Baptist preacher's son to explore, demonstrate, and engage the spiritual discipline of resilience. I draw the basis of my lifelong resilience using stories about the Baptist retirement home, growing up in poverty, playing marbles, my childhood faith, being born in the middle of a big family, free-range children, education, baptisms, working-class ethics, and emergence in high school. Now I invite you to consider your own source of resilience.

Questions to Encourage Conversation

1. How do birth order and family size impact the author's sense of self?

2. How does the author react to his family's poverty?

3. How does his parents' own upbringing transmit from generation to generation?

4. In what way does playing marbles illustrate his approach to challenges?

5. Can you resonate with the author's childhood faith? How similar or different was yours?

6. How does the author's reaction to being left behind as an eight-year-old show his growing resilience?

7. What is the distinction between being truthful and beloved by God?

8. In an age of planned activities and helicopter parents, how does the author's 1960s childhood compare to yours? How does it compare to your own children's childhood?

9. The author turned thirteen in 1968. The turmoil of that time deeply shaped his life. What was going on the year you turned thirteen? How did it affect your life?

10. Did you have a Mr. Robinson radically change the trajectory of your life?

Reflection

As a group, reflect upon the sources of spiritual resilience in your own lives.

DISCIPLINE TWO:
SURRENDER

This being human is a guest house. Every morning a new arrival. A joy, a depression, a meanness, some momentary awareness comes as an unexpected visitor. Welcome and entertain them all! Even if they are a crowd of sorrows...

—Jalaluddin Rumi (Coleman Barks translation)

Into the Maelstrom

Buddhists tell a story from the early days of Buddha's ministry. A mother approached the Buddha following her husband's death. Her only human connection was her baby—who now also lay dead against her breast. She wanted the Buddha to restore this child to life. Her arms were full of embracing these deaths, leaving no room to embrace any other reality.

Buddha took compassion upon her and suggested that to be saved she must find a mustard seed from a household that had never experienced death. Searching day after day, she never found such a place. As a result, she awakened to reality, to that which is.

Trying to reverse her child's death was a natural and even admirable assertion of ego-self in the face of an unpleasant reality. Even Buddha could not change that reality. Yet even to have the possibility of awakening to reality, she needed first to surrender to what is. Upon awakening, this young mother became a disciple of the Buddha. Many years later, she was one of the first women disciples to become fully and truly enlightened.

At eighteen, my ego-self encountered the world—and lost. But in surrendering, I too attained the possibility of awakening. But it didn't begin that way.

When my father drove me to New Haven, all my clothes and possessions, except my books, fit in one large and one small suitcase. I had never been away from home for any extended period.

My father still had strong reservations about my college choice. He said the only person he ever knew to go to Yale, the smartest person he knew, flunked out his freshman year. Dad told me not to be afraid to come home when I flunked out. He shook my hand and headed home.

I determined then and there to graduate from Yale or die trying or else move to another part of the country. I was completely alone for the first time in my life. Thrilled. Terrified. Perhaps my dad was right. I had no idea what lay ahead of me. The next five years would shape me in ways I never could have imagined. I would never return to Tiverton again except for brief, infrequent visits.

Yale encouraged freshmen to arrive early to orient themselves to college life. I am not sure what algorithm they employed to choose roommates, but my quad consisted of public school kids on loans and scholarships: a white swimmer from Milwaukee, a wrestler from Puerto Rico, a Puerto Rican political revolutionary from the Bronx, and me. The two athletes arrived first for their athletic training regimens. Both having early morning training schedules, they decided to bunk together in one bedroom of our quad. The political revolutionary had chosen the bottom bunk in the other bedroom. I ended up on the top bunk in the small dark bedroom.

My bunkmate and I took an immediate dislike to each other, which only deepened as we lived together in this confined space. He dressed very primly, kept his stuff very neat, and was immaculately clean. I often felt like a somewhat dirty, white working-class slob who sometimes drank too much beer and degraded the space simply with my presence. I decided to spend my nonclassroom, nonsleeping time alone in the library. My experience with these roommates helped shape my environment at Yale.

I began Yale as a Rhode Island country bumpkin. I had never slept in a hotel, ridden a subway, train, or airplane, or eaten in a fancy restaurant (except in the kitchen). My Rhode Island accent was so heavy that students from other parts of the country would engage me in conversation just to hear me talk, then often would not understand me unless I talked really slowly. Rhode Island accents seem to have this thing about the letter *r* that amused my classmates.

Student (bringing a friend): Say something!
Me: Waht?
Student: Anything.
Me: I drink watuh from a bubahlah. And pahk the cahr in Hahvahd Yahd.

Yale offered a preregistration freshmen summer camp weekend that included canoeing, swimming, volleyball, and speakers on Yale community life. I desperately wanted to belong, so I went, even though I couldn't really afford it. Those few days were glorious. I hung out with kids from all over the world, including a lot of international students. They made fun of my heavy Rhode Island accent. Often I couldn't understand their accents either. We swapped stories. We sang, played guitar, and socialized over meals and into the night. This was the college environment everyone dreamed about. All the fun with none of the homework.

Still, I desperately missed home. Our residential college was Trumbull—a smaller, modest college built to house scholarship students. With Yale's unlimited meal plan, I gained thirty pounds that first year. Our dorm room was on the second floor of Durfee Hall, on the

Old Campus, where most freshmen lived. Our downstairs neighbors smoked marijuana from morning to night. Billows of smoke came from their room. You could get high just passing through the hallway. The dorm next to ours was Wright Hall. There was an unfortunate tradition where students passing between these two dorms would exchange cries of "Durfee sucks!" and "Wright bites!" well into the night.

Everyone seemed stressed out. The stress levels were especially enormous for poorly prepared working-class kids from mediocre public high schools. We disproportionately would not graduate in four years, if at all. Yet I decided to make the most of it. I wrote my parents that I was "busy, boggled, strung-out, overworked, overconfident, happy, and behind in most of my classes." I assured my parents and myself that "at least 80 percent of the freshmen were behind in their classes almost immediately."

A month after settling into Yale, I got a phone call from my brother David, a junior at Boston University. He invited me to a party he and his roommates were throwing on my birthday. My eighteenth birthday found me on my first train ride from New Haven to Boston. I arrived at BU's Myles Standish Hall late Saturday afternoon.

David's roommates were some of the best-dressed and best-looking guys I had ever seen. Party preparations were in full swing, so I pitched in to help. As the evening wore on, I was introduced to exotic drinks, and new guys kept arriving, but only guys. These were the most effusive and affectionate men I had ever met. I found them delightful. We talked about everything from Nietzsche to the Upanishads. These were men fully engaged with life.

I began to wonder about the absence of women at this party. David caught my eye and said, "We'll talk in the morning." The party continued well into the night. After everyone left, we cleaned up and went to bed.

The next morning, David explained how he had suspected something about his sexual orientation in high school, but it wasn't until he was at BU that he came out as gay. And now he could never go home. In 1973, New England small-town sensibilities had no place for homosexuals. Certainly the Baptist church didn't, and we suspected neither did our Baptist minister father.

David told me he had already come out to each of our three older siblings but only after they promised never to tell my mom and dad. He wanted me to keep his secret as well. Of course, I would keep his secret. It was just one of many things I would never tell my mom and dad, and how cool was that?

Exploring Romance

You meet the most extraordinary people at a place like Yale. I met some extraordinary women my freshman year. Mary, the first girl I dated, had been recruited by Yale because she was a gifted violinist. She played first violin in the Yale orchestra. Mary was also a gifted kisser. But she was much more deeply committed to her music than our relationship. We broke up quickly. Mary went on to become one of the first female conductors of a major symphony orchestra.

Sophia was in my political science class, the daughter of a Swedish diplomat at the UN. She was both brilliant and beautiful. But it took only one visit to her family's three-bedroom Park Avenue apartment to see we could never cross this chasm of expectations based on our social classes. Often she spent more money in a day than I did in any month. But I loved driving her Mercedes with diplomatic plates at very high speeds down Interstate 95 to New York City.

I started hanging out a lot with Rebekah, a friendly Lebanese woman whose parents were international diplomats. We would become close college friends, but there was no sexual chemistry there. I dated Amy, a cute blond premedical student, but she was far more interested in dating upperclassmen than in me. Erica was an attractive New England WASP in my residential college and active in the Yale Christian Fellowship. She seemed to like me, a lot, but she didn't like my friends. I was pretty sure she would not love my having a brother who was a homosexual.

I was searching with no particular common thread other than being interested in girls who were interested in me. I seemed to be the least sexually experienced person on the entire college campus, but I was determined that would not be for want of seeking experiences.

The first weekend at Yale, I met Cathy, a very smart but unstable hippie from Maine who decided to introduce me to sex, drugs, and rock 'n' roll. Her friends seemed promiscuous with both sex and drugs. Being very sexually active and experienced, she was already on the pill. Corrupting this small-town boy seemed almost a badge of honor for her. I enjoyed it immensely! We experimented. I learned things I hadn't even known there were to learn. While most freshmen lived in quads like I did, she had somehow wrangled what was commonly called an "insanity single" room her freshman year. This should have been a warning sign. But I started sleeping there with Cathy instead of my top bunk in the quad.

We got involved with the Yale Political Union, particularly its most libertarian group, the Party of the Right. Finding a group that accepted me made Yale less intimidating—even if it turned out this was not the best group for my mental health or academics. I was determined to take Yale on my own terms. To live the life of the mind. Never surrendering to the expectations of my classmates, my family of birth, or the broader culture.

In high school, I had won the WALE Radio Outstanding English Student prize, the Brown University prize for ability in English expression both written and oral, and the Claiborne Pell American History Medal. So following my freshman advisor's suggestion, I took an advanced English class: From Chaucer to Eliot. I bombed.

The prep school kids were well versed in forms of literary theory I'd never heard of. They knew how to study and when to speak up in class. I also found myself drowning in Literature of Greece and Rome, as these were not topics taught at Tiverton High School. I didn't know how to study them, what the professor wanted, or even how to ask for help. I was thickheaded and working-class enough to try figuring it out entirely on my own—and too ashamed to seek help. I was humiliated.

Yale became a contest to see what I was made of. I did well in my history and political science classes, so I chose them as my double major. By living in the library for the next several months and diligently attending all my classes, I eked out a C or better in each of my classes that first semester, at the expense of having an extracurricular life, which seemed increasingly boring.

So that winter, I started spending a lot of time with the Party of the Right, whose political philosophy centered on libertarianism and the life of the mind. These were kids who took Ayn Rand, Milton Friedman, and Friedrich Hayek very seriously. We would dress up, drink port or sherry, and have debates into the wee hours of the morning.

Someone would announce a game of Risk or a night of drinking or card playing, which could easily last all night. Many days we would begin a bridge game at lunch, which then took precedence over afternoon classes. I quickly learned, however, at some financial cost, that I was out of my league playing poker at Yale, so I gave up playing for money.

Climbing East Rock as the sun began to rise became my transcendent escape from too much anxiety and drinking. I picked my way along the path in the predawn light as the first birds awoke and began to sing. I crested the ridge just as the sun rose in the distance. The dawn rising from the fog was transcendent! I usually walked alone, though sometimes invited friends who had been up all night. The cool morning air and quiet had a gentle healing quality.

Even when I lived in the city, nature was my balm and my comforter. Half the joy of attending Yale football games was the long walk out to Yale Bowl along tree-lined city streets. At Yale, there was usually a place to be alone if a person knew how to find it, including the underground steam tunnels, so I became intimate with a new and different urban geography.

Beyond a few times smoking marijuana, I avoided drugs because they seemed to make people unfocused. Instead, I sometimes drank too much to ease my anxiety. Getting drunk regularly was messy and pretty working-class, though it came in handy when it helped me talk my way into an unpaid legal internship.

I dreamed of becoming a lawyer and a politician. Ed, the managing partner at a local law firm, was interviewing sophomores and juniors for an unpaid legal internship. I had barely begun freshman year but pestered the student taking sign-ups for interviews until she added me as a final entry at 5:00 p.m. on Friday. I went down to the law firm, arriving 4:45 p.m. The secretary was just packing up to go home. She said she thought Ed had already found his candidate. I told her I'd wait, and she went home.

I was alone in the waiting room when Ed escorted the previous student from his office. Disappointment showed on his face when he saw he had another interviewee. So I pointed out there was a bar on the first floor of his building and suggested we do the interview there. Ed bought the first round, I bought the next, and we sat and talked for hours. Ed offered me the job, claiming I was the first college kid ever to outdrink him. He stumbled off to his weekend, and I stumbled back to campus.

Through diligence and hard work, I would eventually turn that unpaid position into two years of paid legal clerk work for the firm. And it really helped me understand what it might be like to be a lawyer one day. But in the beginning, the internship was long hours for no pay.

My financial aid package with Yale required cash payments of $5,500 each year. It assumed I'd draw on my savings, do work study ten hours a week, work every summer, and receive a $1,500 contribution from my parents each year. However, I knew my parents would contribute nothing. And because of my internship at the law firm and my political activities, I hadn't done any paid work my entire freshman year. I had dug myself into what felt like a deep financial hole. I had saved enough in high school to pay for my first year of college, but now I didn't have enough left to pay for my entire sophomore year and beyond.

I hoped to earn up to $2,000 my sophomore year working at the law firm as a paid legal clerk. But even if I did that, and even if I used up the last of my savings, I would still need to net $2,000 during the summer—or I'd have to take a semester off to earn money. And if I took a semester off, I might never return to Yale.

Staying at Yale would require finding a summer job earning at least $6 per hour (equivalent to $29 per hour today) at the age of eighteen. Such jobs did not exist for teenagers in Tiverton in those days. I prayed, "Dear God, whatever job will yield $2,000 for school next year, please show me now. For this I pray, amen." God sometimes listens. But God seldom responds in the manner we expect. Truthfully, I only half expected it to work, but I was desperate.

Walking across campus about fifteen minutes later, I began to notice mimeographed signs stapled to trees: "Earn $2,000 net this summer. Come to Harkness 202." I prayed, "Thank you, God," and headed for Harkness 202. Turned out it was a job selling reference books, dictionaries, and books on New Math door to door. Training was in Nashville, Tennessee, and our territory in Houston, Texas.

I thought to myself, I couldn't sell books door to door if I tried. I had never traveled outside New England. I was sure to fail. But I had already thanked God, so I took the plunge. This small-town boy was encountering the wider world with both trepidation and hope.

Selling Books Door to Door

June found me traveling to Nashville in my manager's car along with four other rookies as we collectively took the plunge into the void. I hated it. If I failed at bookselling, I would still need to take a semester off to earn money. What if no one understood my accent?

Despite my concerns, I applied myself diligently to selling books. I kept to my schedule, working eighty hours a week, 8:00 a.m. to 9:30 p.m. Monday through Saturday. On Sundays, I learned my trade at our team meetings. I overcame my fears and anxieties, eventually becoming a decent salesman. If I could avoid a slammed door in my face, engage people in conversation, and talk really slowly and clearly, then I found people would buy books from this Yalie—and sometimes even come to like me.

Knocking on one door in a wealthier Houston neighborhood, a man answered and asked where I came from. I said Rhode Island. He turned around and yelled, "Mildred, we have a foreigner at the door!" He had never heard of Rhode Island. I couldn't persuade him it actually was one of the United States.

I developed quite a following in some working-class neighborhoods. I would keep track of the best students in the school and whether their family bought books from me. I would then refer to these students by name as I made my way from house to house.

By the end of the summer, after delivering all my books, collecting all my receipts, and paying all my bills, I had $2,700 to take back to school, even after taking my first flight home from Nashville. I was now a successful entrepreneur! My parents couldn't believe it. I couldn't believe it.

Earning my own way in a strange and alien part of the country, having a growing circle of friends, having already survived two semesters at Yale, I now felt ready for whatever the future might hold. I returned to Yale feeling like a conquering hero.

Thus began my sophomore year. To save money, I moved two blocks off campus with two of my best friends. It was a rundown house in a difficult neighborhood. Our monthly rent split three ways was $50 each, heat included. The house was furnished entirely with heavily used furniture left behind by previous students. Our landlady ran the local liquor store. She accepted rent in cash only and hadn't been inside the house in decades.

I bought a third-hand waterbed. Now Cathy and I could enjoy ourselves in my private bedroom. I focused my studies on history, political science, and philosophy. Work at the law firm was rewarding and provided much-needed cash flow, though it required conscientious attention to legal matters.

Given my experience with the Rhode Island Model Legislature, I was recruited to join Yale's team for the Connecticut Intercollegiate Student Legislature (CISL). I rose to lead the team my junior year and become Connecticut State Chairman my senior year. To get involved in local Democratic Party politics in New Haven, I formed the Yale Political Action Group, serving as its president my sophomore year and executive director my junior and senior years. This led also to my serving on the First Ward Democratic Committee my sophomore and junior years.

New Haven Democratic Party politics were notoriously corrupt. When I registered to vote from my new address, I discovered sixty people were registered from this rundown three-bedroom house. Many of their names matched those in the local cemetery. But my thriving in student and local politics helped offset any feelings of inadequacy in academics.

My political activities at CISL, as president of the Yale Political Action Group, and as a member of the First Ward Democratic Committee, consumed what little free time I had, but they were a major source of my growing self-esteem. I pretty much gave up drinking entirely. I didn't have the time or interest for the hangovers that resulted.

I continued to get up every Sunday morning and walk across the campus to attend church. Cathy had introduced me to sex, so to make an honest woman of her, to please my parents and hers, and to reconcile my sense of morality, I proposed to her that fall. She accepted. We spent that Christmas break in Maine meeting her parents, who seemed very nice and somewhat relieved she had met a nice boy. We went to Tiverton to spend Easter with my parents. I was taking on new responsibilities.

Living among the poverty of New Haven's inner city, however, was never easy for this small-town white kid. Many of the poorest parts of New Haven's inner city were within a mile of the Yale campus, sometimes running right up to the campus gates. The poverty and despair in these largely black inner-city neighborhoods were beyond my comprehension.

It was my first experience of seeing the vacant stares of drugged-out, burnt-out people seemingly living without hope. When we returned to our rented house on Howe Street after one summer away selling books, we found bullet holes in our front door. Our landlady reassured us that it had been a gang shooting, so we had nothing to fear, unless we somehow crossed the gang.

This poverty and despair, especially among poor families of color living in 1970s virtual inner-city ghettoes, seemed so much more debilitating than my white New England small-town poverty. Many black people appeared trapped by their circumstances, with no real options for building a satisfactory life, and no way out of their despair. I understood that my coming to Yale represented an enormous privilege most people would never experience. I would help if I could from my privileged place. Yet I could not find a suitable way to connect or make any meaningful difference in their lives.

The fall of 1974, I became a Big Brother to a ten-year-old inner-city boy who himself had never been to a movie or a play, eaten out in a restaurant, or been anywhere other than New Haven. I was determined to make a difference for someone as naïve as I had been at his age. I took him to museums and movies and out for meals, just being an older friend and ally. We mostly just hung out together. I could at least make this small difference.

One night that winter, I was walking with a classmate in one of New Haven's poorer neighborhoods when four black teenagers pulled over and jumped out of their car. They demanded our watches and our wallets. My classmate removed her watch from her wrist and handed it to them, along with her purse. I told them I was too poor to own a watch or even a wallet. The largest of these four teenagers shouted at me nervously not to be messing with them. I just shrugged. They looked at one another, then jumped back in their car and drove away.

My friend couldn't understand how I had lied under such circumstances. My watch was on my wrist and my wallet was in my jeans pocket. The teenagers seemed as scared as me, but I couldn't let them rob me. I was not going to be a victim.

I spent the next summer selling books door to door in Duncan, Oklahoma, a town about the same size and with the same economic demographics as Tiverton, but racially segregated. I was told, to my disbelief, that no Native American or African American had ever stayed in town overnight. Any nonwhite remaining in this small town after dark was, by law, considered a vagrant and arrested by the police. In order to succeed that summer, I was financially dependent upon the townspeople's goodwill and book purchases, but I detested their racism.

All the kids in town went to the same public high school. I drove my beat-up, rusted Toyota Corolla I had purchased for $300. I worked hard to develop a following to boost my sales. By the end of the summer, I came to be liked by most of the kids, many of their parents, and many local business owners.

They learned to understand my accent. I learned to love country western music and cowboy boots. I thrived in the most racist place I have ever lived yet never told them of my true feelings. I decided to change what I could, accept what I could not change, and to love all people, no matter how flawed. The spiritual discipline of surrender allowed me to make my way, surviving and then thriving in all circumstances.

I learned how to fit in. Few people complained about my knocking at their doors too early in the morning or too late into the night. Everyone knew that in the heat of the day, it could well go over 100 degrees. Even dogs went looking for shade.

I was the smart, friendly, dependable, and ambitious kid every parent in town wanted his or her son to be or daughter to marry. I was shocked at the low levels of education, the lack of aspirations, and the young age at which couples married in rural Oklahoma. I met one nice Christian girl of fifteen who already had two babies from two different husbands but was now getting divorced from her second husband because he beat her. This was a summer of culture shock.

I returned to school with new confidence and over $4,000 after paying all my expenses. I also returned with growing doubts about being a lawyer or politician. I felt there might be something more significant to do with my life, but life would unfold. I knew with God's help, I could always find my way as long as I willingly surrendered to divine mystery.

Pain and Heartbreak

Cathy and I had been apart all summer. We tried to resume where we'd left off. Though by now, her drinking, partying, and staying up at all hours—often with heavy drug users I neither knew nor wanted to get to know—changed our relationship.

Along with my normal course load, I enrolled in Edmund Morgan's American History seminar, which required reading one thousand pages a week in primary sources and summarizing them in a weekly ten-page paper.

I also plunged back in at the law firm. I was delighted when they closed the office one day and bought the entire office tickets to Bob Dylan's Rolling Thunder tour. My first live rock 'n' roll concert! I was less impressed, though, when invited to a cocktail party with defense attorneys, prosecutors, and judges, where marijuana was freely shared. The same people who convicted and sentenced New Haven's poor people for marijuana possession were smoking it among colleagues.

I didn't want to be racist like the folks I lived with that summer or hypocritical like the legal professionals seemed to be in New Haven. I needed to find my own basis of integrity, independent of the surrounding culture, in order to feel good about my role in life as a moral being.

After the late-1960s student riots, the university had installed locked riot gates at its residential colleges. Cathy's room was in Morse College, which had an enormous entrance, to which they had added a large spiked gate to be closed only in times of riots. Once triggered, it could be opened only by the college master or campus police.

One rainy night, I was heading home from a party at Morse, but someone had found a way to trigger the riot gates, locking us in for the night. I never liked limitations. Without thinking of consequences,

I climbed the gate and jumped over. But my foot slipped on the wet gate, and I fell. I tore the palm of my right hand wide open on one of the spikes, severing a nerve and pulling a tendon completely out of my hand. I never felt such sheer pain. I was in shock but knew enough to get campus police to take me to the emergency room.

After many days of pain and agony and many sleepless nights, I had reconstructive surgery at Yale New Haven Hospital. The orthopedic specialist sewed my hand back together, but I would be in pain and lose the function of my right hand for months. It took many years for the nerve to grow back, but the tendon never fully did. I could not type using my right hand. So I was forced to drop Morgan's intensive, even though I had loved that class. I was miserable and downcast, and I began drinking way too much.

Cathy and I started having enormous fights. We were making each other miserable. After a fight one Saturday night at my place, Cathy was drunk, so I left to sleep on Rebekah's couch. Returning early Sunday morning to get my suit for church, I found Cathy having sex in my bed with one of our friends from the Party of the Right. I hated her from that moment. I have never come so close to wanting to kill somebody, either her or him or both. Fortunately, I didn't own a gun.

We broke off our engagement. I entered a deep depression, struggling mightily to save my career at Yale. The future had never looked so dark. Cathy had broken my heart. All my plans and dreams were gone. I was empty. In despair.

I began to seriously examine what kind of person I was or could be. I wouldn't date for months and then always cautiously, never again putting my broken heart at risk. I got more heavily involved in my political commitments, even though they didn't help my self-esteem as they once had. I worked through the pain and agony of my crippled hand to attempt to complete all my various coursework.

Through pain and despair, I was learning to surrender my ego-self and preconceived notions of control. I immersed myself in my classes, trying desperately to get on schedule to graduate in four years. I spent most of my free time in the stacks of Sterling Library, exploring the emerging spiritual side of my nature. I still sought to live my life in Technicolor and transcendence, even if it didn't feel real.

A good friend suggested I try Transcendental Meditation (TM). TM was popular at Yale, as was the Hare Krishna path of adoration and the Bhagavad Gita. I tried TM for months, but these paths didn't seem to take me where I needed to go. Chanting, especially in public, made me feel silly. Sitting meditation, even following Maharishi Mahesh Yogi, felt like an exercise in futility. I could sit for twenty minutes—or an hour—and my heart rate would decrease, my relaxation response would kick in, but it wouldn't last. I would end up simply feeling achy, sore, and bored.

Mahayana Buddhist teachings have always made sense to me as a reformation of ancient Hinduism, especially the path of knowledge—awakening through coming to understand the true nature of reality. This worked for me, but I couldn't hold onto this state of reality. I had a similar experience with the ancient Chinese teachings about the Tao, "the Way," which insist our minds are capable of perceiving the divine mystery. I was not yet ready to live in that state of being, but the necessary seeds had now been planted for later cultivation and fruition.

Then there was this Catholic girl from one of the Connecticut colleges. She was active in the CISL. She said she was fascinated with the tantric sexual exercises of Hinduism. I started memorizing all the sexual positions in the Kama Sutra. I never mastered any of them properly, but for the first time, especially sexually, I was in the role of spiritual teacher. Tantric sex empowers the feminine while balancing masculine powers. She invited me to escort her to her junior prom and to spend the night at her dorm. We had to be very quiet, as her roommate was sleeping in the same room.

A few weeks later, Yale was hosting CISL's annual gathering, and she was a delegate from her college. As the head of Yale's delegation, I had a very prominent role. So I invited her to stay with me in my house off campus. This was not love but simply hedonistic sexual experimentation, exploring the divine mystery through physical ecstasy, the yin and yang of sex. Yet I was hungry for deeper meaning.

I needed to find a spiritual path. Like many college students, I often fell into deeply spiritual conversations about what gives life meaning and worth. These sexual exercises, deeply intertwined with another human being, brought at least momentary joy but did not lessen my burden going forward. One of my friends was in Skull and Bones, the Yale secret society. He introduced me to the concept of examining your life, preferably in a circle of supportive friends, to discern what the universe is calling you toward. I discovered that as an extrovert, I best understood my experiences and feelings when explaining them to friends.

I found a group of Quakers happy to teach me their contemplative form of discernment. I began again to attend Sunday morning worship in the Yale Chapel, becoming one of their most reliable student participants. A joyful spiritual seeker, I said *yes* to every spiritual path as long as it had heart and could help me become the person I dreamed of being.

Joys and sorrows are woven fine together. I knew from my spiritual reading and practices that we often grow closer to God during the most difficult passages of our lives. I was beginning to feel like a mystic in my heart as well as in my head, and this brought comfort in these stressful times.

Salvation

Just before school ended, I met a remarkable woman who attracted me immediately. Loretta sparked something in me, making me want to be my best self for her, and I didn't even know her yet. She was a Chinese American freshman, running for treasurer of the Yale Political Union. She was lively, generous, a natural debater, and quite lovely.

Her parents were highly educated Chinese immigrants. Loretta thought of herself as a California girl, yet had her mother's hardheaded Shanghai commercial acumen. She was running against a rather annoying, squeaky-voiced liberal. Loretta was fearless, having been a California extemporaneous debater. She was articulate and sincere, with a strong sense of character. She was also quite attractive and full of life!

When she spoke to the Party of the Right caucus, she won my heart. She was unlike any girl I had ever met. This was the kind of person one could build a life with. I wanted to be my best self in order to catch her attention and win her affection. When she left the caucus, I spoke boldly on her behalf. My rhetoric perhaps swung some votes her way. She won the election easily. I then asked her out on a date, but she had other plans, so we went our separate ways for the summer. I am sure she didn't think any further about me, but I sure thought of her.

That summer, I led a team of book salesmen in Houston, Texas, where my personal sales doubled again. My customers introduced me to southwestern Christian pop theology, which centered on surrendering oneself to Jesus or some form of a higher power. This theology was later captured brilliantly in Carrie Underwood's popular 2005 crossover Christian pop hit "Jesus, Take the Wheel." I took home $9,000 after expenses, making me the thirteenth highest-paid summer salesperson at the Southwestern Company.

That summer, however, I also learned my former tantric sex partner was pregnant. We hadn't used or even thought about birth control. She was in despair. She wanted me either to marry her or, preferably, pay for her abortion.

I was devastated. I could neither imagine ending this emergent life nor committing my life to someone who didn't love me. This had never been about love. But there didn't appear to be any other options. So I paid for her abortion.

I was humbled and forever changed by these consequences of my thoughtless actions. I would never think about sex, drugs, or careless activities the same way again. I wanted to be a better person. I was now seeking salvation, returning to God as the prodigal son.

There is no salvation without surrender. From now on, my spiritual aspirations, rather than my lusts and desires, would lead me. *Jesus, take the wheel.* Failure is painful, especially to our sense of identity, but from every failure something new can emerge. I began the long, slow spiritual process of learning to surrender myself to life and thereby find deeper meaning.

I entered my senior year determined to get serious about academics, graduate from Yale on time, be accepted into law school, and get on with my life. However, life seldom follows our plan. My life would take an entirely different path.

I planned my fall schedule with only three classes in order to focus on my required departmental essay in history. I hadn't learned how to research and write such a large project. My right hand was still healing, which made typing for long hours painful and difficult. I wanted to research and write about how Admiral Perry's 1853 approach to opening Japan had contributed to the fall of the Tokugawa shogunate and led to the rise of the xenophobic Japanese military leaders who would in 1941 attack Pearl Harbor. This paper would demonstrate that US military entanglements are often the results of our own earlier military actions. My senior project had grown out of a discussion we had in my Games Nations Play class that spring.

Unfortunately, the professor who had encouraged me in this topic received an offer to spend the 1976–77 academic year in Tokyo as a visiting professor. I was randomly reassigned a reader for my thesis, an assistant professor who was also dean of Morse College, which happened to be both Cathy's and Loretta's residential college.

Leading up to the November 1976 presidential election, I was state chairman of the CISL, executive director of the Yale Political Action Group, and heavily involved in New Haven Democratic Party politics. This felt like the most important presidential election of my lifetime. A chance to fight government corruption and violence.

Richard Nixon had resigned in disgrace two years before, and now there was a chance to elect Democrat Jimmy Carter as our next president. We thought it might set the country's direction for the next decade and beyond. Yet Connecticut was leaning toward Republican

Gerald Ford. With all the spare time I could muster, I campaigned for Carter in New Haven's first ward. I counted it a personal victory when he won the presidency.

It seemed everywhere I went on campus, Loretta was there: walking between classes, at the library or dining halls. Loretta had her own group of friends who did not overlap at all with my political friends. I was that provincial Rhode Island working-class kid who didn't really fit into Yale culture. I aspired to being worthy of Loretta's love, but I needed to get Loretta's attention to have any hope of exploring a relationship with her.

So I asked her and one of her friends out for coffee. We were all coming from a Yale Political Union meeting where cartoonist Garry Trudeau was the key speaker. They ignored me completely and talked only about Garry Trudeau the whole time.

Finally came Halloween, with parties happening all over campus. The most popular was at the Yale president's house, way up Hillhouse Avenue. I offered that I had a car on campus, so instead of the president's party, we could go to Lighthouse Point beach just outside New Haven and watch the moon come up. Being a California girl and having traveled only by foot around urban parts of New Haven, Loretta was surprised that New Haven had such a beach. She readily accepted my offer to watch the moon rise.

The night was glorious and clear. The moon three-quarters full. We talked for hours about our families of origin, our deepest joys and fears, the presidential election, and so much more. By the time I drove her home, we were dating, and I had found new purpose for my life.

Six weeks later, we moved in together at my house off campus. I was full of joy! I have never loved anyone the way I loved Loretta. Even though there were many aspects of this Chinese California girl that were beyond my understanding, I wanted to spend all my time with her. And there were many aspects of me she didn't understand, such as my white working-class culture, yet Loretta opened her heart to me and loved just being with me. We had our share of disagreements and misunderstandings, but I was my happy self again.

We studied together, ate together, and slept together. (Loretta went on birth control.) It seemed so right. In the midst of my despair, on a cold dark night, I had finally found my soul mate. I would surrender my independent being and ego-self for such a love. My love for Loretta would trigger my second spiritual awakening. By January, I was reducing my political activities and aspirations as well as my hours at the law firm in order to spend more time with Loretta.

There were significant barriers to our long-term relationship: I was white working-class, and she was the daughter of highly educated Chinese immigrants. I was a swamp Yankee, and she was a California girl. I was quite religious, and she was a secular humanist. When Loretta and I grew up, whites dating Asians was strongly discouraged.

Until 1967 such marriages had even been legally prohibited in large parts of the United States. The laws had changed after a Supreme Court ruling, but when we began dating such marriages were still extremely rare, barely more than 1 percent of marriages, and the majority of Americans were morally opposed to such relationships. There was always an interracial backdrop to our love relationship, but our love would transcend all barriers.

My friends, particularly those who had seen Cathy break my heart, could readily see how good Loretta was for me. Loretta had a multiculturally diverse group of friends, most of whom accepted us as a couple, more or less. She introduced me to the Yale Asian parties. These were far more interesting to me than the typical upper-class, WASP-dominated parties or even the spirited Party of the Right gatherings.

Not all her friends, though, were as convinced this white guy would be good for her. Loretta was an honor student with an A- average, while I struggled to maintain a B- average. Her dean, my newly assigned senior-essay advisor, didn't think much of my scholarship. She gave me an incomplete for the fall semester's work on my essay.

So to graduate in May 1977, I had five months to complete four political science classes and two history classes, plus completely rewrite my departmental essay. I got serious. Studied. Went to classes. Managed my anxiety by spending more time with Loretta.

I took Loretta home to meet my parents with some trepidation at spring break. The year before, I had stopped home with three Yale friends, one of whom was a black woman. My mother had taken me aside and advised me not to consider dating that woman—she said for the sake of the mixed-race kids that might result. Her discomfort was clear. I wondered if my mother would feel the same discomfort about my dating Loretta. As it turned out, I needn't have worried. Loretta won my parents' hearts nearly as fast as she had won mine.

Of course, seeing the squalor in which I had been raised, with sharp nails protruding from open walls in the stairway, Loretta began to understand why I was such an indifferent housekeeper. To this day, my awareness of my living conditions is very low, nearly nonexistent. The unkempt condition of our shared home will almost always bother Loretta long before I actually even notice it. Yet we have learned to accept this as differences in our upbringing.

After that visit with my parents, we drove back to campus with our housemate, Josh, in snowy and icy conditions. Suddenly my car went into a skid on the highway. I tried to brake and steer us through the skid, but we went up over a snowbank and a guardrail. I closed my eyes, opened my heart, and let Jesus take the wheel. The car sailed through the air, then lightly flipped over on its roof before flipping again and landing on all four wheels in the median strip.

It happened so fast. It seemed improbable that we weren't seriously injured. A witness pulled over to say he wouldn't have believed it if he hadn't seen it. We said a silent prayer of thanksgiving. The front windshield was cracked, but the car was drivable. Shaken, we continued on to New Haven.

God seemed to be watching over us. Good fortune seemed to be following us, as if we had come together to do something important in this life. Or were simply receiving grace or serendipity, or we were as blessed as we appeared to be, but for me it was salvation.

Doing Better Together

With this blessing, we faced the ultimate test to our socially unacceptable relationship. When Loretta's mom came to visit, she asked whether we were sleeping together, and Loretta confessed. Even though Loretta was the third daughter of four, she was the first to live with a guy out of marriage, much less a white guy. Loretta's mother was extremely displeased. But Loretta loved me no matter what, and I loved her. We still had the full support of my family, my friends, and many of hers, and how our relationship transformed us would win over the rest in time.

We survived negative societal attitudes with our relationship intact. We knew that together we could survive anything—which turned out to be a good thing, because despite my earning solid Bs on my six classes that semester, Loretta's dean still flunked my departmental essay. In order to graduate, I would need to stay in New Haven one more year to rewrite my essay. I would surrender to even this if it meant a life built around loving Loretta.

Loretta came with me to sell books that summer in Knoxville, Tennessee. I was finally the organizational manager of a fairly large crew of salespeople from Yale. It was one of the most racially and socioeconomically diverse student sales groups in the history of the Southwestern Company. We included fifth-generation upper-crust WASP Yalies, first-generation inner-city black Yalies, and everything Yalie in between.

Loretta was a fabulous salesperson, selling more than I had in my first two summers combined. I had my most successful summer yet. We were falling ever more deeply in love. And we learned something important about our working styles that has stayed with us throughout our lives: Loretta is happiest and most productive when she works by herself.

Loretta is wonderful at leading others, but she prefers to do her work herself. I, on the other hand, thrive when managing others. I am fine as an individual salesperson but never enjoy it as much or feel as productive as when leading others by example to improve their own results. We each have our preferred comfort zone.

I would eventually come to understand that my working style is basically my personality type, which is Enneagram Seven. I can be overly idealistic, fixated on planning and avoiding pain through sublimation. But I am also outgoing and chatty, frequently using storytelling to find meaning and taking great joy from life just as it is.

In *Archetypes of the Enneagram*, Susan Rhodes says, "Sevens are also mentally quick, full of ideas, and up for a good time. They are naturally enthusiastic about life and adaptable to changing circumstances." That sounds like me. My Jungian archetype seems to be the Chinese immortal Budai, or Putai, a joyous old soul who has come to be known in the West as the Laughing Buddha. He is often a wise fool or trickster figure.

In my subsequent spiritual adventuring, I would discover this is a rare personality type among spiritual seekers, often depicted as a rogue wisdom teacher, with a long scandalous history in many religious traditions. Sufis might classify Shams of Tabriz, Rumi's soul mate, as an example of this archetype. Chinese Taoists might think of the wandering at ease of Chuang Tzu as opposed to the teachings of Lao Tzu. In Judaism, perhaps King David as opposed to Moses. I set forth on my distinctive spiritual path in the company of prophets, disreputable rogues, and wisdom teachers, as a Laughing Buddha type.

As we returned to campus—Loretta for her junior year, me for revising my senior essay—we fell into an idyllic pattern of life. When Loretta went to class, I would head to the Sterling Library.

As it turned out, flunking my senior essay proved fortuitous. It led to one of the best years of my life. I started to read widely through the stacks, feeling as if I had been given a great gift. Never again would I have such ready access to a world-class library and all day to read. I was in heaven.

I began reading world histories, especially from non-American perspectives. Then I moved deeper into political economy, which led me to philosophy and a broader study of the nature of reality, or I should say consensus realities. These eventually led me into studying world religions, not merely from a Western Christian perspective but through the perspective described by participants, especially the mystics, in each of the major religious traditions.

I began to understand and appreciate the varieties of Christian religious experiences—and the enormous diversity of beliefs, yet each with its pronounced profession of orthodox Christian faith. I studied the discourses between the Taoists and the Confucians, explored the distinctions between Theravada and Mahayana Buddhism, examined the historical differences between the Sunni and Shia branches of Islam, and eagerly read the Sufi mystics of the Middle Ages.

I was reading ancient manuscripts, many dating from the eighteenth or nineteenth centuries. Deep in the stacks, some had not been checked out of the library in a hundred years. I checked out these beautiful old books and read them under shade trees.

Much to my amusement, when I returned the books, the Sterling staff would often send them off to the Beinecke Rare Book & Manuscript Library rather than return them to the stacks. The next time anyone wanted to read these books, they would need to wear gloves and turn them on a book stand. So my self-directed reading not only gave me a broad education but also helped unearth Yale's rare old books.

I would never again feel less educated than prep school kids or anyone else. I began to have a scholarly understanding of life. Reading widely allowed serendipity to guide me through one of the world's great libraries. I began to understand multiple perspectives and realities across geographical space and time.

Rereading my senior essay after all these decades, Loretta's dean was right to flunk me. My writing and perspective were sloppy and immature. When my original professor returned from Tokyo, he looked at my earlier drafts but also at how I was spending my time these days immersed in reading. He recommended I accept a D on my senior essay in order to graduate. A simple rewrite addressing the specific comments made on earlier drafts would be more than sufficient. That would free me to focus on my self-education and still be considered as Yale class of 1977 graduating in May 1978.

That left only the decision of what to do after Yale. Loretta saw a posting for the MBA program at Harvard Business School (HBS). I had never considered a business degree. I don't think I had ever even met a Harvard MBA. But I went to the session, and they seemed like nice people. Perhaps an MBA would give me the wherewithal to achieve all my dreams. The program looked quite interesting and challenging.

So I took the Graduate Management Admission Test (GMAT) and miraculously aced it. Grounded in God, I prayed about it and decided to trust God's grace. I applied only to Harvard. Fortunately, I didn't know at the time how rare it was for HBS to accept anyone without full-time work experience directly from college, especially someone with such a low grade point average. Sometimes ignorance is bliss. By Christmas, they had accepted me, and my path was becoming clear. I was going to succeed in business! It looked as if this would solve my problem of being poor.

I asked Loretta to marry me, and she accepted. Our joy was even greater now than before. We planned our wedding for March of 1979 during my one week off for spring break at HBS.

That spring of 1978, when I was twenty-two and Loretta was twenty, was among the happiest of our lives. The earth was awakening with new flowering blossoms sharing our joy. Our relationship was blossoming as well. I often walked Loretta to her class, then read or took a long walk around New Haven just to contemplate and meditate gratefully on my incredible life. I'd arrive back in time to walk her home after class. Young love is blissful.

That final summer, we took an even larger and more racially diverse group of Yalies to sell books in Birmingham, Alabama. We earned enough money that summer to pay off most of my college debt before heading off to HBS.

Though one traumatic experience that summer still haunts me. Loretta had bought an old green Chevy so she could get around Birmingham, where there was little public transportation.

After a Sunday sales meeting, Loretta rode in my car while two Asian American and two African American guys from our team drove her car just ahead of us. Suddenly three police cars came screaming in with sirens wailing. They surrounded Loretta's car with guns drawn. We pulled my car up behind the third police car and jumped out to see what was happening. The nervous police officer threatened to shoot us if we came any closer.

I had always been able to talk to the police. It seems they had received an all-points bulletin to be on the lookout for two young black men in a green Chevy, potentially armed and dangerous, who had robbed a store a few counties away. As my heart beat frantically in my chest, I convinced the police officers that these four young guys were friends of ours, driving my girlfriend's car, and that we had been together all day at a sales meeting.

I explained we were all Yale college students, working together for the summer. After the police checked our Yale IDs, they apologized and left. Our friends were convinced our intervention saved them from wrongful arrest—and in the Deep South of the 1970s, perhaps even saved their lives.

Harvard Business School

To save money, I rented a room in a boarding house with other impoverished Harvard graduate students in Allston, about six blocks from campus. Loretta arranged her classes so she could get all her work done between Monday and Thursday, leaving her free to drive up to join me in my Friday afternoon classes and then have the weekend together.

Of course, studying with the business elite caused some cognitive dissonance with my small-town, working-class worldview. These people assumed a high level of privilege and prestige setting them apart from average people. I abhorred yet also lusted after such status. I wanted to be like them. But as a person of faith, I also really wanted to help make the world a better place for the poor and oppressed. As Jesus taught, "whatever you did for the least of these, you did for me."

Walking to classes, I always passed a poor housing project at the edge of campus. One snowy evening, black kids were out, throwing snowballs at passing cars. As I walked past with my case notes and brief-case, I became the target of their snowballs, of their anger. Soon I was being pelted with ice and rocks as well. I responded in anger, swing-ing my hard briefcase at them as they taunted and targeted me, which only made it worse. Finally I ran off to campus, where some classmates helped me clean my open wounds and bruises. I was not seriously hurt but shaken by their anger at me and by my reciprocal anger at them. How could I make sense of this?

My older brother Donald was studying socialist economics in the PhD program at the New School for Social Research in New York City. We had some interesting discussions about the morality of capitalist economics and labor—the very idea of deserved and undeserved privi-lege, who gets to decide, and what about those who don't have enough. These would be lifelong questions for me and would help shape the busi-ness executive and person I would become. I was learning to thrive in the world while helping to imagine and create the world that could be.

In each class, we were graded on a curve, with 80 percent receiving Satisfactory, the top 10 percent receiving Excellent, and the bottom 10 percent receiving Unsatisfactory grades. Any student who received most-ly Unsatisfactory grades "hit the screen" and was dropped from the pro-gram. Everyone wanted to avoid hitting the screen, but there was a much smaller group of us who aspired to be the best. Any student who received mostly Excellent grades would be in contention for highest honors. The Baker Scholars were roughly the top 5 percent of all students.

I thrived on competition. I was always ready for any challenge! We formed a small study group to improve our prospects of succeeding at HBS. Between my case preparation, my classes, and my study group, I ate, breathed, and lived business-school cases nonstop Monday through Friday.

Half our grade was based on class participation. This was an environment in which I could really shine. Of course, I had learned to build intellectual arguments during our Sunday dinner discussions growing up. With the help of my study group and my own preparation, I always had an answer for any issue. The professors usually accepted my answers as reasonable, partly because I was so confident and partly because our study group supported one another in class.

Thanks to all this hard work and preparation, I received highest honors. This was an inflection point in my life. I would never be poor again.

When Loretta finished Yale in December, we moved into a furnished basement studio apartment in Allston. This was the cheapest place we could find. Loretta started looking for a job. Given her honors degree from Yale and her proven sales ability, she quickly found a job paying $14,000 a year (equivalent to $45,000 today) as a group-insurance sale representative for Prudential.

That March, we married in a small ceremony at First Baptist in Boston. We catered it ourselves to keep costs low, and my dad co-officiated. Our wedding started late, as my father's car broke down as they drove up from Rhode Island. Yet nothing could mar the joy of that day. Our friends from Yale and HBS were there to help us celebrate. Loretta's parents hosted a Chinese banquet for us at a restaurant in Lexington. We were still poor but were heading toward prosperity. Marrying Loretta was my salvation in so many different ways.

I desperately wanted to start seeing the world, but I still had a problem with my pronounced accent and poor knowledge of other languages. At Tiverton High School, I had studied French for three years with a teacher of Portuguese descent. I could read French somewhat, but the effect of my teacher's pronunciation combined with my Rhode Island accent made my spoken French incomprehensible.

One of my best friends at HBS was Martin, a French count whose family lived in Paris. He invited me to stay with his family in Paris for a week before starting my summer job between my two HBS years. This was a wonderful chance to learn more about the world.

He picked me up at the Charles de Gaulle Airport in his Aston Martin and we sped away. I felt like a country bumpkin all over again as we navigated the streets of Paris and turned into the courtyard of his family's mansion, which occupied an entire city block overlooking the Seine.

He threw a big party to introduce me, his American friend, to his friends who seemed to me to be European sophisticates. They wore beautiful clothes and had an air of sophistication and charm I couldn't imagine achieving. They talked of country estates, ski trips in the Alps, and months spent on the French Riviera, all fantastically new for me. Later, we wandered through the Sorbonne and the Louvre with these friends, and each seemed to have a favorite work of art.

Everyone appeared to be at least trilingual—except this poor provincial American. Since childhood, I had traversed great chasms of identity, but I was beginning to discover how much farther I had yet to go.

When walking Les Champs-Elysées alone, I noticed a sign offering all the chocolate mousse one could eat for about $5. I love chocolate mousse. So I consumed five bowls and watched as the shopkeeper took the sign from his window. I am afraid the French weren't ready for the insatiable appetite of this small-town American.

For me, sleeping in a count's chateau, talking to my internationally sophisticated friends, and walking Les Champs-Elysées were all delightful treats. This was the good life I wanted but never imagined possible.

Bain & Company

I enjoyed doing market research that summer at a data management company. During my second year at HBS, I began looking for a post-graduation job. With my first-year honors and the rapid growth of the strategy-consulting industry, I garnered interviews with the three leading firms: Bain, Boston Consulting Group, and McKinsey. Bain made me an offer at $40,000 a year (equal to $120,000 today), twice what manufacturing firms offered. This was a lot of money for a twenty-four-year-old, small-town, working-class kid.

They also gave me a $5,000 signing bonus on the condition I used it to take on the look of an upper-class WASP. The partner told me to go to Brooks Brothers to buy blue pinstripe and gray flannel suits, to the Custom Shop to have white shirts tailor-made to my build, to Louis's for red silk ties from France, and to Church's to buy English black oxford leather shoes. He told me how to cut my hair and to shower every morning, which would have been inconceivable in my working-class childhood home with twelve family members and only three showers. He also taught me how to present a certain stiffness and reserve in conversation. This was an American social class makeover.

I took to it with the same enthusiasm as I did everything else.

Two or three years earlier, I might have angrily objected to this subjugation of my small-town, working-class self. I was proud of my heritage. However, this $5,000 makeover paved my entry into 1980s Fortune 500 boardrooms, so I was eager to comply. I surrendered my arrogant sense of self for the opportunities it brought.

Loretta pointed out it was easier for me to pass as an educated upper-class WASP than it was for most of her friends. Neither of us recognized then that my mother came from a long line of educated WASPs and had grown up as one herself. How many of my class struggles were actually just in my own head? How much had my sense of identity shaped who I could become? By my early twenties, in under four years, I had passed through a maelstrom and been transformed. I was saved by the love of a down-to-earth California girl. We would go on to have incredible adventures together.

With Bain's offer letter in hand and Loretta's W-2 to show her income, we went to the bank to prequalify for a mortgage. We bought a house with three bedrooms and two and a half baths on an acre and a half in Framingham, Massachusetts, for $86,000. We borrowed 80 percent from the bank and the rest from Loretta's sister and our HBS friends. It was pure joy! The first night in our new house, Loretta and I went out on the front lawn following dinner and did a happy dance of joy and thanksgiving.

We commuted to Boston together each weekday. We worked on the house and yard many weekends. I still recall those first years of our marriage as among the happiest in my life.

At twenty-four, I was so excited about starting at Bain that I barely slept the night before my first day. With butterflies fluttering, I couldn't stomach my breakfast, so Loretta made me some herbal tea, wished me good luck, and dropped me off as she went to her office.

I was about to start my dream job, but I was worried they may have made a mistake in hiring me. What did a small-town, working-class kid understand about international business? Bain had hired me straight out of HBS with no experience working for large corporations. Even dressed in a starched white shirt, a tailored blue suit, and the red tie of a strategy consultant, I was scared to death.

I worried they would take me aside to explain that my job offer, signed by Bill Bain, was a clerical error—that they hadn't really hired me. I was afraid they would quickly discover I lacked the work experience to do this job, even though that had been clear on my resume. I was also afraid they could, reasonably, decide I was too young or too unsophisticated to command the respect the job required.

I had been instructed to arrive at Bain's headquarters in Faneuil Hall Marketplace at 8:30 a.m. Marking the western edge of Boston's financial district, Faneuil Hall Marketplace is a series of interconnected brick buildings with shops on the first floors and offices above. It surrounds tourist shops and a food court. I was anxious not to risk arriving late, so instead I found myself at the entrance to their building around 7:45 a.m.

Now I was afraid this was too early, so I walked several times around the block to burn off some time and nervous energy. The morning was cool, but in my nervousness, I was sweating profusely. My starched white shirt was already damp against my back. My newly purchased black oxford dress shoes were stiff, and my feet began to ache. I still couldn't get my stomach to quiet down, so I drank more coffee.

By 8:15 a.m., I decided it was now an appropriate time to report to the receptionist at the front desk. She asked me to be seated, and I waited another twenty minutes for someone to come greet me. The whole time, I flipped through the *Wall Street Journal* and various magazines on the table in front of me, trying to look busy but unable to focus on the words on the page.

Finally, a sharply dressed, sophisticated-looking fellow perhaps two to three years older than me introduced himself as my manager. He took me through a labyrinth of corridors to my desk. My desk faced a brick wall at one end of a large room that housed six consultants grouped around two secretaries.

In 1980, Bain's headquarters was a hodgepodge of work areas, partners' offices, and conference rooms spread across two different floors of three interconnected buildings. At first sight, the walls and corridors seemed to go on forever in a completely random pattern. I was not sure I could find my way back to the receptionist, much less ever locate my desk again if I did. Everyone seemed friendly enough, but I didn't want to appear obtuse by asking any questions.

Over the course of the morning, I was introduced to a partner, my manager, and two consultants with whom I would be working. It was immediately apparent this was no place for the meek. People talked over one another, interrupting one another's ideas and intellectually competing to show who was the brightest. It seemed intellectual arrogance and quick wits were the preferred communication style.

I began to relax. My older siblings had long ago taught me how to impress with wit and intellectual displays. Competing in family dinner discussions with four older siblings—three of whom would go on to earn PhDs and teach at the college level—prepared me for such competitions. My younger siblings Pat and Steve had been prepared in the same way, helping them to earn PhDs and tenured positions in academia.

Through the case method, HBS had finely honed these skills for me as well. Success required only preparation, ally building, quick wits, and supreme confidence. In such a setting, I could dazzle! My life, thus far, had prepared me for this new role.

By lunchtime, I was starved, exhausted, frazzled, and thoroughly disoriented—but also a little less nervous because no one had yet questioned my right to be here. My manager offered to take me to lunch, and I gratefully accepted. I could easily consume a steak or perhaps a large fried chicken dinner.

As we came down to the now-bustling food court, I was amazed at the wide variety of lunch options. My manager stopped before a counter and purchased a banana and yogurt, which he explained was his usual lunch. He then watched to see what my choices would be. Obviously, efficiency was more important than quality of experience. I agreed to eat the same.

He next explained he usually ate at his desk to save time, but because it was such a beautiful day, we opted to sit on a park bench outside. The banana was underripe. I had never eaten yogurt before. It was watery and lumpy, tasting like milk gone sour. Did people willingly eat yogurt?

I survived lunch, but I was sick to my stomach a mere ten minutes after we returned to work. I threw up in the bathroom about an hour later.

By the end of the afternoon, however, I was nearly certain I could accomplish what they expected of me. The intellectual duels and critiques were actually kind of fun. It was brilliance as a competitive sport. I had the skills to do this kind of work. I knew I might grow to be good at it.

I left the office around 5:15 p.m. and went to the food court to devour an entire roasted chicken with a large plate of french fries. Stress perhaps would make me eat too much, but otherwise I knew I might actually enjoy this job.

Driving home together to our newly purchased house and overwhelming debt, Loretta anxiously asked me about my first day at work.

"How did it go?"

"They seem to like me," I said. "I think I may be good at this."

"They are lucky to have you," she said.

"Only time will tell, but at least I'm well begun."

I surrendered another piece of my perhaps overly developed narcissist ego-self to better make my way in the wider world. So began my traumatizing career in international strategy consulting, which would propel me to early success in the world of big business.

That first year, I helped refine the production processes for a textile company. They had too many product lines with different colors, shapes, and sizes, so short production runs were killing their profitability. Sales forecasts changed regularly. In those days, complex mathematical analyses were done on mainframe computers. For this company, the variables in their production schedules were so numerous that they tied up their mainframe computer for hours.

Using an early version of VisiCalc on the newly introduced Apple II, I helped create what I think was Bain's first personal computer-based spreadsheet. It allowed the plant supervisor to easily change the sales-input parameters and reschedule the machines, so the right combination of products was made with the longest production runs possible. Their profits increased 30 percent. I was beginning to discover that any process could be radically improved if one had the audacity to undertake it.

I joined a Bain case team, restructuring a steel company to exit from money-losing plants. Their most unprofitable plant was the largest employer in Weirton, West Virginia, with a book value of $80 million. However, due to very high union labor costs and a competitive steel market, they lost money on everything they made. We calculated that even with reasonable process improvements, they would lose $120 million running this plant for another ten years. But due to unfunded pension liabilities, it would cost $150 million to close the plant immediately.

Everyone in town knew the plant was at risk of closing. When we approached the unions to renegotiate, the unions hired McKinsey to advise them. McKinsey suggested the unions buy the plant with debt. We sold the plant to the unions for $30 million plus the assumption of all unfunded liabilities, and we walked away. We were making money for shareholders at the expense of other stakeholders.

I was also invited to work on a case to reposition a Swedish label-making company in response to innovations from their American competitors. For this project, I crunched all the data to support our conclusions. When it came time to travel to London to present to the Swedish company's board chairman, the newly elected Bain partner—three years older than me with degrees from Yale and HBS—asked me to come along. The partner and my manager would do the presentation, and I would sit quietly, unless asked otherwise.

At the Boston airport, however, my manager discovered his passport had expired. I flew overnight to London alone with our proposed presentation. Showering and changing at Heathrow, I headed straight to Bain's office to finalize the presentation over breakfast with the partner. This was my first time in London. The sights and sounds of the city thrilled me. This was also the first time I was the most knowledgeable member of a Bain case team in a client meeting. Under my hairline, my scalp began to break out in hives.

The partner had dictated what he wished the presentation to show, but before leaving Boston, I had developed some helpful additional slides. At our breakfast meeting, the partner discarded these additional slides, but I quietly retrieved them from the trash.

When the partner gave our presentation to the board, the chairman asked a key question, one that could only be answered by my analysis. When the partner looked at me, I handed him the discarded slides. At his urging, I explained the slides to the board chairman, who was delighted that we had anticipated his question and provided this key information.

Moving to London

So six months later, Loretta and I rented out our house in Framingham and began yet another life adventure by moving to London to join Bain's only European office. Never again would I feel like a country bumpkin. Now we would become more like those international sophisticates who had so impressed and intimated me since college.

We had some vacation due, so on our way to London, we traveled to Egypt and Israel as well. My favorite picture from that trip is of Loretta and me, twenty-three and twenty-five at the time, sitting on the back of a camel with big grins in front of the Great Pyramid. We were having the time of our lives.

Bain got me a work permit, but since Loretta couldn't work in London, she went off the pill that summer we moved to Europe to see if we could start a family. Our daughter, Sarah, was most likely conceived one hot night in Israel, not far from Jerusalem. Loretta arrived in London newly pregnant.

Living in London was a dream come true. We rented a flat in Hampstead, which was something of an American enclave—the only place in London, it seemed, you could buy American peanut butter. We would walk on the Hampstead Heath, in wildness and wilderness, with occasional gorgeous views back over the city of London.

I was working crazy hours, but loving the work—and who would have ever thought I'd be living and working in London! Every weekday morning, I would hop aboard a double-decker London bus for the twenty-minute ride to my office. Loretta organized the domestic aspects of our lives while I worked seventy to eighty hours a week. We were living in heaven.

I worked for a Swedish publisher, which took me to Stockholm several days each month to stay at the Grand Hôtel Stockholm. I also worked for a Düsseldorf-based glass bottle manufacturer. I focused on process improvements. Our turnaround of the glassmaker's manufacturing plants was written up in *Manager Magazin* as if a phoenix had risen anew from the ashes.

But my favorite client was the Guinness Park Royal Brewery just outside London. I was tasked with improving profits at this ancient Irish brewery. Looking through their records, I saw productivity rose throughout the morning, as men recovered from hangovers, but then fell off sharply in the afternoon. The workers were encouraged to drink Guinness while working but were not allowed to take any home. Many were drunk by midafternoon.

We negotiated with the unions so no one could drink anything alcoholic while at work but could take up to a six pack home each evening, making them very popular in their neighborhoods. The afternoon production rates improved so greatly we almost doubled the plant's profitability through process improvement.

We had a growing group of American expats and Europeans among our friends. For most weekends we had free, Loretta organized outings with friends or trips around the United Kingdom. My boyhood self could never have even imagined such a life. We spent Thanksgiving at a country inn in Wales. We ate scones with clotted cream in Devonshire. This was a great time and place for young love and Loretta's pregnancy.

For the winter solstice—our first Christmas away from our families—we headed to a country hotel in a small town in Sweden's Dalarna province. The short winter days provided just four hours of bright daylight, but at night, the arctic northern lights were spectacular!

The innkeeper lent us his car, and we headed out to explore. Snow was everywhere, with few distinctive landmarks to guide our journey, so we got lost. We pulled well off the road and got stuck in a snowbank. With the failing light of this short day and with fruitlessly spinning tires, we opened the trunk of the car to see what we had to extricate ourselves.

Pulling out an old burlap sack for traction, we closed the trunk—only to discover we had just locked the keys in the trunk.

Suddenly, we looked up to see a car driven by an elderly gentleman skidding straight toward us. I pushed my pregnant wife into the nearest snowbank and jumped out of harm's way. Fortunately, his car all but stopped before lightly hitting the back of our car. But the impact was enough to pop our trunk so we could rescue the keys.

Perhaps with an overabundance of caution, we took Loretta to a local hospital to have her and our baby checked out after falling into the snowbank. We had to pay the equivalent of ten US dollars for a Swedish ID card, but we got an ultrasound. Mother and child were both fine.

The next day, a nice boy at our hotel who spoke English showed us the local newspaper in this small Swedish town. It featured the heroic story of the young father who saved the life of his wife and unborn child. I did feel somewhat heroic in my role in saving my wife and baby!

Bain was a hothouse work environment, where my salary was reviewed every six months. I received my third substantial raise that winter. Given the difference in salary practices among American and British firms, and given the exchange rates, I was now paid as much as the fifty-year-old general manager of the Guinness Brewery. With such strong financial winds in our sails, it was easy to live the good life.

By February, Loretta was tired of the dreary London winter weather. We booked a surprisingly inexpensive beach holiday in the African country of Gambia. The weather was fine, and the hotel was decent, if somewhat rundown and only half full. The beaches were lovely but mostly empty, with bombed-out military equipment left to rust in the surf. We learned we had this paradise largely to ourselves because tourism had been down ever since the coup attempt the previous year. We loved walking these African beaches together. The sunsets were spectacular.

While still in Gambia, we received horrible news. Loretta's father had died of a heart attack back in California. Loretta was devastated. At twenty-six and twenty-four, we didn't have much direct experience with death yet. It hit us terribly hard.

Loretta had always been deeply attached to her father. He had suffered enormous stress in leaving rural China, where he could ride water buffalo, to move to the United States. He never mastered English fully. He had worked as a mining engineer, then a civil engineer, always being passed over for promotions due to his language limitations. After being laid off during the aerospace downturn, he launched a new career in northern California real estate, going in with his friends as investors in apartment buildings in the early 1970s. These had been very stressful but extraordinarily successful investments.

We made flight arrangements to California for his funeral. He looked at peace lying in his open coffin. The graveside internment, for immediate family only, was deeply tearful and very secular humanist, reflecting Loretta's family. Life gave us another opportunity to surrender what we had planned our life to be.

Loretta stayed to comfort her mother for two more weeks, then flew back to join me in London while her doctor would still allow her to fly. A few months later, our daughter Sarah was born. It turns out giving birth to new life was a wonderful counterpoint to grieving the death of a parent. Perhaps becoming parents for the first time was the ultimate surrendering of self to another. We were once again in heaven!

Sarah, however, was a very active baby, often having trouble falling asleep. We discovered she loved to sleep lying on my bare chest, wearing only a diaper. We were bonding—heart to heart, warm skin to warm skin.

My youngest sister came out to stay with us and assist with the baby's first few months. Loretta's mother came out to visit as well with Loretta's sisters and their husbands. We gratefully showed off our new urbane European lifestyle to them all.

My parents came too—their first trip outside the United States. They borrowed our car to travel from one bed and breakfast to another around the English countryside. Then we took a ferry north for a summer holiday in Sweden's Värmland with our baby and my parents. This was Ed's first experience of the country that had formed the immigrant culture that so greatly affected his upbringing in Worcester.

Bain Munich

My work for German companies had been growing so fast that we were becoming a big part of Bain's European practice. My boss persuaded Bill Bain that a small group of us should open Bain's first German office together. He asked me to justify a Bavarian location.

Most of our German clients were located around Düsseldorf and Cologne, and most international flights went from Frankfurt. McKinsey had located their German office in Frankfurt, for ease of traveling, but the best and brightest European MBA students wanted to live in Munich. We chose Munich for its lush greenness, dark forests, and high-tech culture in the midst of traditional Bavarian arts and crafts. Just walking the city streets or the quiet neighborhoods could make anyone a romantic idealist.

To help prepare for our move, my boss and his wife, along with Loretta and me, were assigned German tutors to teach us the language. My tutor began by engaging me in a long conversation, after which she stated the following:

Tutor: To teach you German, we must first correct your speech impediment.

Me: I don't have a speech impediment!

Tutor: You are mispronouncing the letter *r* in your speech or dropping it altogether.

Me: I'm from Rhode Island. That's a regional dialect.

Tutor: In America, that may be a regional dialect. But in Germany, it is a speech impediment.

Me: But I don't know how to speak otherwise.

Tutor: Then you will never speak German like a Prussian.

We agreed to do the best we could. I worked diligently every day to master this new language. After six months, she had me speaking German with a soft *r*, like a Dutchman. Now I had funny accents in three different languages. My clients didn't seem to mind very much. In fact, some told me it helped them focus more upon what I had to say.

After less than a year in London, our small family packed up our belongings and moved to a new adventure, living in Continental Europe. We found a three-bedroom row house in the leafy upper-class neighborhood of Solln, on the south side of Munich. A five-minute walk from my breakfast table would bring me to a twelve-minute ride on the high-speed S-Bahn train directly to the Marienplatz center of the city, where our offices were located. The train always departed exactly at the same time, to the minute listed on its posted schedule. I loved not having to wait on the platform for the train.

We fell in love with this family-friendly pastoral neighborhood setting for some of the most relaxed hours of my week. Loretta and I spoke English with each other and a mixture of German and English with our neighbors, so baby Sarah developed a better ear for languages than either Loretta or I have.

Loretta made some new German friends who took us walking down to the Isar River, where our local biergarten offered jazz on weekends along with local beers, fried potatoes, various German sausages, and roast chicken. Our new friends taught me two rules of etiquette when drinking with others. First, if there is beer in your glass you should drink it down. Second, if you see someone empty his or her beer glass, you should offer to refill it. With only these two rules, you could enjoy a very pleasant afternoon!

Guinness continued to be Bain's largest European client, and I would often be brought onto projects for their expansion into international markets. Guinness stout often goes flat if shipped too slowly or stored too long, yet transportation costs were too high if shipped by air. So Guinness formulated draft beer in a can under pressured carbon dioxide, such that it would pour smooth and foamy into your glass. This product was a great hit virtually worldwide—except in Australia, where beer culture insisted you shoot any beer directly from the can into your mouth. Australia stayed old school.

Nigeria had the third highest per capita consumption of Guinness in the world, three times the next highest African country. Guinness asked Bain to discover why. Guinness's worldwide marketing slogan was "Guinness is good for you!" This slogan highlighted both the stout's taste and superior nutritional value. The Nigerian translation, however, had used a word for *good* that in slang meant "virile" and "potent."

We found people were drinking Guinness to enhance their sexual fertility. While drinking large quantities of Guinness probably did result in increased births, we advised a more nuanced translation for future marketing. Mistranslations or using words with ambiguous cultural connotations was a frequent source of both pain and amusement during the 1980s era of internationalization.

My favorite project for Guinness happened that winter. Over the previous five years, Guinness had helped provide financing to launch Irish pubs in most German cities. As a result, Guinness sales in Germany had soared. But some pubs had sales that were many times higher than comparable pubs' sales after adjusting for market demographics, pub sizes, and even quality of the Guinness served.

So for six weeks, I traveled all over Germany, spending five nights a week in Irish pubs, drinking Guinness, and assessing the cause of these successes or failures. It turns out, success was mostly determined by the quality of the Celtic music played. Young Germans flocked to Irish pubs for a particular experience and drank lots of Guinness as part of that experience. But what they were most looking for was lively Irish or Celtic folk music. If the music was good, they would stay and talk for hours. When it was not so good, they would drink up and leave rather quickly. My report changed Guinness's German distribution strategy and dramatically increased sales and enjoyment as well. This assignment was great fun for me while improving Guinness's profits.

Demand for our consulting was growing rapidly, so we kept hiring German, Swiss, English, and French consultants to work with us, more than doubling in size that first year. Hilda, our office manager, was completely fluent in German and English. I would draft my presentation slides in English, and she would translate them into business German. All the key German words would be right there in front of me as I presented to my clients. I seemed even more fluent in German than I was.

American strategy consultants became essential for helping emerging German multinational companies plan their international strategies. My typical eighty-hour workweek might consist of six twelve- to fourteen-hour days in my office with meetings and conference calls, but it could also include meetings in London, Stockholm, Paris, Boston, New York, or San Francisco on short notice.

This completely disrupted Loretta's ability to count on my physical presence at home and was a particularly difficult time for her. She took over most household responsibilities, especially taking care of baby Sarah, while I submerged myself in the role of international management consultant. This was a far cry from our more balanced relationship in regard to domestic matters and work when we were first married.

This pattern of Loretta handling all aspects of our domestic life would more or less stay with us the next twenty years. She, and to a lesser extent I, paid a huge cost for this arrangement. But our marriage and the partnership we nurtured together made these things possible. It allowed me to pursue entrepreneurial and financing opportunities others perhaps couldn't. But again, this was another form of surrendering our expectations to achieve something even better.

Increasingly, our friends were European sophisticates such as those who had so overwhelmed my sense of self just three years earlier. My clients, especially the middle-aged Prussians, thought a Chinese American wife was exotic, far more interesting than their German wives. This was living in a style and manner I couldn't even have dreamed about.

Loretta and I developed a great fondness for four-star restaurants with five- or seven-course gourmet meals. When we first moved to Munich, we stayed at the Hotel Vier Jahreszeiten, one of Germany's finest, and ate in their four-star restaurant with the sleeping baby at Loretta's side. The meal took so long that Sarah finally woke up and began to cry, making us anxious and disturbing other guests. The manager relocated us to a private dining room and assigned a young waitress to care for the baby so we could relax, settle back with a fine cognac, and simply enjoy our meal and wonderful conversation. The Europeans know how to enjoy luxury.

Sometimes we made a game of fine dining. We often had ten to twelve pieces of silver placed in front of us. We would guess which pieces were intended for which course. Playing uncouth Americans and making a game of our ignorance dismayed some of our European dining partners, but the wait staff seemed to take it in stride. A waiter would quietly replace a piece of silver we had prematurely used but needed for a later course or remove the clean silver we had not used for the course for which it was intended.

I always left room for the crème brûlée or chocolate mousse that so often ended these meals. I continued to gain weight and my girth expanded. Constant work stress led to my growing metabolic disorder. Eating too much and not exercising enough only made it worse. But too much stress and inactivity was the price I felt I must pay for success.

At least once a month, we would travel to a different European city, gradually expanding our reach out to Eastern Europe as well. We came to know the continent as well as many European natives did. We had both learned German, with my vocabulary stronger in business German and Loretta's vocabulary better for domestic matters. I knew a smattering of French and Swedish, and Loretta could speak some Spanish. We immersed ourselves in European culture, traveled widely, and started to become sophisticates in our own right. Traveling to new places has been one of our favorite family pastimes ever since.

That winter, Loretta and I wanted to experience skiing the Alps. So Loretta found a small Austrian inn willing to look after Sarah, offering us a ski-and-stay package that included all our meals plus childcare for our daughter. So we skied, spent time together with friends, ate well, and simply enjoyed our life.

Living in this part of north-central Europe introduced me to new and radically different forms of mysticism. Christianity came late to northern Europe. The deeper roots of German spirituality far predate the arrival of Mediterranean Christianity. The ancient Nordic gods still hold a firm grip on the local imagination. The waves of Celtic, Saxon, Aryan, Gothic, and Germanic tribes that had so long populated these deep northern forests left their imprint on the land and its people. German spirituality was deeply connected to the land and its *volk*, or people.

Christian mystics such as Meister Eckhart or Hildegard von Bingen drew more on this nature-based spirituality than they did on the teachings of the desert fathers. I became fascinated with the Bavarian Illuminati (the illumined or enlightened ones), especially because they seemingly disappeared into the Masons, which then had such an influence on the founding of the United States. Eastern Orthodox Christianity offered an entirely different sense of what it meant to worship, to be in the presence of the divine mystery, and invoke oneness with God through praying continuously, a practice begun with spirit guides found in German mysticism.

German idealism, English romanticism, and American transcendentalism all sprang forth from these ancient European roots in nature and still carry its scent even today. For me, it seemed to connect my nature experiences of the Godhead as an adolescent with my Christian upbringing, my philosophical understanding of Kant and Hegel, and the impact of the first German and then English translations of ancient Chinese and Hindu texts—all of which resulted in an American formulation in Concord's transcendentalists.

There seemed to be a hidden stream of wisdom traditions offering living water for my spiritual journey, which I sought to explore more seriously, even as my career accelerated. I was traveling, slowly and elliptically, from spiritual naïveté to sophistication, from spiritual adolescence to the beginnings of maturity. I would learn to surrender my New England Christian perspective, which was becoming too narrow for me now, as I began to see more of the world.

World Tour

Work had become crazy stressful. Bain's German office turned out to be far more successful and profitable than anyone had expected. When the Bain US-based senior partners refused to let the Bain European partners receive bonuses so much larger than theirs, half the European partners, including my boss and closest friends, left to set up a competing firm. The new firm invited me to join them in London. Bain, however, wanted me to stay and help anchor the decimated German office while they trained new consultants.

After two years of being unable to work in Europe, Loretta just wanted to move back home. Bain offered that if we stayed for three more months of transition, they would offer three additional months' severance pay as well as transfer us and all our goods back home to Boston business class.

For what Bain was offering, we figured we could travel around the whole world tourist class. We decided to take Bain's severance package, but instead of heading straight home, we spent seven weeks traveling in an easterly direction, completing our international education and seeing the world with our own eyes. The timing was perfect, as our Framingham house was rented out until the end of September.

We traveled through Liechtenstein and Switzerland. We flew to India to visit Bombay (now Mumbai) and New Delhi. India was a wonderful kaleidoscope of sights and sounds.

I was inspired by barefoot monks in Kathmandu. Hinduism and Buddhism were attractive paths, but I wasn't yet spiritually mature enough to pursue the rigors of Tibetan Buddhism. For a young husband and father who was still materially ambitious and had a strong sense of self, that spiritual path was not yet for me.

We vacationed on the beaches of the Maldives, sampled the tourist sights of Hong Kong, and explored the intricacies of Zen Buddhism. Buddhism, in its many forms, would eventually become a key aspect of my spiritual journey, but I was first introduced to it through Zen Buddhism.

We traveled to all the usual tourist cities in Mainland China, with the high point being a visit to Loretta's aunt and cousins in Shanghai. As a mixed-race couple with a baby, we were quite the novelty in 1983 China. Having endured occasional racist remarks in the United States because of looking Chinese, Loretta looked forward to visiting China, where everyone looked like her. Instead, the Chinese all viewed her as American. We didn't fit in.

Not until we landed in Hawaii did our marriage begin to look anything like the norm. Especially on the Big Island of Hawaii, racial mixing was everywhere and seemingly completely accepted. When we attended the Hawaiian Congregational church and told them I was directly descended from their missionary founders, they treated us like long-lost cousins.

We spent a week relaxing on Hawaii's broad beaches, then traveled to California to visit Loretta's mom, and finally back to Boston to introduce our daughter to America. We were tired of traveling and eager to return home. We had learned to surrender ourselves, over and over again, to whatever life had to offer us, and we discovered it was far more remarkable than anything we could have imagined for ourselves. It fixed in my mind a determination to follow my bliss, wherever it may lead, even when it means surrendering that which I have always thought I wanted.

Added to resilience, surrender was the second spiritual discipline I needed to learn in order to discover who I was born to be. I determined to gratefully accept what life had to offer.

Blessed be.

AUDACIOUS SURRENDER

Chalice-Lighting Words

This being human is a guest house. Every morning a new arrival. A joy,
a depression, a meanness, some momentary awareness comes as an
unexpected visitor. Welcome and entertain them all! Even if they are a
crowd of sorrows...
—Jalaluddin Rumi (Coleman Barks translation)

Check-in: How does spiritual submission or surrender factor into your
life today?

Additional Reading from *The Joyous Cosmology* by Alan Watts

Listen, there's something I *must* tell. I've never, never seen it so clearly.
But it doesn't matter a bit if you don't understand, because each one of
you is quite perfect as you are, even if you don't know it. Life is basically
a gesture, but no one, nothing, is *making* it. There is no necessity for it
to happen, and none for it to go on happening. For it isn't being driven
by anything; it just happens freely of itself. It's a gesture of motion, of
sound, of color, and just as no one is making it, it isn't *happening* to
anyone. There is simply no problem of life; it is completely purposeless
play—exuberance, which is its own end. Basically there is the gesture.
Time, space, and multiplicity are complications of it. There is no reason
whatever to explain it, for explanations are just another form of complexity, a new manifestation of life on top of life, of gestures gesturing.
Pain and suffering are simply extreme forms of play, and there isn't anything in the whole universe to be afraid of because it doesn't happen to
anyone! There isn't any ego at all.

Questions to Ponder

1. How was the author's crisis in Yale's maelstrom necessary or helpful to his spiritual progress?

2. How did selling books door to door every summer help him learn to surrender his ego?

3. What does it mean to live in Technicolor? Have you experienced it?

4. Why does the author describe his relationship with Loretta as his salvation?

5. What, if any, is the relationship between business success and developing spiritual maturity?

6. How does living in Europe contribute to the author's spiritual development?

7. What effect did their world tour have on the author's and Loretta's relationship and spiritual development?

Closing Words

We had learned to surrender ourselves, over and over again, to whatever life had to offer us, and we discovered it was far more remarkable than anything we could have imagined for ourselves. It fixed in my mind a determination to follow my bliss, wherever it may lead, even when it means surrendering that which I have always thought I wanted.

AUDACIOUS SURRENDER

Author's Comment

This chapter begins with my going off to college at seventeen and ends with my family's successful world tour at the age of twenty-seven. It includes my description of being overwhelmed at Yale, my brother coming out as gay, my academic struggles, my fiancée's betrayal—and how I barely managed to hold it all together throughout. My life turned around when I met and courted Loretta, went to Harvard Business School, married, moved to London with Bain, and welcomed the birth of our daughter. There is a constant second theme here of my emergence as a spiritual seeker. After living in Munich for a year, our family completed a tour of world spirituality before returning to Boston.

Questions to Encourage Conversation

1. Did you go to college? How did your experience compare to the author's?

2. Would you have been comfortable keeping David's homosexuality a secret?

3. Can you imagine selling books door to door to pay for college?

4. Jim describes Loretta as his salvation. Would you? Why?

5. How does growing up white working-class help shape Jim's career trajectory?

6. How would you describe Jim and Loretta's view of the good life? How would you describe yours?

7. How would you describe Jim's trajectory from bumpkin to sophisticate?

8. What does all this have to do with spiritual surrender?

Reflection

As a group, reflect on how spiritual surrender has helped enable your own spiritual journey, or alternatively, how failure to submit or surrender has blocked your progress.

DISCIPLINE THREE:
GRATITUDE

Grateful people experience higher levels of positive emotions such as joy, enthusiasm, love, happiness, and optimism. The practice of gratitude as a discipline protects a person from the destructive impulses of envy, resentment, greed, and bitterness.

—Thanks!
Robert A. Emmons, PhD

Resurrection

I never really appreciated the deeper spiritual mystery of death and resurrection until it became a metaphor for transformation in my life. Now my heart swells with gratitude. When I was twenty, I was in utter despair, physically unable to pursue my dream, betrayed by my fiancée, depressed, verging on flunking out of college, overwhelmed, with no clear path forward.

Then, miraculously, with deep resilience and surrender of my ego-self, so much had changed in so few years. Imagine my joy and gratitude at twenty-eight as we settled back into our house in Framingham. I was happily married to Loretta, we had a baby daughter, my work paid extraordinarily well, and we had just completed the trip of a lifetime.

Our Framingham house was set deep in the woods on an acre and a half. We were surrounded by neighbors with even more acreage, giving us a sense of living in nature. Yet we were less than ten minutes from restaurants and shops and less than forty minutes to downtown Boston and all the cultural life of the city. I loved our winding country road, its sense of woodsy peacefulness, and the nearby Quaker church. I could walk over there on a Sunday morning and just sit quietly with the Quakers.

Our life was good beyond imagining. On crisp autumn days, we would work in the yard, restoring its sense of order after our two years away. I so enjoyed lazy mornings with my wife and daughter, so different from our life in Germany. We had accomplished so much, lived so much, in such a short time. Life was bliss. Now I could seek spiritual deepening.

I had time and mental space to resume my meditation practice. I began to devour spiritual texts at a tremendous pace—two or three a week—often breaking open new insights into the nature of being and becoming. I got to play with my sixteen-month-old daughter, teaching her how to roll down the gentle slope in our back yard, to appreciate the small miracles of nature, and to greatly expand her vocabulary and verbal repertoire. This was a form of householder spirituality in which I could luxuriate as long as it lasted.

I was deeply grateful for the life we had, even though Loretta and I were beginning to feel a little anxious about my finding a new job. We only had about five weeks' severance pay left before we would begin eating into our savings. But all would be well. For I still had access to Bain's research library and extensive network to find my next job.

Serendipity, what many call grace, came once again to save us. When we were down to only two weeks' severance pay left, a former Bain consultant called to ask if I was willing to take on a half-time consulting assignment in Leominster, Massachusetts, and if so, what would be my hourly rate. It was a four-month project to help Foster Grant, a sunglass manufacturer, transfer manufacturing from Leominster to its new plant in Mexico. I told him Bain Europe had been billing me out at $300 an hour—with one third going to me and the rest to Bain overhead and profits. When he readily accepted $300 an hour, I found myself working part-time at high pay on the kind of process-improvement project I'd often done for Bain. And all the while, I still had time to research where to work next and simply enjoy this wonderful life.

I have always worked very stressful jobs at considerable personal cost to my health and sense of well-being. Struggling with weight issues and getting too little exercise, I would often break out in hives, usually behind my ears and under my scalp, when under extreme stress. I wore my hair a little long to hide my erupting skin. But this very stressful work style was the only way I knew how to succeed. It didn't feel possible to do the kind of work I did, to have the kind of life we had, without that stress. This felt like a necessary cost for our happiness and well-being.

This four-month interlude, however, was a sweet exception. Loretta and I rediscovered the joys of spending lots of time together and with our daughter. Loretta became pregnant again as a result of our lovely interlude from stress. Our son, Robert, would be born the following summer.

Yet I still hungered to achieve. I needed to find the right industry. Biotechnology looked to be the most interesting. I could likely generate considerable wealth while doing very worthwhile things, and it seemed to be a fun place to work. Biotechnology was predicted to grow rapidly over the next decade. I quickly discovered the nicest thing about a rapidly growing industry is that it can be like playing reverse musical chairs: every time the music stops, they add, not subtract, a chair. There are always more opportunities to pursue.

I hoped biotech would be what Buddhists call Right Livelihood, as compared to my earlier work on proposing process-improvement or manufacturing-efficiency schemes. Biotech felt like something I could give my heart, mind, and passion to for a lifetime. As it turned out, I would spend the next twenty years of my life deeply involved in biotechnology.

Biotechnology had taken off first in California's Silicon Valley, but there were now half a dozen biotech startups in the Boston area. Nobody had a reasonable business model yet. So I set my heart on joining one of these startups. Based upon my Bain experience, I hoped this infant industry would accept and respect me as a senior manager at age twenty-eight.

Thanks to Bain's incredible network around Boston, I landed interviews with three promising startups. The newly appointed president of Genzyme offered me the position of their chief financial officer. It paid less than half what Bain had paid. Loretta pointed out I was making more money working part-time as an independent consultant. Yet we knew if Genzyme succeeded, it could generate substantial wealth in stock options.

The position would require stressful eighty- to ninety-hour weeks, making short work of my role as a family-centered householder. But luckily, Bain had taught me how to work that kind of schedule. It was with enormous gratitude that I would embark on this next stage of my life. I would start on February 13, 1984. So I set my spiritual texts aside and began to read everything about biotechnology while wrapping up my consulting project for Foster Grant.

Loretta was also anxious to get back to work herself. It had been two years since she had worked, and our financial picture was different now that I had accepted a job with half the pay as before. Given her reputation at Prudential, Loretta was able to negotiate a part-time position at a local insurance brokerage firm. Now we were grateful for two professional incomes once again.

Given my new work role, Loretta remained primary parent, which limited my parenting responsibilities mostly to nights and weekends. Weekend mornings, I often took Sarah out for breakfast while Loretta slept in. That became our special father-daughter time each week.

My brother Steve and his wife moved in with us. My sister-in-law attended medical school in Worcester, and Steve took care of Sarah and Robert in exchange for room and board. Steve and Sarah are still particularly close today! Work-life balance became an important subtext of all those years, but extended family makes more things possible. Whatever life might send our way, we were grateful for the opportunities, for each other, and for our families.

My new boss was Henri, a Dutchman who was a former senior manager for Baxter International in Germany. He didn't mind at all that I spoke German like a Dutchman. Henri was a brilliant strategist. In high school, he had been a world-class chess player. Now he was a great manager and leader of people.

I was grateful to have found another mentor figure. Mr. Robinson had set me on my intellectual path. The Bain partner who recruited me to London and then had me learn German to open an office with him in Munich was another mentor, guiding me in becoming an international business professional. Now Henri would become my third important mentor.

I would need his guidance. I didn't know much about finance, beyond my Harvard MBA, and nearly nothing about biotechnology. I committed to do whatever was necessary to succeed with integrity in this career. I would need to come down a very steep learning curve. And it began even before my first day.

The week before I started, Henri had called me at home to confirm my starting on Monday. More importantly, he asked me to fly to London that Sunday evening and join Sam, Genzyme's chairman of the board, at an important meeting with the company's banker. It seems Genzyme was out of cash, in default on a $1.3 million line of credit. Sam disdained English bankers and business protocols.

So I flew overnight, rented a car, and picked up our chairman. Sam was a serial entrepreneur. He had become a multimillionaire and then had gone bankrupt twice before founding Genzyme. Beginning something new was his major gift as an entrepreneur. He knew how to spot opportunities and buy them with other people's money, but he didn't really know how to manage them.

Sam was dressed in blue jeans and a bomber jacket. I nearly got us both killed by momentarily driving on the wrong side of the road, exiting our first English roundabout. Talk about a terrifying beginning to a new job. But without further mishap, I drove us to Maidstone in

Kent, where Genzyme's angry bank manager was awaiting our 10:00 a.m. appointment.

We were ushered into his presence. Over coffee and cookies, he asked how we would repay the overdrawn bank line. Sam said we wouldn't—in fact, we needed to draw even more to avoid bankruptcy that week.

My spirit sank. The bank manager grew very still and pale.

I asked Sam to wait in the outer office, then I threw myself on the bank manager's mercy. I told him this was my first day on the job. I gave him references for European CEOs who could vouch for my abilities. I asked for ninety days leeway to pay the credit line in full. I had no idea how to do so but trusted we could find a way. The banker agreed on the condition that once we paid the loan in full, he would never deal with Sam again and preferably never even hear the name Genzyme again. I was grateful for the challenge to discover what we could do.

I arrived back in Boston later that evening. After a sleepless night, I went to my office to begin imagining how we could emerge from this crisis. While inspecting the company's employment files that day, I discovered that two weeks before offering me the job, Henri had hired someone else in this same position. The previous hire was a Harvard MBA certified public accountant with CFO experience for this job. But his first morning on the job, he quickly saw how precarious the company's financial position was. He quit that day.

Perhaps I should have done the same. But I was too inexperienced and naïve to know any better, not to mention I was incredibly optimistic and sure of myself. Rather than quit, I gratefully relished my new responsibilities and decided to meet the crisis head on. Audacity can be extraordinarily helpful in such circumstances.

During the previous two years, Sam had completed two acquisitions in England: one an enzyme-manufacturing plant in Maidstone, Kent, financed by this credit line, and the other a specialty-chemistry manufacturer financed by our first round of venture capital and now bankrupt. Neither deal had been fully vetted and approved by the board in advance.

Genzyme had a small Boston headquarters and a ten-person enzyme-research lab. We were very financially leveraged. Sam had leapfrogged the competition, growing the company as a whole from 21 employees to 150 employees, with most of our employees now in England. But he had put the company on the verge of bankruptcy in doing so.

The board had hired Henri to clean up the mess, and Henri had hired me to help. My introduction to biotechnology became a trial by fire. I exuded confidence in the midst of confusion. The stress hives erupting under my scalp had me frequently scratching my head.

The venture capitalists on the board were willing to invest $2.5 million more to support our research and development (R&D), but not to pay down the bank line. In order for the company to survive, this situation required risk arbitrage.

A loan officer at Bank of Boston had graduated from HBS two years behind me, and he was attempting to lend to the biotech industry. The venture capitalists agreed to invest the $2.5 million to fund our R&D, on the condition that Bank of Boston gave us a $2.5 million line of credit to fund our working capital. Simultaneous closings on the equity and debt investments would lessen the risks all around. The loan officer decided that with the infusion of venture capital, this was a deal he could do—especially when we added a sweetener of warrants on our common stock.

So Genzyme survived its first cash crisis. However, we were unable to raise more than about eighteen months of forward cash. We were growing from crisis to crisis.

Building Genzyme

To imagine Genzyme in its earliest days, you need to know that our world headquarters occupied half of the fifteenth floor in an old textile warehouse in Boston's Combat Zone, so-called because of the drugs, prostitution, and violence in the neighborhood. The area was dirty, dangerous, and disreputable. Genzyme had a research laboratory, a blood-processing laboratory, and a small suite of executive offices. We initially shared a men's room with a fur retailer and a gay bookstore. As we grew, we quickly took over the entire fifteenth floor. We were on the edge of Boston's Chinatown, so Chinese food was plentiful and cheap.

In such a location, Genzyme's line of interleukins—particularly IL-2, which could be used for cancer research or to treat drug addicts—raised some eyebrows about our shipments. Three months after I began as CFO, my secretary nervously walked into my office to say we were the subject of a Food and Drug Administration (FDA) raid. Men in blue jackets with "FDA" in big letters started seizing all our financial records.

Biotech was new to them. They thought we might be selling to local drug addicts. We had to prove that 100 percent of our production was sold to legitimate research laboratories worldwide before they released my staff and let us continue our shipments. Many residents of Boston had also been worried about the potential health impact of biotechnology's genetic engineering, but we convinced the FDA we were legitimate suppliers of research materials.

We were conducting leading-edge research on a bootstrap budget. Senator Ted Kennedy had recently shepherded the Orphan Drug Act through Congress to incentivize development of therapies for often-overlooked diseases. We were one of the first companies to focus on orphan diseases. Developing life-saving treatments for rare orphan diseases would become our core competence.

Our enzyme-processing lab collected and processed 150 human placentas a week from births at Boston hospitals. Our technicians ground the placentas up to extract a rare enzyme called glucocerebrosidase; the enzyme was needed to treat a rare genetic disorder called Gaucher's disease. This disease leads to bruising, fatigue, anemia, low platelet counts, and eventually an enlarged spleen, liver malfunction, skeletal disorders, and painful death.

Our founding scientists produced large research quantities of this enzyme under contract with the National Institutes of Health (NIH). At the same time, we were also searching for a means to scale its manufacture and, under the Orphan Drug Act, seek approval from the FDA for the enzyme's use as a therapeutic. Our best estimates were that less than ten thousand patients worldwide needed this therapy, which was why large drug companies didn't pursue it. But for those ten thousand patients, it could save their lives.

Given existing technology, we couldn't make enough Ceredase, our purified extracted enzyme, at any reasonable cost. We would need to clone the cell line for glucocerebrosidase and scale it up to over one thousand times our current production levels while maintaining its purity and efficacy in transport as well as creating a delivery mechanism to get it into all the body's cells that needed it. And then we would need to take it through three phases of FDA testing and approval. This would require at least $100 million in R&D over a decade.

A computer-aided design and computer-aided manufacturing (CAD/CAM) startup was located on the fourteenth floor below our placenta-processing lab. One summer Saturday morning, six months after beginning at Genzyme, I was returning with Sarah from breakfast when I received an angry phone call from the CAD/CAM company's head of research. He wanted to know whether the "red goop" dripping from his ceiling and mucking up his continuously operating computers was contagious and how quickly I would be there to clean up the mess.

One of the recirculating lines in our processing lab had come loose and was now spewing semi-processed blood products all over the floor of our lab. They then dripped down through the ceiling into the CAD/CAM computer lab. It was impossible to know for sure, but I assured him that at this stage of the processing, it probably wasn't contagious. And of course we would clean it up as soon as possible.

I called the scientist running the processing lab, explained our situation, and met him there to clean up the goopy red mess. Such was the nature of the biotechnology industry. Even my summer Saturday mornings with Sarah weren't sacrosanct.

This was a small example of how the world of blood processing and products was in deep turmoil. In 1984, the Centers for Disease

Control and blood-processing industry were only beginning to understand blood-borne diseases and how to contain them. The emergence of acquired immunodeficiency syndrome (AIDS), which researchers later identified as coming from human immunodeficiency virus (HIV), had recently cast into doubt any certainty authorities had about the true biological safety of blood-derived products. Most blood products, and certainly these human placentas, were not routinely screened for HIV.

We were largely working in the dark. Most chemical purification techniques would damage the enzymes we were trying to preserve. In those days, extracting and purifying involved a lot of calibrated heating and cooling, recirculating fluids between filters, and hoping to kill the viruses and organisms that could harm someone while preserving the enzymes needed to be therapeutically useful. In 1984, this was very much a hit-or-miss proposition.

I asked Henri how two business leaders trained in the humanities could ever understand the science enough to know what to fund and when to discontinue funding. To run the business, we senior managers needed to understand the emerging science. So Genzyme created our first Scientific Advisory Board (SAB) made up of leading scientists at MIT and Harvard, including the chair of chemistry at Harvard, chair of chemical engineering at MIT, and leading molecular and cellular biologists. Genzyme gave them collectively a 10 percent founding equity stake in the company in return for their scientific expertise and access to their scientific ideas.

That first year, we started a monthly Saturday morning sharing of ideas between the academic scientists, our company's scientists, and our company's senior management. They taught me about genetics and Maxwell's equations; I taught them how to perform business-process improvements and the capital asset pricing model (CAPM). This was an intensive course on scientific and business education, and we all began to better understand the risks and possibilities as we built this biotech company. This bonding between scientists and businesspeople was critical to our success. We each did for the other that which we could not do alone. I learned the core science of biotechnology from some of the world's best scientists.

Nine months into my job, our founding scientist asked me to fire his longtime laboratory head. Bob had just turned sixty and hadn't kept up with scientific advances. The younger scientists we were hiring from MIT and Harvard did not respect him.

When I called Bob to my office and told him he was fired, he crumbled, even though he had known it was coming. We offered six months' severance. It was far more than we had offered anyone else, but it seemed so little for someone who had worked so hard and now seemed unemployable as a molecular biologist. I felt horrible as he left my office.

Six months later, Bob was back in my office. I greeted him somewhat anxiously, but Bob was a new man. For decades, his hobby had been making wooden furniture and sculptures. Now he was selling them at fairs around New England. He was doing something he loved and making more than he needed to live on, given his simple desires.

He told me he wished someone had fired him six months sooner. Ever since, whether I'm doing performance reviews or firing someone, I remember this: the inevitable is best done firmly, with fairness and loving compassion, but never delayed. I am grateful to have developed my business ethics while working in a company with integrity. Capitalism can be a source of human flourishing.

As CFO, it was my job to report how we were doing financially and help to raise additional funds as needed. Our annual bonuses and jobs themselves depended upon hitting our numbers. The board of directors agreed that if our revenues for 1984 exceeded $5 million, and we became profitable for the first time, Henri would become chairman and CEO in 1985. If we were successful, Sam would resign as chairman, and we would be the team in place to prepare the way for our initial public offering (IPO) in 1986.

There were three key senior business members of this team: Henri, David, our senior vice president of sales and marketing, and myself.

Henri and David had their offices on either side of mine. They were my closest friends at Genzyme. We were all underpaid but eligible for large bonuses if we hit these 1984 targets. Our ability to raise more funds and the value of our stock options depended entirely upon positive results.

But just after Thanksgiving, David walked into my office and said we had a problem. My heart sank as he described the situation.

Our Maidstone enzyme plant had been contaminated with a virus. A large production order could not be completed before year-end, leaving a hole in our revenue targets for 1984. He had been assured the contamination was a temporary problem, readily fixable in early 1985, but not by the year-end cutoff date.

Following industry practices, we could send the contaminated product to the customer so we could record the sale for 1984, but the customer would likely return it upon discovering the contamination—or worse yet, contaminate their own product by using our contaminated product. Or we could ship the product to them on December 31 to record the sale and profit in 1984, then immediately tell them about the contamination in early 1985 and ask them to return it.

But strictly speaking, American accounting rules would not legitimately count either type of sale as being completed in 1984. Granted, we all knew technology companies that violated these rules without blinking. But that wasn't who we were. David and I knew missing our year-end targets over a production issue beyond our control could cost the company dearly, perhaps even costing us our jobs. Yet violating accounting rules was unacceptable.

We went next door to talk to Henri. He said of course it was my responsibility to conform to appropriate accounting rules—but he didn't want to miss the year-end numbers for any reason or lose the opportunity to become chairman and CEO. This was a real test of our integrity under pressure. How we responded would set a tone for the entire company, one that would help define what we would and would not do in seeking success.

We decided to make our year-end numbers another way. We instructed the entire sales and marketing staff and most of the accounting staff to call every customer with a January order and ask if they might take product from our inventory in December instead. By the week following Christmas, we had eked out just over $5 million in bookable sales and had generated $10,000 in profit. We had accomplished our goals without sacrificing our integrity. This cleared the way for our future success and made very public our commitment to be a management team that valued integrity as the company grew.

In 1985, I would go on to clean up all the company's accounting, writing off any legacies from Sam's time as chairman. It imbued the company with an ethic of integrity while working for the public good. We were determined to be a company with integrity. We were passionate about helping people and doing it honestly. That cultural context helped recruit some of the finest scientists in the industry. It allowed us to feel good about the products we were developing—we were doing good even while doing well. I have enormous gratitude for being part of creating a company with extraordinary success and integrity over many years.

Gaucher's disease is a recessive genetic disease particularly prevalent among Ashkenazi Jews. The head of the National Organization of Rare Disorders (NORD) was of Ashkenazi Jewish descent, and two of her four children had the disease. We tested her oldest son, Brian. His disease was advancing so quickly that he might die before we had our therapeutic approved. Brian's internal organs were swelling with accumulating lipids, which, if not reversed, would likely lead to a series of painful and expensive surgeries and an early death.

We received permission from the FDA to make Brian the first patient in our phase I/II clinical trial. It's normally primarily a safety trial, but instead, we agreed to give him a big enough dose to potentially save his life. Our scientists worked frantically to collect enough human placentas to make enough Ceredase to clear Brian's accumulated lipids. Finally, we had enough material late on a Friday. Our lead scientist,

Scott, agreed to fly the therapy to Washington, DC to infuse Brian the following Monday.

That weekend, however, there was a power outage in Chinatown. We had a backup generator for just such a situation, but it failed to start as intended. When Scott checked in at his lab on Sunday morning, the frozen therapeutic had begun to thaw—potentially destroying the entire batch.

Scott refroze it and hoped for the best. He flew the therapeutic to Washington, DC, and began Brian's weeklong treatment late the next day with considerable trepidation.

Incredibly, Brian seemed to respond immediately. By the end of the week, we had our first full remission from disease. Brian would need periodic infusions the rest of his life, but his spleen had shrunk to normal size, his liver function was good, and it looked as though this disease would not end his life. We celebrated like never before at Genzyme!

Then we went back to work to prepare enough material to test the next three patients in our phase I/II trial. In the following months, we infused each of these additional patients, but none of them showed the kind of dramatic response we had seen in Brian. This was worrying. And Brian also appeared to be accumulating lipids once again. The follow-up infusions from the newer batches of material were just as pure and potent but didn't seem to have the same ability to clear lipids.

At this point, many experienced clinical research teams would likely have abandoned this as a failed therapeutic. Not Genzyme. Not given our culture. Scott went back into the lab to see whether the power outage had somehow improved the enzyme's ability to be taken up in the cellular macrophages.

It turns out it did. The enzyme has a chain of carbohydrates attached to its surface. Raising it above freezing had cleaved the outermost two, exposing a sugar that macrophages take up preferentially. Modifying the production process to include this new knowledge allowed us to make a product that worked splendidly for all the test patients. They now showed the same lipid clearance and physiological improvement.

We had our first proprietary therapy and had also discovered a whole new therapeutic strategy in terms of carbohydrate remodeling of enzymes to improve therapeutic uptake. Due to our science and our culture, Ceredase—and Genzyme's subsequent recombinant form Cerezyme—would become billion-dollar drugs, creating new lifesaving treatments where none had been possible before.

Biotechnology is an industry where gratitude is in abundance. Gratitude for being able to devote your life to reducing human suffering and diseases. Gratitude for scientists who just will not give up. Gratitude for unanticipated problems that lead to new inventions. Gratitude for the multitude of failures that are necessary along the path to success. Yes, even gratitude for a world that includes such suffering and illness to make overcoming it possible. I am grateful for all.

However, there was such uncertainty with biotechnology research and such enormous costs and time required. We were always underfunded, which is probably why anyone who knew better did not want my job. That and because my position as CFO was always at risk.

Sam told me early on he didn't like me—or any young Harvard MBA, for that matter. But there was little he could do as long as the board liked my work. So he planned to wait until we went public and then propose someone so young didn't have enough experience and gravitas to be CFO of a public company.

I was determined to take the company public as its CFO. Of course, the complexity of our accounting was well beyond me. It required an understanding of US Generally Accepted Accounting Principles (GAAP), American financial and tax accounting, English financial and tax accounting, and emerging biotechnology financial and accounting standards.

Fortunately, with the help of our auditors, I found Theresa, a Southeast Asian British CPA who had grown up in London but now lived just outside Boston. She was doing audits of US GAAP financial and tax accounting. I immediately hired her as our company controller. Theresa knew the applicable accounting standards and adjusted our books for conformity.

To succeed in any emerging field requires a combination of audacity, innovation, risk taking, humility, accountability, and integrity. No doubt I had the requisite audacity, innovation, and risk taking. But now I had to learn humility. I had to admit the limits of my own knowledge to avoid bringing the company to crisis. I was never as brilliant as I could make myself seem.

In this exercise of humility, I discovered I could greatly magnify my productivity by gathering around me highly competent people whom I could trust. Theresa was perhaps the most important hire I ever made. I could trust her to understand from a tax and accounting perspective what needed to be done and how to do it. I knew she always had my back, which allowed me to focus on fundraising and financing.

We grew to be good friends. We frequently played tennis together when the weather was suitable, and we watched our kids grow up. Her daughters were a little younger than our kids. She was yet one more example of proof that the support of my parents, siblings, and friends has been key to my success in business and in life. Such long-term relationships with people you can trust make this kind of intense work schedule and risk taking possible. I have always been blessed with people who care about me. Now I needed to make my circle wider.

Biotechnology Emerges

I started reaching out to other local biotech executives to see if we could all agree on common negotiating positions with our suppliers, bankers, auditors, and others. Marc, a Harvard JD/MBA, played a somewhat similar role at Genetics Institute as I did at Genzyme. He told me such conversations between companies could be construed as illegal collusion of some sort.

So in 1985, we founded the Massachusetts Biotechnology Council (MBC) with just six companies. Operating as a professional association, we could legally exchange such information. In fact, that was the stated public purpose of the council. Marc agreed to be the MBC's first president, and I agreed to be president after him.

We were Young Turks, inventing an industry and learning from one another about the basic science, business development, finance and accounting, regulatory affairs, and all other aspects of building companies. Being the heads of an industry association gave us a platform to help transform the world. It looked awesome on my resume as well.

I loved promoting this new industry because genetic engineering seemed scary to people in those days. For instance, out of fear about the dangers of our biological processes, the Cambridge City Council passed an ordinance that made it illegal for anything that had ever been alive to enter the Cambridge sewer system.

They were trying to avoid "genetically engineered monsters" in the sewers. But of course, almost everything we eat has once been alive. We worked with the Cambridge City Council to create a model ordinance for industry best practices. Then we got other towns across Massachusetts to adopt it.

In my time as president of the MBC, I also spent a lot of time at the statehouse, explaining the risks and potential rewards of this new industry. I was appalled at how often state lawmakers, who didn't understand the science at all, would try to extract donations from us, but I needed to work with the powers and systems as they existed.

Our industry's greatest champion in Washington was Senator Ted Kennedy. I spent a lot of time in Washington, helping raise money for him and getting to know his staff on a first-name basis. Senator Kennedy reciprocated, publicly recognizing my role in helping create the Massachusetts biotech industry. When we finally organized a national biotechnology association—initially called the Industrial Biotechnology Association, but later became the Biotechnology Innovation Organization (BIO)—I was invited to join that board as well. Doing well while doing much good for the world came easily together.

I served as master of ceremonies at the opening of the new biotechnology incubator at Massachusetts Biotechnology Research Institute in Worcester as we awaited Senator Kennedy's arrival as the keynote speaker. Finally he arrived, bounded to the podium, thanked me by name for helping to create the industry—then pulled a speech out of his right pocket that extolled the benefits of silicon to the emerging computer industry.

As he jumped into his limo to head to his next stop, his aide came to me quite embarrassed. The biotech speech had been in his *left* pocket. He hoped the senator would now tell the computer executives at his next stop how important biotech was to their future as well.

This level of influence was quite heady for someone not yet thirty. I was soon invited to join an Office of Technology Assessment (OTA) task force on America's future competitiveness. Economist Robert Reich was chair. Now I was heading to Washington more often and traveling in bigger circles. It seemed like my brilliance was being increasingly widely sought after.

Growing up, I never imagined being part of the establishment. Coming of age in the apocalyptic, mutually assured destruction Cold War era, I never expected to see my thirtieth birthday. Yet I had plunged into strategic consulting and biotech entrepreneurship with the same audacity as I had when learning to play marbles.

The Latin motto over the entrance to my Yale residential college read "*Fortuna Favet Audaci*," often translated as "fortune favors the brave" or "bold." I translated it as "fortune favors audacity." Audacity was both my means and my process. But without gratitude, audacity can easily devolve into just arrogance, and without humility, brilliance can easily lead you over a cliff into the abyss. Hence these spiritual practices.

Now approaching age thirty, I was a person of influence and power, with an ability to use that power and influence to help shape our company and the emerging industry. I determined to do so with appropriate humility and gratitude. We began the process for our IPO just two months after I turned thirty.

Henri persuaded Sam to sell David and me each $40,000 of his common stock at half our expected IPO price. It represented an enormous gain for Sam on his founder's stock, and it nearly doubled my modest ownership stake in Genzyme's future success. Now I needed to work even harder to catch the coming window of opportunity to take Genzyme public.

Loretta had built her employee-benefits practice at the insurance brokerage firm, but now they were in merger discussions with a firm in Boston. She didn't want to work full-time or report to anyone. She wanted more flexibility on how to manage work and family.

With plans to start her own business, Loretta and I began looking for another house—preferably with a swimming pool, in a nice neighborhood, and in a town with great public schools. Loretta even interviewed elementary school principals in order to find one with a compatible educational philosophy. Of all the neighborhoods we looked at, my heart was set on transcendentalist Concord, so we narrowed our search around Alcott Elementary School.

When we told our realtor what we were looking for—and for not much more than $300,000—she just looked at us and laughed. But many weeks later, we got a phone call. It was the dead of winter, but a 1950s California contemporary with a swimming pool was on the market in the Alcott school neighborhood. The owners were divorced, and the tenants who had rented the house had burned down the freestanding garage. We immediately went to look at it.

It was a quiet street in an area called Musketaquid, where the indigenous people's main village had been when the seventeenth-century colonial settlers purchased Concord. The street ended at the Assabet River, along a section that in the 1840s Henry David Thoreau called the prettiest river in America. This was a place we could put down roots and live happily ever after.

We bought it even though we needed to borrow the entire purchase price on a bridge loan from the bank until we could find a buyer for our house in Framingham or get some liquidity from Genzyme's IPO.

Loretta resigned her corporate position and started her own employee-benefits business when we moved to Concord.

Transcendentalist Concord

My parents and Theresa and her husband helped us move in over Patriots' Day weekend. I awakened that first morning to the sound of gunshots from the reenactment of the battle at the North Bridge. This was my kind of town!

The largest congregation in town was First Parish in Concord, the church that had once counted as members Ralph Waldo Emerson, Henry David Thoreau, and Louisa May Alcott. Being Unitarian Universalist (UU), it had a religious orientation wide enough to make room for Loretta's secular humanism as well as my liberal Christian interreligious spiritual seeking.

We began attending First Parish and enrolled our kids in the religious education program. Loretta got involved in their social justice work, eventually becoming Chair of the Social Action Council. This is how we became UUs and transcendentalists.

We repainted our front door red and purchased two Chinese stone lions to guard the entrance. The pool was warm enough for swimming only about six weeks each summer, so Loretta added a gas heater. That way, she could swim most days between Memorial Day and mid-September.

Loretta and I turned our large living room into a library. I still bought and read fifty to one hundred books each year. There was only room in my new library to keep roughly fifteen hundred volumes, so I became a major annual contributor to the Concord library book sale.

We were adapting our settings to maximize our flourishing and create space for a spiritual life. In fact, I was having fantasies of leaving behind Genzyme's intense pressures, perhaps to spend many months in a Buddhist monastery, deepen my spirituality, and make sense of my life.

In response, Loretta booked us on a weekend meditation retreat at a Zen monastery in Upstate New York. I was already exhausted as we arrived on Friday, but we quickly settled into meditation, followed by a vegan dinner eaten in silence and more meditation afterwards. After a short night's sleep, a bell woke us at 4:00 a.m. to begin sitting meditation again. We had walking meditation in the afternoons. Meditation time was interrupted only by simple meals.

Loretta toppled over late morning on the second day, and they helped her from the room. The meditation master threatened to beat me with a stick if I tried to go help her. I was to meditate! Later I would discover they had fed her orange juice and sweet dates, suggesting she relax—all the while, I struggled in torment with attaining inner peace.

Early afternoon on the third day, shortly before we would head home, the guru offered to answer our questions. He had an aura of enlightenment about him. When it was my turn, I asked how long I would need to meditate if I wanted to attain a spiritual aura such as his.

He took a long, deep breath. He said most novices begin around nine or ten years old and must diligently practice their meditation for twenty years or more in order to arrive at a state of spiritual equanimity and peace. But, he added, he had been observing me all weekend and was convinced it would take me considerably longer.

Instead I found my own way. I purchased a canoe and later a kayak to spend long, quiet afternoons paddling alone on the Assabet, Sudbury, and Concord Rivers. I developed a lifelong habit of taking long stomps through the Walden Woods and around the town forest, especially the part known locally as Fairyland, and then crossing over Route 2 to walk around Walden Pond.

I reread all my books by Emerson, Alcott, Hawthorne, and Thoreau, then ordered more. I plunged back into nature transcendentalism and its power to help my soul more fully awaken. This move to Concord helped nourish my emergence as a transcendentalist. My collection of religious artifacts grew as I practiced paths from multiple world religions. These spiritual practices in this setting became both my out-reaching branches and my spiritual roots.

I have had many teachers along my path—which sometimes seems like a pathless path. I am repeatedly surprised and always quite grateful to find the teacher I need at each step along the journey, whether as a human mentor, such as the first three mentors who had blessed me on my journey, or as a book that presented itself to me when I was ready for it. I could never have come this far without the help of so many others, for which I am grateful.

Back at Genzyme, our treatment for Gaucher's disease was doing well in human clinical trials. Genzyme had in our R&D pipeline two additional enzymes for treating other rare genetic diseases. Henri found and acquired sources of hyaluronic acid that promised many medical applications we could separately license to different medical companies.

Our operating companies were growing nicely, with improving efficiencies and profit margins. At most, though, they would offset only about half our annual R&D costs. We would be an unprofitable, development-stage company for many years to come. But for the first time in US history, such companies were successfully going public. I continued to prepare for our IPO, which plunged my life into overdrive, giving me yet another audacious high.

Theresa was as important as I was, perhaps more so, to Genzyme's going public. Preparing for the IPO, I often found myself, along with our auditors and Theresa, in negotiations with the chief accountant at the Securities and Exchange Commission (SEC). These were long, te-dious, technical accounting arguments about how to interpret GAAP in these new emerging circumstances. By some accounting interpreta-tions, we would look attractive to investors; by others, not at all. I am grateful for the SEC's challenges, as they allowed us to hone our very best accounting arguments.

We fought for and won the favorable interpretations that allowed us to go public. However, I couldn't find an accounting treatment that allowed us to capitalize rather than expense our massive R&D costs.

And without that, I couldn't persuade the leading biotech analyst at Kidder, Peabody & Co. that we should absorb such losses on our profit and loss (P&L). Instead, we refocused our business plan to use our IPO proceeds to further develop hyaluronic acid and our operating businesses. I would need to find another way to fund our treatments for orphan diseases.

The IPO was an enormous success, trading up 25 percent its first day. At closing, the banker handed me a check for $27 million to deposit in Genzyme's bank account, since the CEO and CFO were the sole signatories on the account. I felt enormous pride in being trusted with so much money. The character and integrity of individual entrepreneurs matter greatly. This is why I am so grateful to have been part of building a company with great integrity, with strong internal controls to avoid violating ethical boundaries. Investors need to know they can trust you, especially in times of stress, and you need friends and influence at times to succeed.

As outgoing president of the Mass Biotech Council, I gathered a group of CFOs from all the public biotech companies. We would come up with a way to make long-term, high-value R&D projects publicly fundable. We compiled a CFO's guide to finance and accounting for public biotech companies. We wanted to create the new industry standard for financing and accounting that included our high R&D costs. Because no one else had yet done such a thing, it was adopted nationally. In dealing with auditors, this became our accounting bible.

Seeing as we couldn't use IPO proceeds to fund the costs of the Gaucher's program, we used the emerging biotech accounting standard instead and created a novel financing structure: an R&D limited partnership called Genzyme Clinical Partners, modeled on IRS-approved real estate limited partnerships. This structure allowed investors to fund our risky human clinical trials, writing off their entire investment the year it was incurred, and have Genzyme buy back ownership of the partnership for appreciated common stock when and if the product was approved.

This would bring new revenues onto our P&L statement, make us appear better funded, larger, and more profitable, and actually have a less dilutive effect on our equity. Everybody came out ahead. We floated a $10 million R&D partnership that worked so well for all parties concerned that investors asked us to spin off additional R&D financing vehicles for orphan diseases about every other year thereafter.

It gave us better control over our R&D spending and created large tax benefits for our investors. Our stock appreciated enough upon success so we could buy back the resulting therapeutic relatively cheaply. This was a widely accepted, legitimate, and timely use of the tax code. However, within a year, others began to copy us—sometimes with less investor-friendly terms or higher risks that put such financing vehicles at risk.

In response to others' misuses of this kind of financing vehicle, the IRS kept changing what was allowed. By apportioning risk, cash flows, and returns, we continually restructured these vehicles to continue funding our leading-edge research in a highly profitable manner.

We were creating new classes of financing vehicles that better met our evolving financing needs. This was audacious innovation that made people a lot of money and helped to build an industry. I am deeply grateful for such innovation. That year, *CFO Magazine* named me, at age thirty-two, the most innovative public company CFO in the bio-technology sector.

When Henri hired me, he had asked me to promise to stay five years—not under contract, just a moral obligation. Over those five years, I raised over $80 million for Genzyme, helped radically improve our operating performance, created standards and structure for our worldwide financial and administrative systems, and introduced new and robust financing vehicles for new opportunities. I also oversaw the creation of our new corporate headquarters in Kendall Square, Cambridge, and our billion-dollar pharmaceutical protein plant located next to Harvard Business School. A heady success for my first decade in business.

Yet as the company grew, the CFO role would become less about directly impacting the operating businesses and more about focusing on administration and finance. We were hiring growing numbers of experienced executives to lead the diverse operations we were launching worldwide. As CFO, I became more of an umpire, even though I always had more of a general management orientation. I preferred creating solutions and managing people to simply monitoring others. But I kept my promise to Henri, staying five years and six weeks as his CFO—nearly three years beyond Genzyme's IPO—before moving on to my own excellent adventure.

I will always love and cherish the young scientific and business entrepreneurs who built Genzyme together, especially our culture of integrity and possibility. I feel truly grateful to have been in the right livelihood, in the right place, at the right time to make an important difference in the world. The spiritual discipline of gratitude was a key part of my success.

I have been so fortunate to be able to transition my sense of identity as new opportunities have presented themselves—from the small-town, white, working-class boy whose teacher encouraged and prepared him for Yale to the young executive who accepted the manners and mannerisms of the New England WASP business culture in order to have opportunities with Fortune 500 company boards and CEOs. From the heavily accented country bumpkin who, with sufficient training and experience, became a successful international business executive. And now to be a trusted and admired public company CFO. So much of it seems to be about how we present ourselves to the world.

American Heritage

It is amazing how much our lives are shaped by who we think we are, what we think we are capable of doing, how we respond to what happens to us, and who we become. I grew up in small-town culture in Rhode Island. Yet my mom's family had been in New England for over three hundred years. My maternal grandfather had researched these stories and gave them to his children in 1959. Those stories of my mother's family history could have helped shape my emerging four-year-old sense of identity, but my mother put them away for forty years, until my father had been long dead and buried.

On my mother's side, we descend from the Pilgrim John Alden, born in Harwich, England, in 1599. We also descend from John Crandall, a Welshman born in 1609 in Monmouthshire, England. His descendants settled around Tiverton and Little Compton beginning in the eighteenth century. Tiverton's Crandall Road is named after them. We weren't as different from other Central Baptist families as I had thought.

We are also descended from Robert Goodale, who was born in Ipswich, England, in 1603 and immigrated to America in 1634. His descendants established a homestead in Marlborough, Massachusetts. It was at this homestead in 1819 that my great-great-great aunt Lucy Goodale married Asa Thurston, a graduate of Yale College and Andover Theological Seminary. They were one of seven couples sent by the Baptist Missionary Board to be the first missionaries on the islands of Hawaii.

We are also descended from Abner Goodale, who fought with the rebels at Concord's North Bridge, and the loyalist Peter Collicutt, who fled north to New Brunswick, Canada, during the American Revolutionary War.

On my father's side, we descend from Gustaf Sonderland, born in 1858 in Dalarna County in the north of Sweden. He joined the king's guard. Serving at the palace in Stockholm, he met and married Augusta Bergland, a lady-in-waiting to the queen. In 1880, they immigrated to Worcester, Massachusetts, establishing the Swedish immigrant side of our family.

Think how much different my sense of self-identity would have been growing up if I had known we were descended from America's first families as well as recent immigrants. That some of my ancestors had successfully graduated from Yale, Harvard, Massachusetts Institute of Technology, and Mount Holyoke. That some had fought at Fort Barton, fished off Sakonnet Point, fought at the North Bridge, and helped create a country long before I was born. This is my American heritage.

Of course, human realities are socially constructed. Our sense of "us" and "them" makes an enormous difference in our lives. But they need not limit us.

My children have grown up with a strong sense of their own diverse cultural heritage. As Robert described it once to his cousins in China, he and his sister are one-quarter descended from WASP settlers of colonial New England who helped build America, one-quarter descended from Swedish immigrants who moved to New England over one hundred years ago to build a new life, one-quarter descended from Chinese of Shanghai, world renowned as shrewd traders and business people, and one-quarter descended from the Naxi people, a Chinese minority group living in the foothills of the Himalayas. His maternal grandfather came to the United States on a prized scholarship and stayed to make a new life here when the Communists conquered China. This is their heritage, bringing together many diverse cultures into one American life, drawing upon cultures from around the world.

Living and Dying

A big piece of our family story relates to my gay brother, David. David graduated from Boston University with an English degree in 1975. In 1978, he secured a position teaching English literature at a tough inner-city high school in Brooklyn, New York.

David lived in Manhattan and was involved in the gay lifestyle of NYC in the early 1980s. He spent the school year trying to hold his students' attention and teach them some English, and he spent his summers full of art and counterculture in Provincetown. David had a shy sense of humor. Somehow, while openly living as a gay man in NYC, he kept being gay a secret from our parents in Rhode Island for almost a decade. No one wanted to confront what Baptists said about homosexuals or gay men.

We had recently moved to Concord when David was diagnosed with HIV. He was hospitalized with a bronchial infection, and the doctors weren't sure what was causing all these opportunistic infections gay men were dying from. In those days, dying of AIDS was greatly stigmatized. Sarah was four and Robert was two when we first told them their uncle was dying of AIDS. David was one of the first patients in the AZT experimental drug group, and it probably added eighteen months to his life.

My brother Donald also lived in Manhattan at the time. He could support and provide brotherly companionship for David. We helped where we could. David introduced me to *A Course in Miracles* and the other spiritual practices he relied upon. These spiritual practices, along with a close circle of friends, made the final two years of his life bearable.

Finally in 1988, David could no longer keep this secret from our parents. Given homophobia among Baptists, we had no idea how they would respond to his being gay and dying of AIDS. However, we need not have worried. My father said God wanted us to love one another. Everything else was secondary. So my entire extended family—and even my father's Baptist church—welcomed David home to die. This was transformative for my family of birth.

Sarah was now seven and Robert was five as they experienced their first death of a close family member. They heard us talk of the deep prejudices of the broader society, and they saw us cry our tears as we distributed David's ashes off his beloved Sakonnet Point. We played John Lennon's "Imagine" as we scattered David's ashes in the water.

Life is beautiful and real, and so is death. Following David's death, my mother, a Baptist minister's wife, began speaking at gay men's gatherings, leading support groups, and telling young gay men they were loved. Many gay men, some estranged from their own mothers, lined up with tears in their eyes to be hugged by my mother and to be assured that God loved them too. This is the kind of extended family we wanted to bring our kids up within. This is a way of transcending life and death. This is audaciously embracing both living and dying.

My son Robert and I were very close up until he was about ten or so, but then he had a very hard time in middle school. He stopped talking to me. As a Cub Scout, he had always liked to hike in the woods, but he didn't like to camp out. So we began a tradition of father-son hiking trips each summer. We began hiking from inn to inn along the Long Trail in Vermont. Over time, we expanded into western Massachusetts, Upstate New York, northern New Hampshire, and eventually our favorite, Acadia National Park in Maine. Cadillac Mountain joined Fort Barton, Sakonnet Point, East Rock, and Walden Pond as transcendent places for my soul. Mountains, long walks in nature, and being with loved ones restore my soul.

The long drive to the hiking area was often enough to get Robert and me talking just like old times. And days spent climbing mountain trails, followed by a great meal and warm beds, always cheered us up. We've continued our annual tradition of father-son outings for nearly twenty years.

We have a relationship built over many years and over our many experiences traveling together. He is my favorite traveling companion. We've gotten to know the restaurants and bars of Bar Harbor when we hike Acadia. We've walked the entire inner cities of London, Berlin, and Paris over the course of two days each. My very favorite was a walking tour of Scotland—from east to west, Edinburgh to Oban, each night staying at a different hotel and sampling a local single malt distillery. Life is good!

An Excellent Adventure

The late 1980s saw a breakthrough in transgenic science, where genetic information is transferred from one species into another through microinjection into an embryo, thereby mixing human and animal genes together. Suddenly, amazing new models of human diseases, cheaper production systems for human pharmaceuticals, and incredible opportunities in genetically modified food all became possible. The scramble was on.

I was New England's best-known biotech CFO, well regarded for my reputation for integrity and fundraising. My name was in the mix with venture capitalists to become chairman and CEO of a startup by my early thirties. I did aspire to run my own company, but I had promised Henri I'd stay at Genzyme five years. My fifth anniversary of employment wouldn't be until February 1989, so I turned away all offers until that day neared.

Most transgenic opportunities required relocating from Concord. But one opportunity in particular caught my interest: a Worcester, MA startup called Transgenic Sciences Inc. (TSI), led by former scientists from Integrated Genetics in Framingham. Integrated Genetics had explored transgenics, but they decided to focus on the potentially higher value pharmaceutical production aspects. So a few of their former scientists started TSI to focus on other applications of the science.

In 1988 alone, TSI had signed an exclusive research agreement with the Tufts University veterinary school for animal models, licensed in vitro drug-screening technology from MIT, initiated research to create transgenic food animals through a collaborative research and development agreement with the US Department of Agriculture, entered into a collaborative research program on transgenic production of human growth hormone at UMass Amherst, and lined up a small New York investment bank to take them public in 1989. And for their IPO, they needed a recognized biotech leader to lead them as chairman and CEO.

My decision was not as straightforward as it might seem in retrospect. Genzyme was beginning to consider the transgenic area as well, which meant TSI might one day go head-to-head with Genzyme. In discussions of my career, Henri suggested he might one day make me his chief operating officer, but not yet. He expected me to be patient at age thirty-three.

Also, I liked the venture capitalist who had given TSI its first investment, but I didn't trust some of the other founders of this startup, and the NYC investment bank had a pretty awful reputation. This would be a risky venture to lead, yet it had key scientific relationships and initial funding already in place. Plus, it was the most interesting startup within an easy commute from our house in transcendentalist Concord.

After long discussions with my family, Henri, and some of my closest friends in business, I agreed to accept this role in January 1989. I needed to complete Genzyme's 1988 annual audit and prepare the transition of my responsibilities, so I worked for Genzyme through March 1989.

To help manage my extraordinary career risk, I negotiated to be elected TSI's chairman, president, and CEO and to approve at least four of the eight members of the board of directors. This company needed to be built on integrity with its science, people, and external relations, and it hadn't begun entirely in that fashion. With that understood, I embarked upon this excellent adventure. It would turn out to be the riskiest and wildest ride of my already risky and wild career.

We renamed the company TSI Corporation. In a flurry of activity, we completed a small public offering in May 1989 at $1.25 per share, netting $1.9 million after repayment of the investment bank's bridge loan. We doubled the size of our scientific team, even though that meant our IPO cash would last less than fifteen months. The *Boston Business Journal* did a full-page description of our newly public company, featuring a portrait of me as a very well-dressed, serious, and businesslike young chairman and CEO.

With so little cash, we needed to show our success very quickly. I earnestly began looking for ways to leapfrog our competitors in the preclinical drug testing business while also finding a cheaper way to fund our growth. I drew on my experiences at both Bain and Genzyme to make this an outstanding company and to be able to get results quickly.

I found a small unprofitable animal-testing laboratory in downtown Worcester. It was owned by a local multinational conglomerate, but the lab business was no longer strategic. I knew this facility could give us immediate operating revenues. It could provide a platform to utilize our developing transgenic human-disease models on behalf of their existing customers. And given what I had learned at Bain and Genzyme, we could possibly improve the laboratory's operating margins enough to pay off the acquisition costs largely with their own cash flow.

The large conglomerate, however, was more concerned with how the sale of this small division would appear on their balance sheet. It needed to be structured to be nondilutive for stockholders' equity and give them a onetime gain rather than a lot of cash. So I structured a $7 million purchase price consisting of $1 million cash, $2.5 million in redeemable convertible preferred stock, and $3.5 million borrowed from a local bank collateralized by the operating division we were buying. We were borrowing half the purchase price using the lab's own assets.

We scheduled to close the transaction in early December 1989, but over Thanksgiving, the banking environment started to decline, making closing much more difficult. A week before TSI's transaction was scheduled to close, our Worcester bank manager called to say the credit committee had agreed to go forward, despite the deteriorating banking environment—but only if I personally guaranteed the loan and pledged the title to our house, our stock, and our personal assets as security.

I had sold my Genzyme shares earlier in 1989 to diversify our family's finances, avoid any conflict with Genzyme's potential transgenic interests, pay off our mortgage, and set up a small investment portfolio. Our assets wouldn't cover the $3.5 million loan, so if TSI defaulted on the loan, it would result in our personal bankruptcy.

That weekend, Loretta and I had a long conversation about what it means to be a biotechnology entrepreneur. She agreed for us to do this on two conditions: one, when our house's title was returned to us, it would forever after be in her name alone; and two, we would change banks at the earliest opportunity. In taking entrepreneurial risks, there are advantages to being married to such a hardheaded entrepreneur.

Becoming Number One

Boston magazine's January 1990 issue focused on "Faces to Watch in the 1990s" and featured me as their leading technology company CEO, which gave us the ability to raise more money and hire great people. It also fed my ego-self. They held a big conference, and my picture was everywhere: *a face to watch in the 1990s.* They even gave me a mirror for my bathroom with the same slogan, so every morning I was greeted with this affirmation. This was a big deal—and the seed of my ultimate destruction.

At the age of thirty-four, I was on top of the world. As a result of all this publicity, our stock price doubled. I led panels at Mass Biotech Council meetings and gave keynote speeches for the national industry organization. I was invited to speak at Ted Kennedy's events and also honored at the Ernst & Young annual biotechnology conference in Laguna Niguel in Southern California. Loretta did her best to remind me I was not brilliant or superhuman. Rather, I was relatively smart and hardworking but also just in the right place at the right time. She warned me fame was fickle and could easily turn on me as well.

The *Central Massachusetts Business Digest* featured me on its cover, the smiling CEO, standing in our microinjection laboratory. It described how TSI could be part of bringing back the "Massachusetts Miracle" of the 1980s. The national *Businessweek* magazine devoted their cover story to "The Genetic Age" and on page seventy featured a photograph of me in my best business suit with white mice running all over me. My quote: "The first thing you do with a new gene is put it in a mouse to see what it does."

The science was progressing wonderfully, but we were still at a very early stage as a company. There was no good way yet to fairly value our scientific-disease models. Improving the operating business came more readily. It took us only nine months to improve the operations of the business we acquired so that it would be profitable enough to cover a large portion of our research costs and bring us close to breakeven performance overall.

And it took only six months of over-the-top publicity to double our stock price again and trigger an outstanding warrant call, raising $3.3 million in additional financing. That allowed us to pay down the bank loan, convert the preferred stock, and cancel my personal guarantee and pledges. TSI switched banks, and it was Loretta's house now. We would never personally be so highly leveraged, and at such great financial risk, ever again.

During those six months, we focused our transgenic research on four key human-disease models and also explored other preclinical and biological companies we could acquire to capitalize on my experience base. Our board and investors began to dream of building a high-growth, research-oriented, widely diversified, operating biological business with extraordinary shareholder returns, strong values, and shared vision.

We were driven to succeed. Perhaps driving too fast. Literally. I got so many speeding tickets driving between Concord and Worcester that I temporarily had my license suspended. Fortunately, I was able to compensate one of my brothers, who was temporarily available, to drive me to and from work each day. Whether it be in driving, in company-building, or in life, there is such a thing as going too fast. It isn't sustainable. But I was young and in a hurry.

TSI was grabbing market share before anyone else could. But by 1990, there were already a dozen venture-backed transgenic companies presenting at investor conferences. The field was already getting too crowded. I listened to each company's presentation and read their public materials. I felt TSI was one of the three best-positioned companies, but we would still need to find a way to draw press attention and financing to fund our rapid growth.

I met with the CEOs of two other well-positioned startups. We agreed our research areas did not overlap or compete. TSI was the leading company in creating human-disease models, mostly in transgenic mice. The best-capitalized transgenic company was producing genetically leaner pigs in Pennsylvania. A Dutch transgenic company had the strongest science for addressing the larger pharmaceutical markets by producing human drugs in cow's milk.

We each agreed to tell any reporters and bankers that we thought the other two companies were the most exciting opportunities in transgenics in addition to our own. The Dutch CEO even coined a catchy phrase to help investors remember the differences between us. He said, "The Pennsylvania transgenic company is hogging food applications, whereas my story is a bull story, and Jim's is a story of mice and men." Within months, we three emerged in the public imagination as the dominant forces in our respective transgenic sectors with ample funding opportunities.

There are surprise visits you never want to encounter, such as that FDA raid my first year at Genzyme. In my second year as chairman and CEO at TSI, we received a surprise visit from the Federal Bureau of Investigation (FBI). It seems in the 1980s, many molecular biologists kept backup samples of their company's cell lines in their home freezers. After all, a temporary power outage could wipe out a cell line representing many years of work. The companies owned those backup cell lines. When the biologists left their employers, they were required by contract to return any and all such cell lines. Not all of them did.

The FBI had a sting operation, posing as Russian scientists trying to acquire US biotechnology. One of our molecular biologists had a tissue Plasminogen Activator(t-PA) cell line stored in his home freezer. He had offered to sell it to these supposed Russian agents. Now the FBI needed me to confirm this scientist had not stolen any TSI cell lines as well. Fortunately, our safety protocols protected TSI and our cell lines. The scientist went to jail. Integrity still counts when you least think about it.

The following year, TSI doubled in size and scope through three small US acquisitions. At the board's request in March 1990, I developed a strategic plan for TSI Corporation to become a billion-dollar corporation. It tracked the historical revenue-growth trajectories of Walmart, Costco, Sysco, Wang Laboratories, Food Lion, Toys "R" Us, Apple, Nike, Computer Associates, Microsoft, and Lotus Software.

Between 1970 and 1990, these high-growth companies took on average twelve years, during times of tremendous technological change, to go from startup to $1 billion in revenue. Their average annual return to their shareholders varied, from as low as 13 percent for Apple to 122 percent for Costco. In fact, the greater the companies' dependency on technology, the lower their financial return. Based on this plan, our board approved the strategy to assemble a world-class management team to undertake the audacious goal of attempting to become by 2003 a billion-dollar leader in this emerging field of preclinical and clinical testing of biopharmaceuticals.

According to industry sources, total spending on preclinical and clinical drug testing was $12 billion in 1988, of which $2 billion was contracted out to 450 independent labs. The largest of these independent laboratories were international and could offer the latest technology for testing, and one even had annual revenues in excess of $100 million. Yet the average independent laboratory had only $4 million in revenues in one local laboratory. The industry was growing at 6 percent a year and so was forecast to reach $27 billion by 2003.

As the technological sophistication of drug testing grew, pharmaceutical companies increasingly contracted work to independent labs. So our sector was forecast to reach $11 billion by 2003 and to be dominated by a number of large, technologically sophisticated, multinational, and well-financed competitors. Our corporate strategy called for us to be among that small emerging group of companies over the next fifteen years.

Our 1990 annual report featured a picture of one of our transgenic mice on the cover. By 1991, our annual report was able to celebrate our diverse, growing international team of scientists and managers as well as the depth of experience we had recruited to join our mission. In less than three years, we had created and come to dominate an entirely new transgenic biotechnology business sector.

In the midst of this chaotic growth, I focused on my growing international connections and my spirituality. We had two facilities in Japan: a research lab in Tokyo and a contract testing lab in Osaka. Japanese "saving face" culture often prevents executives from saying precisely what they mean. Because I didn't understand Japanese, in negotiations, I always had one person translating the words spoken and another person translating the expected meaning of those words. Gradually I became more comfortable and proficient in Japanese culture.

Long days negotiating with Japanese executives would often end with us exchanging stories over beer in a bar, followed by dinner with sake, and ending at their favorite club in Ginza, an upscale entertainment area that includes private clubs for executives and a red-light district. We developed the kinds of intimate friendships that can seldom be developed in the boardroom. These were not only my collaborators and potential customers but also my friends.

In time, some of them invited me to the hot springs, or public bath resorts. Everyone would marvel at the whiteness of my skin as we sat around naked, enjoying the hot, tepid, and ice-cold baths. Our talk often turned to Zen Buddhism and how I might learn that spiritual path.

Zen descends from Chan Buddhism, a melding of Chinese Taoist mental concentration and Mahayana Buddhist meditation practices. Whenever I stayed a week or more in Japan, I spent the weekend in Kyoto, the ancient capital and spiritual center of Japan, partway between Osaka and Tokyo. Monks were happy to show me the ancient ways of Zen Buddhism and let me rest and concentrate away from the stresses of business and family.

Zen taught me to focus as never before, to establish an island of calm in the midst of the chaos, and to be at one with all that is. There was little enough time in my busy life to meditate, yet being spiritually grounded created focus and concentration, which dramatically improved how much I could get done each day.

At home, I took to rising early to meditate in the quiet of the morning, and I spent evenings reading spiritual texts of one sort or another. So in a busy life, my spiritual practice still thrived. I was grounded in my spiritual practice, even as I led TSI's soaring success.

By 1991, Amgen had become the largest biotech company on the West Coast, with a sixty-one-times price-earnings ratio and a $5 billion market capitalization. Genzyme had emerged as the largest biotech company on the East Coast, with $250 million in cash reserves, a thirty-three-times price-earnings ratio, and a $600 million market capitalization. TSI Corporation was emerging as the fastest growing of the next generation of biotech companies.

Ernst & Young, Merrill Lynch, and *Inc. Magazine* offered an annual prize for Entrepreneur of the Year. TSI Corporation was a finalist in 1990 and again in 1991. Imagine my sense of pride that the company I had built had so quickly emerged triumphant.

But rapid growth takes on a life of its own. Our managers had joined for career growth, and our investors had invested for rapid share growth. Now many of them lusted for more.

In 1991, the *Worcester Business Journal* ranked TSI the number one fastest-growing public company in Massachusetts. Against my better judgment, but again feeding my ego-self, they featured me on their cover wearing a magician's white tuxedo and standing in front of a neon DNA molecule as they described our emerging dominant position in the biotech sector. They saw our incredible growth as a kind of magic. Only in the article's final paragraph did they acknowledge that TSI was the first company to focus on AIDS-disease models partly due to my older brother David's death from AIDS. In May 1991, TSI raised another $12.5 million to complete four more acquisitions of US and international companies.

The *Institutional Investor*'s top-ranked biotechnology analyst issued his judgment in July 1991 that the three best investments in biotechnology were Amgen, Genzyme, and TSI Corporation. Our stock doubled yet again. With our soaring stock price, we completed a unique R&D offering called Exemplar, which funded off-balance sheet the completion of our first four human-disease models, including the one for AIDS.

In a special "Inside Business" feature, the *Boston Globe* championed our strategy. We were on a rocket, following a strategy to take us to a billion dollars. Completely fearless. Fortune favors the audacious! Our management team felt invincible as we cleared hurdle after hurdle and emerged a clear industry frontrunner. Our success both drove and was driven by our rising stock price.

Unfortunately, the accelerating yin-yang nature of our growth was unsustainable. Someone with a little perspective—or perhaps a little more maturity—probably could have seen what was coming.

By the end of 1991, we had completed our international expansion, buying out a competitor's laboratories in France, acquiring the leading preclinical-drug-testing laboratory in Germany, and opening an even more advanced genetic research laboratory in Japan. I was traveling over half of every week just to keep up with our expanding operations.

Our stock doubled again, up 800 percent in less than three years. TSI raised another $28 million in a follow-up public offering in January 1992 to continue our quest to be the number one company in our field. But by annually doubling our staff and revenues for three consecutive years, we had created an environment of enormous corporate chaos. The integrity and coherence of our company culture was at risk. Yet with revenues of $45 million annually, we had emerged as the fifth largest preclinical-drug-testing laboratory in the world.

Embracing Worldly Power

I began to look for opportunities to give 10 percent of our new wealth away or use it to do even more good in the world—when and if I could ever make this newfound wealth liquid.

One opportunity came my way shortly thereafter in the form of a poor black Baptist church four blocks behind my office. They had taken out a mortgage to renovate and expand the interior of the church. When the banking environment declined, their mortgage was sold to another financial group. Now the church was in default and were being foreclosed upon with very little notice. The congregation was at risk of losing their church building if they couldn't come up with the entire amount within a week.

I met with the black pastor, who I must admit reminded me of my father. Then I called the local bank president and offered to collateralize this mortgage with my TSI stock if he would buy out the other financial entity and avoid foreclosure. He was happy to do so. Three years later, when the church was thriving again, they paid down the mortgage enough to release my guarantee. My resources had helped them weather their storm.

I liked this outcome so much that I've collateralized guarantees through banks twice more to give friends and family time to find their way back from dire financial straits. This is an important way to express our gratitude for our many successes in life. Over the years, Loretta and I have gratefully lent or gifted money to over half of my siblings in their times of need. We count ourselves lucky to be able to do so. There is a tremendous difference between simple greed and using your financial success to become a benefactor for others. How you make your money and what you do with it makes all the difference in spiritual terms.

At TSI, our genetic-disease models were among the most scientifically advanced for biotechnology drug research and development. We began to forward integrate our business by acquiring a leading Phase One human clinical trial company in London. I restructured our senior management team to try to restore some measure of control.

To make more time for my international business travel, I finally stepped down from the board of directors of the Mass Biotech Council. They honored my founding role with a very lavish dinner celebration. I felt good about my role in creating an industry, but now I needed to save my company.

I would attempt to reign in the dragon I had created at TSI, without getting singed, while still adhering to the values upon which we had built the company—and still maintaining the stock price we needed to succeed. Our mission became more urgent. My increasingly exhortatory speeches to our employees sometimes got so evangelical that some of our senior managers would feel moved to yell "Hallelujah!" or "Amen!" to punctuate my good words.

We live our days in the midst of living and dying. The year after Loretta and I met in college, my dad almost died. He was diagnosed with aggressive lymphoma and given six months to live. At the time, I was feeling fairly estranged from my father, having left the Baptists along with his dreams for me in ministry. I was struggling, unsuccessfully, to finish Yale on schedule. Still, we headed up to Boston, where he had been transferred to the care of a leading oncologist.

US medicine didn't know much about curing cancer in 1977. But my dad's oncologist found a therapeutic in human clinical trials that showed promise and obtained some on a compassionate-use basis. My father went into full remission. It was a miracle! He was in remission for nearly fourteen years.

But by the end of 1991, he was again hospitalized with lymphoma. His new oncologist went looking for the drug, but it was unavailable, having failed in human clinical trials. It was now too late for my dad, but what TSI was learning with these new disease models could make all the difference for better survival outcomes for other families in the future.

This was part of my motivation to make a career in preclinical and clinical development. I wanted to do well financially, but I also wanted to make a difference. Our disease models helped develop many lifesaving drugs and added many years to families' lives together.

In the fourteen years that clinical-stage drug gave my father, he found a new sense of himself as a teacher; he healed relationships with his children, most dramatically with David; and he watched his first five grandchildren grow up, including Sarah and Robert. He experienced much joy in those years of living. We should all be so lucky as to live a longer life, and one that is more full of living life well.

Even during the long months he spent in the hospital dying that winter of 1991–92, he was a minister of God. Nurses would find him sitting with other cancer patients, hearing their grief and suffering, and offering them compassion as the pastor he was. He remained a faithful minister of God until he could no longer raise himself from his bed. Despite our differences over the years, he has always been a role model for me.

For six more weeks, Ed's doctors hooked him up to ever more machines to keep his bodily functions going—machines that sapped his strength and hindered his ability to communicate. Finally, his doctors concluded it would only be a matter of days. At my dad's request, they disconnected all the machines and let him go home to die.

In his final week of life, Ed was able to set many things right. He was worried about my mother; they were in a very precarious financial situation. But Loretta assured him we were doing very well and would always take care of my mother.

Ed had led a hard life and had risen to many challenges. In the end, he died surrounded by family. Instead of dying young, as Loretta's dad had, Ed lived those extra fourteen years, and we were deeply blessed. However, his estate was in horrible condition. As a Depression-era kid, he was a hoarder. It took seven industrial-size dumpsters to clear out his clutter. The house I grew up in was in poor repair, as were two other heavily mortgaged rental properties he had purchased. Dad had also spent $18,555 investing in decorative plates from the Bradford Exchange. After much effort, Loretta managed to liquidate them for about $10,000. His exotic real estate portfolio—the swampland in northern Florida, a desert lot in Mexico, and the undeveloped scrub brush in southern Florida—all went for little more than the taxes due.

At my parents' wedding, my mother's father had gifted them a collection of blue-chip American stock certificates. In his pride, my father stored them away in a safe deposit box and never tried to cash them or invest them. He had no sense of their value. Over forty-five years, they had now appreciated to more than $100,000. I was once again grateful for a wise maternal grandfather.

After we liquidated my parents' entire estate, and thanks to those blue-chip stocks, my mom had $336,000 to live on for the rest of her life. But she had no place to live. Loretta and I promised her that she would never be destitute or alone.

The year 1992 would be TSI's most successful ever—*Inc. Magazine* even named me a finalist for 1992 Entrepreneur of the Year—but it would also be a dark night of the soul for our personal life. In the thick of everything, when there was no time to consider anything else but TSI, my world was completely shattered. Loretta was diagnosed with an ovarian cyst. Suddenly nothing else mattered. At eight and ten, Robert and Sarah were much too young to understand their thirty-four-year-old mother's life might be at risk. So I carried that worry entirely upon my own shoulders.

The doctors quickly prepped for surgery to remove one of Loretta's ovaries along with the cyst. Thank goodness the cyst turned out to be benign. But the experience still shattered our sense of security and well-being. Our lives were so fragile, subject to catastrophe at any time.

We had struggled with David's long illness and his death at the age of thirty-five, Loretta's father's death at age sixty, and then my father's decline and death at the age of seventy. But the very idea of Loretta's possible death at so young an age completely devastated me. I would gladly trade all my worldly success to keep the love of my life. Fortunately for us, the worst did not happen.

My brother Steve once again came and helped care for the children. With excellent medical care and strong support systems at home, Loretta recovered quickly, and I am eternally grateful for the many kindnesses of our families. They made our living possible.

I returned to my role as chairman and CEO with a new awareness of the fragility of life. Success was sweet, but family was sweeter, and we all lived just one diagnosis from disaster. I needed to find a way to hold onto what was good while doing my job well.

TSI had been racing ahead now for four years, capitalizing on our transgenic technology and my international business experience. We had become one of the five largest competitors in the world in this emerging field, with the expectation that we could emerge with revenues of over $1 billion when the industry completed its process of worldwide consolidation in 2003.

Over this period of four years, we had completed six separate financings and seven more acquisitions, and we had started two operating divisions from scratch. TSI entered 1993 stronger than ever with a budgeted revenue target of $70 million, over seven hundred employees, a fixed-cost base of $55 million, and an expectation for turning profitable on a worldwide basis for the very first time.

A Prideful Fall

My 1993 budget presentation to TSI's board ended with three definitions of success. The first was a definition sometimes erroneously attributed to Ralph Waldo Emerson but actually from Bessie Anderson Stanley, which I had kept on my desk for years:

> To laugh often and much; to win the respect of intelligent persons and the affection of children; to earn the approbation of honest critics and endure the betrayal of false friends; to appreciate beauty.
>
> To find the best in others; to give one's self; to leave the world a bit better, whether by a healthy child, a garden patch, or a redeemed social condition; to have played and laughed with enthusiasm and sung with exultation; to know even one life has breathed easier because you have lived—this is to have succeeded.

The second was what I called Bain's definition of success:

> A superior financial return for shareholders over an extended time period. Finding high-growth sectors to maximize business opportunities, with a focus on relative market share, value creation, and high reward for high performance.

Finally, the third one I called the Genzyme measure of success:
> Building an important corporation faster and better than the
> competition, with great expectations, satisfying but not focusing on
> shareholders, stretching forecasts as far as you reasonably can, and
> then working like crazy to make them happen, because results are
> all that matter.

We wanted to succeed by all these measures. But little did we know that as we approved this budget, the newly elected president of the United States was creating a health care task force that would accidentally destroy our company.

First Lady Hillary Rodham Clinton chaired the task force and in March 1993 announced they would seek caps on drug prices in the United States. In order to put pressure on the federal government, the Pharmaceutical Research and Manufacturers Association (PhRMA) immediately suggested its members discontinue their existing preclinical and clinical development contracts and lay off nonessential R&D employees.

By April, our 1993 revenues had fallen to $34 million, less than half what we had on the books in January. Our stock price was in free fall, and we were hemorrhaging cash. I called an emergency board meeting. We were days from defaulting on our bank lines and needing to file for bankruptcy.

The board decided to go into executive session without me present. After several hours of contentious discussion, mostly about whose fault this was, they voted to fire me.

I was devastated. It seemed surreal.

Our stock had already fallen by two-thirds, but upon the announcement of my being fired, it fell much further. My severance terms were set by my contract, but most of our people were at-will employees. So when the board voted to lay off half of them, I went to bat for them to ensure their families were not too shabbily treated. I spent the better part of the next six weeks assisting severance negotiations, exit interviews, and outplacement counseling for employees whom TSI had laid off.

None of us had seen this coming. Calling upon my industry network, I assisted many of them in this unexpected transition.

For my own family, it was an incredible blow. I had lost my position of honor and respect, my great salary and bonus, and my industry reputation. Our net worth declined by 90 percent over six weeks. My fame, fortune, purpose, and identity were all destroyed in this unexpected cataclysm. I felt like I was a sacrificial lamb.

Yet losing my company was never as bad as losing my wife would have been the year before. Life is precious. Fame is fleeting. I fell from the high wire but did not die. So I gathered family and friends around me and tried to be grateful for yet another chapter in life beginning.

The *Worcester Telegram & Gazette* devoted a large part of its business section to the morality tale of TSI taking on too much concentrated business risk, leaving us vulnerable to this temporary business downturn. The *Wall Street Journal (WSJ)* summarized my obituary in three short paragraphs: bright guy, brilliant plan, destroyed as collateral damage.

Suddenly people who had for years chased me for access would go quiet when I entered a room. Or they'd look away or head the other direction to avoid me, as if being collateral damage could be somehow contagious. Then again, other people who had never made time for me suddenly reached out with kind words of support. My self-identity was on a roller coaster, my self-esteem gyrating wildly.

The week after my termination appeared in the *WSJ*, one prominent Boston venture capitalist called me. I had pitched to him on numerous occasions, but he had never invested. He reassured me there was the potential for resurrection even after public executions. He offered to invest $2 million from his fund in whatever I decided to do next.

I began watching Steven Spielberg's movie *Hook,* where Peter Pan has grown up to be a clever financier who dabbles in mergers and acquisitions, forgetting the essence of his being. That is, until his nemesis, Captain Hook, steals Peter's children and forces him to return to Neverland to remember who he is so he can save his family.

I must have watched this children's movie twenty or thirty times, long after my wife and children grew bored with it. But this felt like my situation. *Hook* became my Delphic oracle explaining my fall from grace. Now I needed to rediscover my true identity, decide whom to truly be, and find my right occupation for the next stage of my life. From every failure comes new opportunities.

New Hope

When I was on top of the world with everyone singing my praises, Loretta would remind me, "I know you better than they do, and you're not as brilliant as they say you are." Then when everything fell apart and the *WSJ* wrote my obituary, Loretta affirmed, "I know you better than they do, and you're not as foolish as they say you are." My family has always understood me in a way that helps us navigate life's challenges together. I am very grateful for Loretta and my family.

While recovering from my downfall, Loretta suggested that once school got out for the year, we go hiking and camping at Acadia National Park with another Concord couple who had kids the same ages as ours. I went reluctantly, but hiking and being in nature always cheers me.

The morning of the second day, I was awakened at predawn by the singing of birds. So I got up, dressed quietly, and made my way to the top of a nearby hill. I watched one of the most beautiful sunrises ever, alone on the hilltop, with the birds singing forth as harbingers of hope, and my family sleeping peacefully below me. I wept. No matter how difficult the fall or how painful it feels, the sun also rises and life begins anew. This was an important step in awakening along my journey to spiritual maturity.

Investors began asking what I would do next. It seems some were interested in me now, whereas before they had felt it was too risky to back someone so sure of himself who had experienced nothing but successes in his first dozen years in business. Others had made a lot of money by following me before and now wished to make more. They knew I could accomplish great things while now being acutely aware of how quickly it could all turn bad. Friends suggested that when knocked off a horse, you leap right back on, or you never would.

I started getting offers for new opportunities as president and CEO of early-stage biotechnology companies, some of which had even better technologies and more funding for treatments and cures for human disease that looked even more exciting for the future.

As I struggled to choose between these attractive offers, I was forced to think about my life. For example, one opportunity looked quite exciting, with excellent science, strong funding, and a great senior management team. But it was located west of Philadelphia and would require me to spend four days a week away from my family for the next several years. Once again, I'd have to choose between family and success.

Sarah was now eleven, and Robert was nine. The strain and stress of the last few years at TSI were already having a negative effect on them and on my relationship with them. I was approaching the age of thirty-eight—much too young to retire, and our finances were in shambles given TSI's collapse. But perhaps I could step back from working eighty to ninety hours a week, from being the person in charge, from putting everything at risk each day.

My decision was helped along when my former mentor Henri called me. He asked to see my final business plan for TSI. Genzyme had bought Integrated Genetics (IG) and had inherited their transgenic business as part of the deal. But IG had focused on producing pharmaceuticals in goat's milk, which was a high-risk, long-term scientific strategy.

Henri said he thought my strategies were generally sound and that Genzyme had plenty of cash in the bank to wait out the return of the pharmaceutical companies. I still owned 5 percent of TSI's now nearly worthless common stock, so I went over to Genzyme to present why TSI was now grossly undervalued.

Two weeks later, Genzyme Transgenic offered to buy TSI for 50 percent above market. To run this new division and implement my strategic plan, Henri appointed a young Yale graduate with an HBS MBA who had worked at Bain & Company.

I felt it was a fitting finish to my days as an entrepreneur. The sale of the company gave me investment capital to pursue my next venture. After anxious years making my way along a tightrope, I had fallen, only to discover that, in truth, the tightrope is stretched barely two feet above the ground. I still had abundant resources to rely upon. I learned that I need not have been so afraid. I learned to greet both success and failure with gratitude as my teachers.

This is the key to the spiritual discipline of gratitude. When good things happen, it's easy to be grateful, even if people sometimes aren't. But our joys and sorrows are woven fine together. If we engage with life, we will experience both. If we live life with audacity, our joys and our sorrows multiply. This is the nature of being human.

This third spiritual discipline of gratitude works best when one has first learned resilience and surrender. It's gratitude for life as it is. Gratitude for the good things we seek for ourselves and others. Gratitude for the pain and suffering we endure along the way. Gratitude that we feel, that we suffer, that we endure. Gratitude in which we sometimes find new hope.

The Buddha says, "Life is suffering." We are not rocks. We are not islands. Because we love, we will inevitably be hurt. But we are transformed in the process, and for that we should be grateful.

AUDACIOUS GRATITUDE

Chalice-Lighting Words

Grateful people experience higher levels of positive emotions such as joy, enthusiasm, love, happiness, and optimism. The practice of gratitude as a discipline protects a person from the destructive impulses of envy, resentment, greed, and bitterness.
—*Thanks!* Robert A. Emmons, PhD

Check-in: What role does gratitude play in your happiness with life?

Additional Reading from *The Joy of Living* by Yongey Mingyur Rinpoche

Imagine spending your life in a little room with only one locked window so dirty it barely admits any light. You'd probably think the world was a pretty dim and dreary place, full of strangely shaped creatures that cast terrifying shadows against the dirty glass as they passed your room. But suppose one day you spill some water on the window. . . . A little of the dirt that had accumulated on the glass comes away. Suddenly a small patch of light comes through the glass. Curious, you might rub a little harder, and as more dirt comes away, more light streams in. Maybe, you think, the world isn't so dark and dreary after all. Maybe it's the window. . . . In truth, you have not changed anything at all. The world, the light, and the people were always there. You just couldn't see them because your vision was obscured. But now you see it all, and what a difference it makes!

Questions to Ponder

1. What are the causes of Jim's resurrection?

2. How does his audacity factor into his business success?

3. How does becoming UU and transcendentalist change his spiritual life?

4. What cultural and socioeconomic identities do you carry?

5. How does his business successes and failure transform Jim?

6. What are your sources of hope and gratitude?

Closing Words

This is the key to the spiritual discipline of gratitude. When good things happen, it's easy to be grateful, even if people sometimes aren't. But our joys and sorrows are woven fine together. If we engage with life, we will experience both. If we live life with audacity, our joys and our sorrows multiply. This is the nature of being human.

AUDACIOUS GRATITUDE

Author's Comment

In many sectors of American society, especially among the more highly educated, it can seem rational to be cynical—the world is such a horrid place. Yet growing clinical data suggests that gratitude is the basis of health, wealth, and long-term well-being. On the spiritual journey, it is even more important. A spiritual practice that does not include gratitude can never achieve peace, love, joy, or awakening. This is why it is a fundamentally important spiritual discipline.

Questions to Encourage Conversation

1. Is resurrection an appropriate term to describe Jim's return? Why or why not?

2. What does Jim's handling of the bank default say about his character?

3. Why do Jim and Loretta join the Unitarian Universalist church?

4. What does it mean to become transcendentalist?

5. How do cultural and socioeconomic identities impact our life choices?

6. How did Loretta's ovarian cyst and David's dying of AIDS transform Jim?

7. What's the impact of fame and fortune?

8. What is Jim's source of new hope? What is yours?

Reflection

As a group, reflect upon the elements in this story that resonate with your own and those that do not.

DISCIPLINE FOUR:
GENEROSITY

Generous *means "freely giving more than is neces-*
sary or expected." So generosity includes the idea of
open-handedness, along with a connection to our
internal experience and spirituality. . . . Generosity
ennobles us; it makes us great souls.

—*The Generosity Path*
by Mark V. Ewert

Beginning Again

Life has its ups and downs. Now as I approached age forty—having lost my job, most of our net worth, and much of my industry reputation—it was time to start again. After having worked seventy or eighty hours a week for most of my adult life, I suddenly had no job and no clear prospects. My career was now apparently in shambles.

I could have easily succumbed to a scarcity mentality, one in which I had to give up my dreams and focus solely on my own needs. But that is not my nature. Instead, I embraced this as a time for deepening my practice of spiritual generosity.

I focused on the sudden abundance of time in my day—time to spend with my wife and my children, time to read all those philosophical and spiritual books I hadn't gotten to read, time to think and reevaluate my life. I took comfort that Loretta's business was doing fine, the kids were doing well in school, and I had learned much from my dozen years in international business. And thanks to Loretta's and my financial prudence over the decades, we had the financial wherewithal for me to contemplate and explore reality.

I reflected upon the fact that Loretta and I have always been willing to live below our means in order to accumulate wealth and financial freedom for the future. When I started at HBS, I lived in a rooming house while Loretta finished Yale. When she moved up to join me, we lived in a basement studio apartment in Allston to minimize our spending.

We jumped at the chance to buy our own house in our early twenties, but we bought just the house we needed, not the most house we could afford. The bank told us that based on our salaries, we could borrow up to twice as much—and a more expensive house would be a good inflation hedge against the 12 percent inflation rate of the time. But a large mortgage at 14 percent annually felt like too much for us. It would have forced decisions upon us about where and how we worked for this next stage of our lives.

We bought our first new car that summer of 1980, a small inexpensive Mitsubishi Champ, for our commute to Boston. Interest rates on car loans were even higher at 17 percent. This added considerably to the cost of the car. So we saved our money and prepaid our car loan in less than a year without penalty. We eventually drove that car all over Europe.

We knew then that living prudently and growing our wealth would bring us financial freedom. We wanted to become self-reliant, free of loans and debts. That was worth far more to us than anything we could have bought with this money. When we did spend money, we always favored life-enhancing experiences and education rather than mere material goods. Financial freedom allows one to live from generosity. In turn, generosity frees the spirit to live into divine mystery.

We shared these values with our children. Both our children had their own bank accounts from a very young age. We also taught them early on to employ generosity to care for the needs of others. Fortunately, they grew up to be admirable savers and have always been very financially prudent.

Robbie seemed to magnetically attract money as a small child. He would explore telephone booths, look under seat cushions, and search any public place for the spare change and occasional dollar bills people left behind. He was happy to buy toys if it was our money he was spending. But he carefully counted and saved his own money.

He was a natural-born economist. As entrepreneurs, Loretta and I often talked about our businesses' financial situations over dinner with our kids. When discussing shorting the English pound sterling or the Japanese yen because they were temporarily overvalued compared to the dollar, Robert at age ten could give as good an explanation as anyone.

It wasn't always easy raising our kids with these financial values in affluent Concord. Many families took a very different approach to how they spent their money and their time. Perhaps this brought them joy, but it mostly seemed to bring them anxiety in the best of times and deep distress during times of trials and turbulence.

I remember one seemingly wealthy Concord family who drove expensive cars and lived in one of those big showplace houses, often called McMansions. Then the father lost his job. Because I had strong contacts in the local venture community, he asked me to help him find another job.

Senior-level positions can sometimes take up to a year to secure, so I asked how long he could afford to be unemployed. He said his house was mortgaged to the hilt, the cars were all leased, and the family had only a small emergency fund. They would be bankrupt if he didn't find a job within six months. I agreed to help him network, and he thankfully found a job just nine weeks later.

Such financial precariousness taught us something about money and meaning. We wanted to live with a spirit of generosity no matter our circumstances. Because of our earlier decisions in life and sound financial values, I knew we would find our way through this challenging stage without resorting to a scarcity mindset. We never lost our spirit of generosity.

In fact, we had called upon that spirit after my dad died in early 1992 so we could be financially responsible for my mother. My childhood home was in such disrepair by the summer of 1993 that we feared for her health and safety. She would need a new home.

Mom loved Lake Boon in Stow, Massachusetts, where she and my dad had honeymooned in 1945 and where we had our rare summer vacations. It also wasn't terribly far from her family's ancestral homestead. In her later years, she was reconnecting with her heritage growing up.

So Loretta and I bought a lakefront cottage for her. It had three upstairs bedrooms for when my siblings visited, but we had an architect adapt the main level for her arthritic single-floor living. This allowed me to generously spend some of my newfound time to benefit our entire extended family. We all became quite fond of that lakefront cottage.

While living at the lake, so near her family's ancestral home, my mom resumed genealogical research on our family. It became her major hobby for the next decade. For the next seven years, my mom was in the water daily all summer. She loved her pastoral view and setting and loved that so many of her children and grandchildren would visit her there. I have great memories of canoeing with her on the lake, watching Robbie go exploring in a kayak, and diving off the dock with Sarah in summer.

By purchasing a home for her, we were free to invest most of her own estate in the stock market. Over those seven years, it appreciated 50 percent despite her modest draw for living expenses. When she was ready, she could afford, with our help, a one-bedroom suite at Newbury Court, our local assisted-living facility.

Balancing the Yang and Yin of Life

As I contemplated the next stage in my career and life—and as I looked back upon my earlier days and decisions—I knew I needed to seek a greater sense of balance. I was approaching my forties, nearing midlife.

It became important to me to change my way of being in the world, to change my sense of self and how I would engage with the world in the second half of my life.

In the early days of Genzyme, I had often headed to my office by 4:30 a.m. and worked through to 8:00 p.m. I seldom met our neighbors. Six weeks after we moved into our new house in Concord, Sarah was playing with the girl next door. The girl asked Loretta if Sarah had a daddy, because she had never seen me.

During that time, Loretta was the primary parent, caring for two kids at home under five years old while building her own business. Yet I chose that living arrangement and willingly paid the price success seemingly demanded.

Part of finding an appropriate balance for my forties would involve finding the right amount of risk in my future ventures. In my twenties and thirties, I had taken on way too much risk. In particular, I thought back to my days at Genzyme, when we came close to losing everything after the stock market crash of 1987.

After leveraging our debt to buy Genzyme founder's stock from Sam, then taking Genzyme public in 1986, I borrowed as much as I could on margin to buy yet more Genzyme stock. I believed that by taking on margin debt and raising the value of our Genzyme holdings, we could better reap the fruit of all my hard work—even if we were heavily leveraged.

Loretta asked me how low the stock could go before we lost it all. Genzyme had gone public at $10 per share and traded as high as $16 per share. I told her Genzyme had never traded below $7 as a public company. We could meet any margin calls as long as the stock was above $5.25 per share, which was less than half its current level and 25 percent below its lowest price ever. On the other hand, if Genzyme went to $30 per share, as analysts predicted, we would become wealthy.

Then came the crash of October 1987. For ten days, stocks were in free fall with no apparent bottom, each day worse than the day before. Genzyme stock fell from $16 to $12, to $10, to $7.50, and then for the first time ever to less than $7 per share.

I was deeply scared, but there was little I could do. One thing I could do was call our major investors to try to lessen their anxiety. I reassured them Genzyme was fundamentally sound. Someone would step in at some point to begin buying again. I hoped this was true.

One large investor said he had seen the reports of my buying stock on margin. He asked the same question my wife had asked: At what point could I not cover the margin call and therefore go personally bankrupt? I gave him the same answer I had given Loretta.

Three days later, Genzyme traded at its lowest point, $5.75 per share. This investor began aggressively accumulating shares. I called a few weeks later to thank him. This prudent investor forestalled my complete financial disaster. He said it was no problem—he made an extraordinary profit when the stock rebounded. Plus, he thought having a bankrupt CFO might hurt Genzyme and his investment going forward.

I learned from this near-bankruptcy experience. I didn't scale back my appetite for risk, just managed it a lot better. I learned to better calibrate and diversify risks and ensure the risks I was taking were well worth the potential consequences involved.

Joining Genzyme as CFO was an incredible career risk, but through hard work and luck we made it work. Joining TSI as chairman and CEO was another incredible career risk, yet I set out to build a team that could make it work. I sold my Genzyme stock and took TSI public in 1989, in my thirty-third year. TSI's miraculous 800 percent rise in stock price over the next four years meant we were "wealthy" when I was only thirty-seven, at least on paper and at least by our modest standards. But we stayed grounded in our values and our integrity.

Looking back at the highs and lows of my twenties and thirties gave me fresh perspective on the career and life I wanted in my forties. Now I was ready. It was possible to be a present and considerate husband and father while pursuing my passions with every fiber of my being. With a renewed focus on seeking balance with the yang and yin aspects of my nature, I was ready to take my next step, whatever it may be.

Seaflower Ventures

I would need to begin again, now with a far more modest fortune, and rebuild our wealth. My former executive assistant at TSI called me three months after I was fired by TSI. She said the new CEO was not a nice person. She asked to come work with me in my next endeavor. I was uncertain what I would do next, but I expected I'd need an executive assistant. So I hired her.

We incorporated as Seaflower, which is what Sherblom, originally spelled Sjöblom, means in Swedish. We rented a small office suite in Waltham, in the center of the biotech-investing ecosystem. Given my reputation, opportunities began to appear, often looking for my advice more than my money. Ben, a talented MD/MBA with biotechnology program management experience, soon joined me with venture catalyst aspirations of his own.

I had joined the board of directors of Alpha-Beta, a carbohydrate development-stage drug developer, and now got more involved with assisting them. I also began to make a series of small investments, $25,000 to $50,000 each, in interesting local startups such as Geltex, a gel-based drug delivery company; EcoScience, an organic pesticide and microbiotics company; and Boston Biomedica, a biotech blood products company. This was a fun way to be involved in the next generation of biotech companies without risking my time, health, and well-being, as I had previously done. This was also a way to build back up our wealth without my being consumed by the effort and to make generosity core to my career and well-being.

A young scientist approached me to help him find funding for his novel contrast agent, which looked to revolutionize endoscopic surgery. I liked his technology a lot. I helped to write him a fundable business plan and then introduced him to the venture capitalist who said he wanted to invest in my next deal. We both invested in this opportunity. When the company went public four years later, we all made an excellent return.

The scientific founder of Aphios, a therapeutics company, approached me about becoming his board chair with substantial additional stock compensation beyond whatever equity I invested. I would serve as Aphios board chair the next six years, helping build a first-rate board and business strategy.

But there always seemed to be an unforeseen setback preventing this company from breaking out. The company never fulfilled its scientific promise. Sometimes the circumstances just aren't right, or the founder seeks to keep too much control, or the situation never really jells. I kept with it, eventually investing over $160,000 of my own money and endless amounts of my time and frustration, but it never succeeded.

Risky opportunities more often fail than succeed. Being able to sustain losses and delays is key to survival in a risky environment. It requires financial resources, a generous spirit, and a strong sense of self to enjoy risk taking.

In 1994, an unusual opportunity presented itself in the form of a Michigan real estate mogul named Brian. Michigan's governor was frustrated that the state was ten years behind California and Massachusetts in this emerging field of biotechnology. Brian was a friend of the governor. Brian had assured him that if he set aside a substantial portion of Michigan's gambling revenues from the Native American casino, that money could catalyze a whole new high-paying biotechnology industry for Michigan.

Brian had visited prominent venture capital firms in San Francisco and Boston. He had heard the two most creative venture catalysts in the biotech field, catalyzers of new ventures, were me and some fellow who lived on a houseboat in La Jolla, Southern California. Brian had flown the other venture catalyst to Michigan in January to discuss the structure of his involvement. The weather was icy and cold. So the other venture catalyst headed home to Southern California.

This left Seaflower seemingly as Brian's best option. But I had no interest. I had refocused my life to spend more time with my family, exercise, and work on my spiritual path. Brian and I talked for quite a while about the importance of family, health, and pursuing one's spiritual path. At the end, Brian asked me to write a proposal detailing the terms under which I would be willing to take on this role he envisioned. Generosity of spirit suggested I at least try.

Just for the fun of it, Ben and I decided to write a proposal we expected Brian would not fund but which would give him a sense of what it might take to succeed. We proposed the State of Michigan hire our small team of entrepreneurs half-time for three years as venture catalysts. We suggested they pay a monthly retainer to cover all our office and overhead costs as well as our modest salaries. Michigan would cover all our travel expenses, and we would spend up to a quarter of our time in Michigan, where he would provide us an office. And we would receive a 10 percent founder's stake in any biotech enterprise we created as part of this venture.

Brian faxed back the State of Michigan's acceptance the next day. So Ben and I accidently became part-time venture catalysts serving the State of Michigan for the next three years. Loretta and I agreed it was prudent to accept this less-risky approach in building Seaflower. Having faced possible bankruptcy in 1987 from the stock market collapse, then again potentially losing everything, including our house, in 1990 when we leveraged ourselves as bank collateral, we were determined never to be so leveraged again.

In this Michigan venture, we created and built a diversified portfolio of companies. We began with a chiral pharmaceutical startup. The second company dramatically improved crop yields. A third offered alternative uses for corn as fuel. The fourth company bioengineered foods. A fifth made bioplastics. As the portfolio grew, we hired an amazing Michigan CFO to help us monitor and keep track of them all.

Our Seaflower team received 10 percent founder's stakes in each company. These technologies were good. But unfortunately, we were unable to find entrepreneurs to continue to build these companies, and we could not find enough early-stage investors to fund them, so too much depended on our limited resources. There wasn't a supporting ecosystem to grow these companies.

Early-stage companies are exceedingly risky and require risk-supportive environments to thrive. These companies suffered from a lack of experienced entrepreneurs to staff their growing teams and a dearth of early-stage venture capital able to sustain the losses of early hurdles and failures. Few companies ever succeed solely based on their original concepts. Without patient early-stage capital, they will generally fail before they find their winning solution. It turns out the biotechnology industry infrastructure I had helped to create in Massachusetts was critical to any startup company's subsequent chances of success.

So despite our optimism and prodigious efforts, most of these companies failed. And it seems even 10 percent of nothing is still nothing. While this three-year contract protected our financial downside as I assembled a small team and learned the venture business, it provided little direct upside. But it did present us with an incredible learning opportunity.

The largest pharmaceutical company in Michigan was Parke-Davis. We got to know them well. Watching us launch so many companies, they hired us for a year as their venture catalysts to help with their product pipeline as well. But they had the same problem: no entrepreneurial spirit for risk taking. We could not change their culture in just a year.

The most interesting technology we found in Michigan was a renal cell-based kidney-filtering system that showed remarkable early clinical results in preventing acute renal failure. I would become a major investor, then chairman and CEO, of this company for the next five years, eventually relocating them to Rhode Island to build their organization with some more experienced people. I gave my best efforts and five years of my life to breathing life into this next wave of cellular-regeneration technology. Creating these companies continued to need and take everything I had to offer. But I approached it all with a spirit of generosity.

Two years into Seaflower Associates, we had proven we could foster innovation. Ben continued to work on corporate development, and Theresa joined us to handle our fund and tax accounting. Chris, our Michigan CFO, created financial systems and controls for our startups, and Alex, with a background in marketing, joined to oversee the companies' product and corporate development plans. More and more people wanted to invest alongside us.

So in 1996, we raised a small $5 million health and technology seed fund to invest in biotechnology and life science startups around Boston and Ann Arbor. I agreed to be founding managing partner with this small team of partners in this seed-stage venture. I would serve on the board, often as chairman, while Alex focused upon business development plans and Chris served as CFO. We were a full-service venture catalyst group and loving it.

We spun a combinatorial-chemistry company out of Parke-Davis. I served as chairman and also initially CEO, and we hired a Michigan project manager. Two of our earlier Michigan deals were struggling but doing well enough to receive follow-on investments from our new fund. I also served as chairman and initial CEO of Synthon, a chiral chemistry company that could control the chirality, or chemical symmetry, of a drug. Controlling chirality dramatically improved efficacy while radically reducing potential side effects. This was breakthrough technology.

It seemed everyone wanted me in every meeting, and everyone seemed to need my attention. Once again, I was stretched too thin. I couldn't be everywhere for everyone, yet as a firm, we were heavily invested in our success. I began to work too much and take on too much personal risk again. But this was all so exciting–I couldn't scale back my commitment.

The most scientifically advanced company in our portfolio was Molecular Geodesics, Inc., a biomimetic-material startup with a $3 million Defense Advanced Research Projects Agency (DARPA) grant for pathogen neutralization. The founding scientist was a brilliant medical molecular biologist teaching at Harvard. I served as chairman and initial CEO as we built a world-class research, development, engineering, and management team.

Our most successful company would come to be called ViaCell. Its scientific founder was so young and lacking in stem cell credentials that no one would fund him. He had created an early-stage stem cell bioreactor that outperformed existing technology by an order of magnitude. So we helped to cocreate this startup company with Zero Stage Capital. This one investment eventually paid back the entire fund with a twelve-fold return on our investment.

Early-stage venture capital requires extraordinary risks. You can't focus on the downside risks or what the company lacks; otherwise, you will never invest. Such investing requires a generous spirit that focuses on potential upsides. You must imagine what the technology might achieve if it works and what the people might achieve if given a chance to do what they have never done before. And you must then create a network of stakeholders, all of whom are willing to be generous with their time, talents, and financial resources to create a company.

For me, this is what Buddhists mean by Right Livelihood. And this was what made Seaflower distinctive in the mid-1990s venture community: our generosity of spirit, sense of integrity, and willingness to work patiently for years to bring new technology to life. We helped create from chaos. This was one of the happiest times of my entrepreneurial life. I was doing important work and bringing forward technologies that could increase human flourishing while working with the small entrepreneurial team I had chosen.

This work also had immediate impact in my own personal life. When one of my nephews was born with a damaged kidney, ViaCell froze stem cells from his umbilical cord and placenta. Now as biological-regeneration technology continues to advance, my nephew might even be able to meet many of his future medical needs from his own stem cells. We did good things while doing financially well. This is the essence of Right Livelihood through generosity.

We were investing on the technological edge. The rest of our portfolio consisted of a company with emerging radiology telemedicine, a company in nanoscale optical device diagnostics, a company that performed clinical trials meta-analysis, and a company with advanced technology for preventing decubitus ulcers. I was bringing along younger partners who assumed an ever-larger role in the fund. This was a well-diversified portfolio of high-risk, early-stage companies that could make a great impact.

This was who I was and what I wanted to be doing with my life. I aspired to be and do more than I had achieved in my first forty years. It drew upon my resilience, my willingness to surrender my own ego, my gratitude for everything that happens, and my growing spirit of generosity.

Living Charitably

In this new stage of my life, I reflected much on how that spirit of generosity had grown over the years. In particular, I reflected upon how our generosity transformed into charity.

Charitable giving has always been a core piece of my life. In contrast, giving to people you didn't know and who were not related to you was not part of Loretta's cultural upbringing. But my birth family believed in tithing, giving 10 percent of everything we received to God's work, however we conceived it. We often gave as much as possible to the church, then gave the rest away to those in greatest need. There was always someone in greater need than us.

So we gave generously. Growing up, I tithed from my own earnings, giving 10 percent of the profits from my minimum wage jobs, book sales, and even marble sales. Tithing produces a sense of gratitude and generosity that makes the other 90 percent of our earnings so much sweeter for our own wants and needs.

In our early married life, Loretta and I were not members of a church community, so we gave generously to other causes. This has been a liberating practice throughout our married life. Generosity is more about the spirit than it is about the money. No matter how little or much we have, we can be generous with others. Now in the second half of our lives, generosity would grow into an even more important spiritual discipline for us.

During our twenties and thirties, we thirsted for material well-being and financial freedom. But we always strove for something more along with it. We could have focused just on ourselves; we were certainly busy enough. But we tried to live generously. We were always active in our various communities, helping others wherever we could. Now that we were entering the more generative stage of our lives, generosity remained at the core of our being, even when we were anxious or stretched too thin or when trying to do too much.

This spirit of generosity blossomed in our forties—and it continues to this day. Over the decades, it's allowed us to be generous givers to our First Parish Church, our Unitarian Universalist denomination, and our alma maters. We've focused the majority of our generosity to help make the world a better place, sometimes through a program Loretta created called Funderburg Scholars, which helps fund college education for inner-city youth. For years, we have watched those youth begin to flourish. This way of being in the world has been an enormous source of pride and joy for us over the decades.

We also devote considerable financial resources to help repair humanity's environment. To help fight world climate change, we have given money to plant a thousand trees on forty acres in the Amazonian rainforest. We also help those in greatest local need by contributing through the United Way or the Concord-Carlisle Community Chest, helping various social service agencies address economic disparities and needs in our community.

This charitable giving is an important aspect of living a life of generosity. At certain stages of our lives, tithing or near tithing was an appropriate level. This spirit of charity and generosity has remained strong through our entire lives. Knowing the meaning of money in our life can make a great difference in our relationship with the divine and our own flourishing.

Into Divine Mystery

Approaching middle age, I yearned to more fully live a balanced and still deeply rewarding life. A major part of that balance would be focused on spiritual deepening. There was a middle way between ninety-hour workweeks and completely giving up work to pursue my spiritual path. This was perhaps my personal variation on the Buddha's Middle Path.

Meditation became a more important part of my spiritual journey. Church also became a bigger part of my family's life. I taught in the religious education program. I became an usher for Sunday worship and joined the church finance committee.

Around this time, a fifty-year-old man who had been a pillar of the church experienced a massive midlife crisis. He was reevaluating everything in his life: his job, his wife, his teenage children, and his very sense of self. He slept in a tent in his backyard as he tried to make sense of his life.

We started a men's group around him to provide emotional support and direction. It was an opportunity for him as well as us to go spiritually deeper. This group met at church most Saturday mornings, when our families might least miss us. We explored how our childhoods and educations had set us on this path for success at tremendous costs to our health, our families, and our sense of well-being. Gradually, the group grew, eventually including as many as twenty-five men. It provided spiritual sustenance and a means to make meaning of our lives.

A small subset from our men's group—professionals and business executives mostly in our forties and fifties, and mostly with wives and kids—decided to take our spiritual lives more seriously. We committed to meeting not only on Saturday mornings but also every Sunday night for two hours to discuss spiritual issues in our lives. Our conversations ranged wide and deep. We met faithfully, including Super Bowl Sunday, when watching the Patriots together turned into a very important spiritual experience.

I realize this men's spiritual contemplation group is perhaps an example of social class privilege. But I also realize so few professionally successful men use that privilege to become more fully themselves. Through this group, we discovered we all had much richer interior lives than we ever showed the outside world. Some of it was magical. Some was painful. Much was fantastical. All of it meaningful.

We shared stories and examined the details of our lives as they passed through the fires of our thoughtful contemplation. We helped one another feel less alone on the spiritual journey. In a sense, we brought salvation to one another. We helped one another heal deep wounds in our religious and spiritual lives, both the scars that were visible and those invisible to others. We learned together to count the number of our days and to consider the meaning of them. We laughed, we wept, we sighed, and we told stories. We were liberated to live lives of deeper meaning and joy, assisting one another on the journey.

After a busy week, I once gathered with these men on a small island called Rattlesnake, in the middle of a large lake in New Hampshire. I wrote in my spiritual journal: "We buy groceries, cook, and eat. We hike, swim, drink beer, play poker, tell stories, pontificate. I pontificate. Yet the most delightful part is that I have no role but to be one of eight men. I am not father, spouse, son, brother. I just am. I am not employer, salesman, fundraiser, or advisor. I just am." It is good to just be.

This was the period of my life when I was most deeply into Jungian symbols and trying to understand the collective unconscious. Jungian archetypes, like Budai, began to haunt my deep meditations and dreams. I began to record more transcendent moments in my spiritual journal. I started meditating on being more present in the here and now.

In my manic world of striving and experience, it became clear: my personal key to inner peace was finding sufficient time for quiet reflection, for noticing, for perspective, so that I could, like Henry David Thoreau, suck the marrow, or essence, from life's experiences. This is very much a transcendentalist way. The unexamined life might not be worth living, but it is equally true that the unlived life is not worth examining. This meditation helps keep life grounded and meaningful.

I was called to live a meaningful life. Yet I knew it was only possible for me to feel whole and at peace when life's concerns were not too pressing. The key, then, to my joy and contentment was balance: to be completely and passionately absorbed in a professional endeavor while also finding time for family, friends, and quiet reflection on the nature and meaning of such a life. This was the pursuit of human flourishing grounded in a spirit of generosity.

This was how I engaged the world as an Enneagram Seven. Or speaking more spiritually, this was my Budai nature. Budai is the Chinese or Japanese immortal often associated in Buddhism with the future Buddha. He is always smiling and laughing, loved for his impish generosity. Carrying all his material resources in a sack on his back, he shares them with children and those in need in order to make a better world. He is a good and loving character.

A deeper sense of spirituality gave me a deeper perspective on my career as well—in particular, on the large role it had played in my life. At that stage in my life, I was mindful of the mixed messages I sent my family by choosing business over family time. But this was part of my being and becoming.

It wasn't just a matter of money. Loretta always said my passionate drive to succeed couldn't be justified in strictly financial terms. It required great sacrifices by me, my kids, and my wife—especially my wife—that wouldn't ever be repaid in financial terms.

Then why did I do it? Because I wanted to contribute meaningfully to this world, and this was what life seemed to have trained, prepared, and called me to do. I helped create those companies, and I deeply cared about their success. Only through following my calling in life could I ever find contentment. When my children were grown, I wanted them to remember a loving father who made time for them, but I also wanted them to understand the importance of doing one's life's work well.

That was who I chose to be at that stage of my life. That was my life's work. I had a sense of purpose, yet my life was a mystery. I was passionately immersed in the present, and the path led on. This was immanence encountering transcendence, both heaven and hell, in my day-to-day life.

I wrote a typical spiritual journal entry that year while stranded at an airport: "I notice brilliant lightning streaks across the sky. The rain comes down in torrents. After an intense fourteen-hour day, I am sitting in the Detroit airport surrounded by delayed and tired passengers. My plane home has been rerouted to Dayton, leaving me indefinitely delayed. Patience. Calm. Nothing can be done. This too can deepen the soul. So let it be. Let me experience the present fully."

Another journal entry: "Sun rising. Running late. Mist rising off the Concord River, and fog slowly lifting off the fields. I overslept. Afraid I'll miss my plane. Can't afford to miss these important meetings. Also am afraid I'll miss the beauty of the early morning. Please, God, let me always take the time and attention, even in the stress of life, to truly experience the glory of the early morning. But please, God, let me catch my plane today."

Such is the nature of becoming momentarily awake. It doesn't change what happens, only how we experience it. Our lives will be miserable if we try desperately to control everything in our lives or if we experience life as a victim of circumstances, from a sense of entitlement, or with a scarcity mentality. However, our lives will be good if we can find resilience in the face of failure, surrender our ego-self to the greater good, greet everything that happens with a sense of gratitude, and bring our generosity to our encounter with the world. The choice is always ours to make.

Deepening Family Ties

Any spirit of generosity begins with our families of birth. After my father died, my far-flung birth family stretched from Florida to Texas to Maine, and everywhere in between. Still, we continued gathering once a year, either at Thanksgiving or Christmas.

Different families took turns hosting what could be twenty to twenty-five people at a gathering. I eagerly looked forward to it each year. Whenever it was our turn to host, I loved helping buy and cook for such a large group.

Unfortunately, our time together was often too short. Everyone's lives were full and complex, and we increasingly had families of our own. Sometimes the last sibling to arrive would sit just as dinner was put on the table, and the first to leave would rise immediately following dessert.

Each year, Loretta's family gathered for a week, usually in California or else some exotic Caribbean location. They had more means than most of my siblings to afford such travel. Over cooking and conversation, they managed to renew family ties. They continued this practice annually for several decades, and it seemed to create a much greater family bond.

So in 1996, Loretta and I decided to see if it would work for my family as well. We rented a big house at the beach and invited everyone in my extended family to join us for a week. That was one of my most enjoyable times with family. Nothing to do, nothing to say—we just got to spend time together. Generosity of spirit helped to bring my birth family closer together.

After that, we decided we could afford to make it an annual thing. Each summer, Loretta and I would rent a large beach house somewhere in Rhode Island and invite everyone who could to come spend the week with us. It helped that my oldest sister and her large family lived in Rhode Island, so they would visit as day trips, reducing the size house we needed to rent.

We often walked the beach before breakfast, played in the sand and waves with the kids during the day, and walked the beach again at sunset. My brother Steve said this was why all large extended families needed a "white sheep" of the family. I asked what that was. He said the white sheep was the one person who did well enough in business to host everyone else for an annual family reunion at the beach.

As our families grew and these gatherings became more popular, we began to focus them around Scarborough State Beach in Narragansett, Rhode Island. It was easy to get to. We could rent two or three houses in different configurations to sleep everyone. It gave everyone some flexibility and privacy in the midst of this large annual gathering of the tribe.

My mother particularly enjoyed these gatherings. She used to take long walks on the beach, each time with a different one of her children, to talk about how we were living our lives. It was magical—especially seeing how well the cousins in the next generation got along year after year. This deepening of family ties became an important part of who we were and who we were becoming.

A New Calling

Seaflower Ventures was doing well enough for me to transition to a less active and more advisory role. In 1998, we raised Seaflower II, a $10 million fund from many of the entrepreneurs in the Boston area who had made money investing with me in the past but also from some small institutional investors for the first time.

In early-stage venture investing, every two to three years, you must raise a new and generally larger fund in order to support your portfolio companies. These companies often must go through several rounds of capital raising over five to seven years before there is any financial return. If you're not reinvesting in your portfolio, it means you're disinvesting—sometimes at the worst possible time and valuations.

After we raised the 1998 fund, I continued to serve as managing partner, but I encouraged my younger partners to take on larger roles in sourcing deals, monitoring investments, and serving on boards of directors. This allowed me to stay involved in the business while enjoying a more balanced family life and deepening my own spiritual exploration.

Recognizing the growing impact of computer advances and the Internet, we added a computational biology company, an Internet-based clinical trial management company, an e-science information and genomic data company, an Internet-based medical imaging company, and an Internet-based medical records company. This was all in addition to continuing to support our existing portfolio companies. The world of technology was rapidly changing around us, and we shifted our investment focus to adapt to it.

But increasingly, I felt like a stranger in a strange land, trying to keep up with vast areas of information science without the time or training to do so. I never attained the same level of scientific understanding and comfort with these newer information technologies that I had with the biotechnologies we had previously funded. In my twenties, I had been a Young Turk in biotechnology—I could get my mind around anything and everything. Now twenty years later, the technology began to leave me behind.

Ongoing changes in the venture industry and growing syndicate sizes meant that by the spring of 1999, we had to begin fundraising for Seaflower Fund III. It would be four times the size of Seaflower II. We were raising the money based upon my track record, which meant I had to remain as managing partner for at least the ten-year life of the fund, at least at half time, and to be the primary rainmaker for this new fund.

But after two weeks of pitching the fund in Europe and the Far East, I came home tired, jet-lagged, and grouchy. I wasn't enjoying this anymore. The venture industry was changing from building new and exciting biotechnology companies to flipping life science private equities. The newer investors were less interested in long-term success than with what we reported quarter to quarter.

I didn't want this to be my sole professional focus, my primary means of making the world better, for yet another decade. It was time to consider a change.

The following week, I received a postcard from Andover Newton Theological School (ANTS), my dad's old seminary, inviting me to spend a day with them. My calendar never had an open day. But I looked at the day they suggested, and it was wide open. I took this as a sign and went to visit the school.

I loved the classes, professors, and students. Loved talking about things that had real meaning. I remembered how much I envied my father's line of work.

Now I knew what I should do with my life. I called Loretta and told her I was enrolling at ANTS part-time in order to become an ordained Unitarian Universalist parish minister. There was a long pause. She said, "You could take up golf. Many men deal with their midlife crisis by taking up golf."

But now in my mid-forties, I knew again what would make my heart sing and how to live into my bliss. Perhaps my life's journey had been leading to this all along.

In 1997, at the request of my UU minister, I had helped found the Wright Tavern Center for Spiritual Renewal. I became a governing board member and would eventually serve as board chair from 2001 to 2003. I also became one of their more popular teachers. Based upon what I knew and loved, I created and taught three courses: Business Ethics under Chaotic Circumstances, Introduction to the Sacred Texts of the World, and How to Discern Your Spiritual Path in Life. This was a way to generously share my growing wisdom.

Seeing a new path ahead of me now, I began to practice intentional meditation each morning using Tibetan incense and prayer beads for journeys into the realms of spirit. During meditation one morning, a guardian angel, Michael, appeared.

Michael said he had always been with me. He showed me how he had assisted me in dealing with life-threatening events: when I almost lost my hand falling from the riot gate, when we skidded out of control on the ice returning to college, when I was dealing with Loretta's ovarian cyst, or when we were almost hit by a driver who ran a stop sign while driving to church. He also showed me how to distinguish between spiritual beings that could help me on the journey and those that could do me harm.

Given my Jungian inclination, I rationally understood that Michael and the other spiritual apparitions I encountered on the journey were Jungian symbols of our co-creation of reality. Yet they seemed so real and important to my spiritual journey. Serendipitous manifestations of spirit, which many call grace, were helping guide my path.

But having a guardian angel presented me with a dilemma. I couldn't speak about him to anyone without seeming to assert a certain specialness for myself. Yet I wasn't special—as many bad things happened in my life as in everyone else's lives. Michael didn't prevent any of my suffering and struggles. Yet he did ratify my feelings of being blessed, of being a child of God, of having a purpose in life that went well beyond simply making a living. I felt beloved, resting on the breast or chest of God.

Over the next several months, I had many long metaphysical conversations with Michael, usually but not always during deep meditation trances early in the morning. We came to an understanding. He would be my Jungian manifestation of my cosmic consciousness until my faith belief system could sustain such an understanding in a nonanthropomorphic form. Michael was like training wheels as I developed a robust, multilayered understanding of divine mystery. He taught me many spiritual things, and then one day, he simply stopped appearing. I was again on my own pathless path, finding my own way.

A new chapter of my life emerged and began to take shape, one that integrated my father's dreams for me along with my own spiritual journey and intuitions while also honoring the decades of my professional life and training. God indeed works in mysterious ways.

The success of our various investment funds meant that by 1999, Loretta and I were financially secure once again. All this was possible because of our hard work, our good fortune, and our careful values about money and meaning. The opportunities and options we had now in the second half of our lives were largely due to how we had lived the first twenty years of our married life. I will always be grateful for the love and caring of a good hardheaded woman.

I began at ANTS by taking New Testament Foundations and Introduction to the Hebrew Bible. With my Baptist upbringing, I figured Bible classes would be the easiest. I was not well prepared, however, for the diversity of Christian beliefs among my classmates.

There is a greater variety of beliefs *within* Judaism, Christianity, and Islam than there ever has been *between* these three Abrahamic faiths. An extreme example was a young Southern Baptist classmate from Tennessee who had accepted a full scholarship to attend ANTS despite his pastor's warning that a northern seminary might put his faith at risk because the devil lived in Massachusetts.

In one of our first New Testament classes, the professor explained when modern scholars believe each of the four Gospels had been composed, for which kinds of emerging Christian faith communities they had each been written and the different perspectives they offered the early Christian communities.

This young man grew more and more agitated, eventually raising his hand and asking the professor: "Didn't Jesus preach from the same Bible we do, the Authorized King James Version?"

The professor suggested they meet after class. The young man was gone the next week, suggesting his pastor might have been right.

Despite all the different perspectives among my classmates, there seemed to be very few mystics at this Protestant Reform seminary. So I mostly kept my intimacy with the divine mystery and complexity of my own spiritual journey to myself.

Householder Responsibilities

Now that I had a greater capacity for serving others, opportunities to do so increasingly presented themselves. I began to take on a greater role providing care for my mother, Rae. That winter of 1999, she had a bad fall on ice and was hospitalized with a hairline fracture of her hip. She decided it was time to move into Newbury Court assisted living. We had kept her on their waitlist these last seven years, anticipating this day would come.

Loretta and I lent her money for the down payment. We negotiated a one-bedroom with a woods and river view. This would become her home for most of the last twelve years of her life. This was a safe and supportive community as she aged and healed through her cataract surgeries, knee replacements, and eventual hip replacement.

Once mom moved into this new home, her energy and sense of well-being rebounded! She organized Newbury Court's library, making it far easier to get the books residents wanted. Mom volunteered in the office at both West Acton Baptist and First Parish in Concord. She liked writing cards for the grieving and shut-ins. Mom even went with the Baptist pastor on home visits with the elderly.

When her Baptist pastor had a problem on the Fourth of July, my mom decided I could help. American Baptists serve Communion the first Sunday morning of the month. Yet the first Sunday in July that year was the Fourth of July, and the minister needed to be away at his wife's family reunion. According to traditional Baptist theology, his deacons could serve Communion, but they weren't comfortable doing so. He was unable to find another Baptist pastor free to lead worship and serve Communion for his congregation that Fourth of July Sunday.

So my mom offered my help. She knew I loved serving Communion. Being desperate, the pastor agreed, only asking me please not to mention my preparation for the UU ministry. I offered a very inclusive, very Universalist Baptist Communion and was told by the matriarch of this congregation how much like an old-fashioned Baptist Communion service it was.

I visited my mom frequently and accompanied her to various doctors' appointments and surgeries. Loretta and I had dinner with her most Sundays. Her health declined gradually over the years, but never her spirit. She organized quilting for AIDS Project Worcester, collections of housewares for the homeless, and a newcomers' table to help introduce people coming to Newbury Court. Helping other people is what made her heart sing.

Caring for my mother, providing to her some of the love and caring she had provided to so many, was just part of my new balance in life. I spent mornings as managing partner at the venture fund and afternoons and several evenings a week on my theological studies. Our family life found a new balance as well. With Sarah in college and Robert getting his driver's license and the freedom that gave him, Loretta and I were more focused on being a couple again.

I also took on new denominational roles. The president of the Unitarian Universalist Association (UUA) asked to see me. I offered to go to UUA headquarters, but he wanted to meet at the venture fund's office, saying he wanted to visit the dragon in his lair. I soon joined the UUA President's Council, a small group of UU families that provide much of the funding and support for our movement. I have remained active on the council the last fifteen years.

He asked me to look at the UUA's $100 million endowment, managed by an investment committee with the advice of a socially responsible investing (SRI) committee. I joined the SRI committee, and two years later, the investment committee. In total, I served eight years on the investment committee, the last four as chair. Over those years, we raised the endowment's returns from the bottom quartile to the top quartile while lowering its risk and increasing its SRI character. This improvement in returns yielded an additional $5 million a year in investment gains for the UUA.

The UUA president also asked me to intern in his office during my second year at seminary in order to develop and lead workshops for UUs who had senior roles in the world, including CEOs, senior vice presidents, managing partners, and even a US senator. The workshops confidentially and intimately explored the individuals' ethical and spiritual lives within their positions of power.

This was rewarding work. Many of these successful people had never been able to be vulnerable among peers, to learn from one another, and to come to terms with their own doubts and fears. None of us are exempt from doubts and fears. I very much enjoyed leading these transformative workshops focused upon resilience, surrender, gratitude, and generosity.

The men's spirituality group at First Parish began taking weeklong vision quests every summer. We would fast for four days and have extraordinary visions. Each time we returned, we told folks about our experiences, and they were eager to have such experiences—but without the hardship of fasting for four days. There was a yearning among some in the congregation for a mini vision quest in Concord.

I pointed out that one can go only so deep in a day. But I realized the value of any spiritual practices and always beginning within your personal comfort zone. In many ways, my private visions and meditations as well as group vision quests served as pivot points in my own process of becoming. Even the exercise of journaling can be of extraordinary value. I will always cherish the spiritual journals I kept describing my journey and refer frequently to them as a source of spiritual deepening.

So I agreed to help others experience even just a taste of such things. With another popular teacher at the Wright Tavern Center for Spiritual Renewal, I offered a twenty-four-hour fasting vision quest and transcendental walk for spiritual seekers.

We prepared with a simple Friday meal at sunset, the beginning of the Sabbath. Through guided meditations, we explored and focused the participants' intentionality. Then we each agreed to fast and be in complete silence for the next twenty-four hours until gathering together again as a group at sundown the next day. The heart of those twenty-four hours was to be spent meditating in Concord's Estabrook Woods.

This would give everyone a chance to experience being alone with his or her thoughts and meditations in nature. We gave everyone a map and sent each one on his or her own way.

It was cold and blustery in Estabrook Woods that late-October Saturday. Other walkers in the woods were bundled against the cold. Runners wore grim determination on their faces. The world rushed by us as we meditated in silence.

I found a quiet spot off by myself. As my meditative state deepened, people looked right through me as if I cast no shadow, and dogs ran by me as if I had no scent. Perhaps in my quietude I passed beyond space and time. Perhaps I was not recognizably there. Perhaps I was real and they were merely spectral images, as in Plato's cave allegory.

More likely, we were just occupying two distinct realities—like ships passing each other in a dark night, neither impinging on the other's progress. I sat there for hours. When I relaxed and breathed out, two dogs sniffed me and began barking. We were clearly sharing reality again.

That meditation experience was just one example of how I was now living the more balanced and generative life appropriate to midlife. Creating Seaflower Ventures had helped me rebuild our family fortunes over a decade. Preparing for Unitarian Universalist ministry had allowed me to integrate what I loved best from my Baptist upbringing with my emerging sense of the divine mystery. The five weeklong vision quests with my men's group had given me comfort in practicing the presence of God through fasting and deep meditation. Now I was more able to take on householder responsibilities while still making my contribution to the world—and doing so with generosity and joy, increasingly living in divine mystery.

Befriending God

I was moving forward on my new career path to ministry while still fulfilling my obligations to our final ten-year fund in the venture business. Raising the Seaflower III fund in the changing institutional venture environment had been even more difficult than I had anticipated, but we finally closed at $40 million at the end of 2000. It allowed us to continue supporting two of our existing companies as we identified two additional startups.

I still served as managing partner, though I was no longer the largest investor or working full-time at it. I would let others take a much larger role in this fund. Because of my reputation, I also served as chairman of the board of another new company I helped found in 2001, and I served on the board of directors of two other new companies as well.

This final portfolio would grow to be eleven companies by 2004. But given the changing market conditions, when we finally closed out the last of our fund positions in 2011, the portfolio had returned less than two-thirds of its original capital. I am told this was about average performance for an early-stage technology venture fund invested during this period following the 9/11 terror attacks. But now I was called to other things in my journey of becoming.

Preparing to be set aside as a man of God requires psychological preparation as well. At the request of the UU Regional Subcommittee on Candidacy, I underwent six months of Jungian analysis. I found an analyst who specialized in treating ministers and set up a weekly appointment.

We began with stories about my parents, my siblings, and my childhood. I never cried so hard as when reliving traumas of growing up in poverty and the overwhelming maelstrom of Yale. I had been carrying deep pain and suffering—never told, unexamined, and full of meaning about who I was and could be. Many sessions included funny stories, laughter, and reasoning, but many also seemed to end in cathartic tears. It was tremendously healing.

Eventually we got to more positive stories about joys and successes, about my love for Loretta and our kids, about my friendship with God. I told him of angelic Michael and my various spiritual adventures. I never felt as beloved as when I was reliving my direct experiences of divine mystery. I felt lightened and perhaps even enlightened. I began to look forward to what each session might disclose about my life stories. I was being psychologically resurrected to my best self.

I learned to claim my heritage, both the joys and the sorrows, and to make peace with my complicated history. I learned to befriend God in all his awesome majesty and also in his everyday presence. This was an important milestone in my becoming who I was born to be. My sense of self, which transcends my ego-self, felt at home in the universe at last.

At the end of the six months, my therapist suggested we were done. Because I enjoyed our meetings so much, I asked to continue. He said he also enjoyed our encounters and was happy to hear my stories and take my money, but he didn't think it was necessary because I was clearly psychologically healthy and firmly grounded in my faith. With his strong affirmation, my sense of my higher self began to soar. I decided to focus on being a good friend of God.

Preparation for UU ministry also required completion of clinical pastoral education (CPE) at a hospital. Given the complexity of my schedule, the only way I could manage this was through nearby Emerson Hospital in Concord. I applied for their CPE program, but they refused me. Their program fell under the auspices of the Jesuits and was for Roman Catholic novitiates only.

Nevertheless, I appealed to the head of the program, an Irish Catholic Jesuit priest. He agreed to admit me because Unitarians had been one of the few groups who helped the Irish immigrants coming to Boston in the nineteenth century. As an Irish Catholic, he felt he owed the Unitarians something. His was a generous spirit.

Over the next ten months, I would spend fifteen hours a week training as a chaplain at the hospital and one weekend a month at the Jesuit center in Weston. The hospital was two miles from my house and the Jesuit center only seven miles, so I could fit this program into my busy schedule.

CPE brought me face-to-face with pain, suffering, and death. This CPE training is a critical period in our preparation for becoming ordained clergy because we learn to first transform our own suffering before reaching out to help others. Healers must be able to deal with their own pain.

I also learned about being a spiritual companion—to journey with someone in times of suffering and pain and to do so faithfully by coming to terms with my own demons. This included the misery of David's dying of AIDS, my father's slow, painful death from lymphoma, the pure terror of Loretta's ovarian cyst and of my potentially being a single parent bereft of my life partner, and facing my own mortality. My spiritual director also helped heal me from the spiritual pain of growing up in poverty. As a result, I was finally able to leave much of that behind me.

A student chaplain learns to look upon joy and suffering with equanimity but never with indifference. One must be able to sit bedside with the former business leader facing his imminent death, to play with the child dying from leukemia, to laugh with the athlete recovering from broken bones, and to bring hope to the alcoholic finally dying of his failing liver. Each person has stories of a lifetime. Each can be redeemed through these life stories. A chaplain learns to bring what they each need—to pray, comfort, laugh, make conversation, help make meaning from pain and suffering, or just offer a physical presence. A high compliment for a chaplain is he "prays well with others."

I befriended the nurses. I received a daily printout of patients and medical conditions, but the nurses would tell me who on the floor might most welcome my attention.

One time, I approached a patient's room, but a nurse waved me away. The nurse said the patient was bitter and mean. She was wasting away and dying. Still, I entered her room, led by divine mystery.

She would not talk to me. She refused to have me pray with her or for her. So we sat for thirty minutes in silence. She was in deep pain.

I came back the next day. And the next. Finally, she began to trust me and told me her story.

"When I was young," she said, "I fell in love, married, and gave birth to a son. I loved my husband dearly, but over time, he became increasingly erratic, abusive, and finally died of a brain tumor."

I winced. "To endure such pain and loss so young is painful and difficult," I offered.

"So I raised our son as a single parent. He was a great student. He earned an undergraduate degree from Yale and a medical degree from Dartmouth. On the very weekend he was awarded his medical degree, he was killed in a car accident by a drunk driver."

I grimaced. "How horrifying!" I said.

"My Methodist minister told me this was God's will."

I shook my head. "What a horrible notion of God's love!"

"I'm angry with God," she said. "I couldn't change that if I tried, yet I feel guilty in my anger."

I became angry too. "Faced with such suffering, you're right to be angry with God," I replied. "Let's be angry with God together. Let's curse how miserably life has dealt with you!"

She looked at me in surprise. "But aren't we risking eternal damnation with such anger?"

"Not at all," I reassured her. "I'm on excellent terms with God. I know God was right there crying with you at the deaths of your husband and your only son. The God I know is particularly close to those in pain and suffering. These are his special beloved children whom he wishes to gather to his bosom, and hold close."

So we railed against the injustice of it all. We complained about her Methodist minister's inadequate theology, which let her down in her time of need.

Eventually, we even began to laugh through our tears. She told me stories of her son through the decades of their life together. She remembered the joys of new love with her husband when they were first married. She had so many wonderful, joyful stories, but they had been oppressed by the weight of her despair. As she remembered them and lifted them up, her health improved. After several weeks, she went home to resume her life again.

My role as a healer was to help make room for her to experience her pain and righteous anger and then use that experience to help bring her back to God. A chaplain learns to exude generosity of spirit.

This CPE program required me to attend Sunday Mass with the Jesuits whenever I spent the weekend on retreat with them at the center from Saturday to Sunday. But because I only lived seven miles away, I chose to spend the night at home in my own bed, arriving at the center just after Mass ended and just before our program started. I could not bear attending Mass–I knew they would not extend the Eucharist to me, and that would be too painful.

Skipping Mass resulted in a prompt reprimand from the Jesuit who headed the program and who served as my spiritual director for those ten months. I asked him if I was part of the body of Christ. He affirmed I was. So then I asked, shouldn't they extend the Eucharist to me, a recognized part of the body of Christ, to be a truly catholic church?

He paused and looked very thoughtful, as if consulting God. He said that under original Catholic doctrine, the Eucharist was intended for all God's children. He affirmed me as a child of God. Such was his generosity of spirit. So I agreed to attend Mass the next weekend I was with the Jesuits.

I had tears in my eyes when they placed the wafer on my tongue. The Jesuit abbot noticed and asked me to help with scripture readings whenever joining them. In their Eucharist, my Christian faith was redeemed. This was a spiritual awakening! I wanted to tell everyone I knew. But they asked me not to, at least for a few years, for fear they might get in trouble with American Catholic bishops who had forgotten God's purpose and withheld the Eucharist in order to enforce Roman Catholic political positions upon the laity.

In every Communion to this day, I come face to face with God. I love the experience. One Sunday, I celebrated Mass with the Jesuits after spending the weekend with them, then raced to Boston Common after lunch to celebrate Episcopal Communion with homeless people at *common cathedral*, where I served as treasurer of the board, and finally celebrated Communion that evening with United Church of Christ Congregationalists, where a classmate was leading her first Communion as a minister.

Three different chances in one day to embody divine communion. I felt the joy of embodying the divine presence, even while linking together three different traditions. I'd like to think that through my love of Communion and through my body I helped to mystically align these three faith traditions with Jesus's initial intent in creating the rite of Communion.

Generosity in Community

As part of my training for UU ministry, I was also required to spend two years working half-time as a ministerial intern in a congregation. The UU New England Regional Subcommittee on Candidacy suggested that because my home congregation, First Parish in Concord, was the largest UU congregation in New England, and because I was coming to ministry from a secular background of wealth and power, the best location for my ministerial internship would be a smaller and poorer congregation. Serving in a very different kind of church setting would help my ministerial formation. I would learn how to be a generous minister in a new context.

I chose First Parish of Watertown, where their minister, my supervisor, was a working-class former hippie and leading UU historian. As a UU humanist congregation, they encouraged me to scale back my references to God. The minister also suggested I eliminate entirely any reference to my mystical experiences of the divine or spiritual beings or my many privileges associated with graduating from Yale and Harvard. I removed any mention of running public companies or active investing as well.

My public presentation of self was again being tailored to meet other people's expectations. I was putting on masks, playing with my identity, to better serve their needs. But this was a gift freely given by me to them—to adapt my sense of self in a spirit of generosity.

This congregation encouraged my young ministry. I thrived under their encouragement. When the minister went on sabbatical during the last six months of my training, they asked me to be their sabbatical minister. Once again, I responded, "I am here Lord. I'm ready. Send me."

One dark and stormy night, I dreamed I was drinking beer and playing poker with many wild cards with Divine Mystery. In such circumstances, it's important to remember God's omniscience. You might as well play with your cards face up on the table, but you can also count upon God's love and justice.

I was having a good night, so the pile of poker chips in front of me continued to climb. Then God dealt me a hand I thought could not lose—a royal straight flush.

I grinned, and God grinned back at me. I pushed my entire pile of chips into the middle of the table. God called. It seems he had dealt himself five aces, which trumped my royal straight flush. We both started giggling, then laughing, then rolling on the floor with laughter.

Having won and lost a fortune, both in my dreams and in my lived reality, I now could speak generously of money and meaning. It seems this dream—and life—was preparing me for yet another calling. Mine would be a distinctive Unitarian Universalist ministry, with a focus on money and meaning. I would help others see that generosity is a key ingredient for success on the spiritual journey, that it is integral to our enjoyment of life.

Generosity is perhaps the most important public, or community, virtue of the first four spiritual disciplines. Resilience, surrender, gratitude, and especially generosity create the atmosphere for awakening to divine mystery and growing spiritually in community into the human beings we were born to be.

The foundational spiritual discipline is resilience. In terms of resiliency, Loretta's Chinese immigrant parents and my highly educated but impoverished parents had each prepared us for finding the resilience that made us such a good match. Spiritual resilience became our platform for learning to surrender our ego needs to the greater good. And because we started with so little, developing the discipline of gratitude was quite natural—even gratitude for complexities and suffering within the context of a life well lived.

So while the spiritual disciplines of resilience, surrender, and gratitude are built upon one another, they alone will seldom bring us into a spirit of abundance and joy. The spirit of generosity, how we contribute to the world's abundance, also has to be present from the very beginning. It is not only how we manage our own thoughts and feelings but also how we treat others that brings us joy. Especially in the second half of life, generosity is foundational to our sense of well-being.

Much of this we learned from our parents, of course, but we also had to validate generosity's power as a spiritual discipline in our own lives. We always lived well below our means. We had the audacity to prepay our loans to create a generative attitude toward money. This was our disciplined way to live a life of worth and meaning over decades, and it has made all the difference. Generosity interconnected our wants and desires with the world's needs.

However, our generosity had very little to do with the absolute level of our income or finances. Rather, it has much to do with how we feel about money and how we behave with whatever level of wealth comes our way. Generosity takes different forms, depending on our financial circumstances. But finding our way to a generous spirit, no matter what our means, is key to living a life of joy, peace, and well-being.

Jesus expressed this in his story of the widow's mite. She had very little and therefore could give very little. Yet what she gave was everything, so far beyond the large gifts of the rich man.

This is the gift of spiritually transcending scarcity. You can't practice generosity while feeling insecure about your finances or operating from a scarcity mindset. Likewise, you can't practice resilience while feeling victimized by circumstances, or practice surrender while holding tightly onto self-control, or practice gratitude while feeling self-entitled.

Scarcity can be a psychological trap for some people. It sucks the joy out of life. I am often shocked at how many families with household incomes of $70,000 or $100,000 a year operate from a "scarcity" mentality that keeps them from expressing generosity. Yet particularly admirable are those families who manage to live within their means and practice generosity on household incomes below $30,000 a year.

Scarcity need not be a trap. Everyone can have a generous spirit. Most of us can learn to be generous no matter what our income level. Families living in poverty must be especially creative to find ways to express their generous spirit, but opportunities exist for even them to transcend a scarcity mentality. A generous spirit makes for beloved community.

My mother maintained a generous spirit most of her life, including the decade she raised a family in poverty and the two decades she spent in retirement living on less than $30,000 a year. Loretta and I were generous people when we were just starting out and deeply in debt. We were even more generous through the period when our fortunes soared and plunged, and we remain so now that we are financially secure.

Each of us chooses how we will live, and that choice alters our spiritual opportunities. So choose abundance. All religions teach some form of this wisdom. Generosity enhances the joy we receive from living. This has always been true. No matter how rich or poor we are at any point, a generous spirit creates opportunities that scarcity won't.

AUDACIOUS GENEROSITY

Chalice-Lighting Words

Generous *means "freely giving more than is necessary or expected." So generosity includes the idea of open-handedness, along with a connection to our internal experience and spirituality. . . . Generosity ennobles us; it makes us great souls.*
—*The Generosity Path* by Mark V. Ewert

Check in: How has generosity helped shape your life and well-being?

Reading

Generosity takes different forms, depending on our financial circumstances. Jesus expressed this in his story of the widow's mite. She had very little and therefore could give very little. Yet what she gave was everything, so far beyond the large gifts of the rich man. This is the gift of spiritually transcending scarcity.

Questions to Ponder

1. How is your relationship with money reflected in your spirituality?

2. Are you free to live the life you choose, or do you feel trapped by financial constraints?

3. Do money conflicts and anxiety interfere with your well-being?

4. How does generosity of spirit relate to Jim's growing spiritual visions?

5. What calling of the spirit might greater generosity call forth from you?

Closing Words

Each of us chooses how we will live, and that choice alters our spiritual opportunities. So choose abundance. All religions teach some form of this wisdom. Generosity enhances the joy we receive from living. This has always been true. No matter how rich or poor we are at any point, a generous spirit creates opportunities that scarcity won't.

AUDACIOUS GENEROSITY

Author's Comment

In our society, we are hesitant to talk about two topics: sex and money. In this chapter, it feels as if I have violated several social norms in order to discuss money and, more importantly, make my teaching and interior spiritual life more transparent. It verges on too much information to discuss how Loretta and I adapted to wealth with generosity, my risk taking and anxieties, our hunger for wealth, and the incredible turbulence of our finances. But at the same time, it felt necessary to illustrate the power of generosity. Likewise, discussing my growing transcendentalism, deepening family ties, guardian angel, and conversations with God perhaps leaves me vulnerable to ridicule. If so, so be it. They all are part of my spiritual journey. Perhaps these stories may be useful on your own journey as well.

Questions to Encourage Conversation

1. Does generosity factor into your life? How?

2. How does talking about money and generosity make you feel? Why?

3. Do you feel good about your income and financial well-being?

4. How do you feel about your expenses and how you choose to spend money?

5. Do you tithe (give away 10 percent)? Why? Why not?

6. What kinds of risks have you been willing to take in order to succeed?

7. Can you recall any transcendent experiences?

8. Have you ever adapted to changed circumstances?

9. Why does Jim's spiritual life explode when his career and householder responsibilities contract?

10. Do more of your resources go to consumption or to collecting life experiences?

Reflection

As a group, reflect upon what prevents you from being more generous than you are.

DISCIPLINE FIVE:
MYSTERY

*The first mystery is simply that there is a mystery. A
mystery that can never be explained or understood.
Only encountered from time to time. Nothing is obvious.
Everything conceals something else. The Hebrew word
for universe,* Olam, *comes from the word for hidden.
Something of the Holy One is hidden within.*

— "Honey From the Rock" by Lawrence Kushner

Idolatry

My childhood faith was formed within a loving, caring small town Baptist community. But as to the nature of God, more was concealed than revealed. As young adults, Loretta and I chose to raise our kids and anchor our faith within the Unitarian Universalism of First Parish in Concord. Its broad, inclusive affirmation of the worth and dignity of every person, pursuit of justice, equity, and compassion in human relations, acceptance of one another, and encouragement to spiritual growth in our congregations fit our sense of the divine mystery.

But what do I intend to convey with words such as God or divine mystery? The existential "God is dead" movement was popular among some Protestant theologians when I left the Baptists. This was the death of the big white omniscient and all powerful "God in the sky when I die" metaphysics. Such anthropomorphizing of the divine mystery no longer felt culturally appropriate. It disavowed our participation in divine mystery while disempowering humanity.

Perhaps like quantum physicists, trying to simultaneously describe attributes and actions at the quantum scale, mystical theologians must accept that any comprehensive explanation of the nature of God limits divine mystery to our human understanding. Any comprehensive description of God is inherently less than fully true and, in some sense, a form of idolatry. A mystic can speak of his or her own experiences or teachings of faith traditions, but neither can fully capture the entirety of what we mean by divine mystery.

From Buddhist mystics I learned that conceptualizing any perfect spiritual figure, whether Jesus Christ, the Virgin Mary, Buddha, or Confucius, often gets in the way of directly communing with our divine nature within ourselves. We contain a spark of the divine within us. Buddhist mystics go so far as to say if you meet the Buddha on the road, kill him! It is an illusion that obscures your own inherent Buddha nature.

The nature of God is a deep mystery. Not like a true crime mystery, where somebody is guilty and your job is to figure out who, but rather in the sense of being ultimately unknowable. To signify this element of the unknown, ancient Jews wouldn't even speak or write a name for God, simply using four consonants YHWH to signify he who cannot be named. In the Torah, when confronted by Moses to provide his true name, God simply says, "I AM." A designation that in that particular context says: enough said.

The *Tao Te Ching* addresses this fundamental mystery in its very opening words: "The Tao (way of integrity) that can be spoken is not the eternal Tao. The name that can be named is not the eternal name... [Divinity and the Way] emerge together but differ in name. The unity is said to be the mystery. Mystery of mysteries, the door to all wonders." That which can be named and fully known is not real, and that which is real cannot be named and fully known.

Our attempts to tame divine mystery can easily slip into religious idolatry. Where we mistake the human finger for the moon it is pointing us toward. Where we sometimes falsely concretize symbols and metaphors for the things they represent. This is why Islam refuses to allow images of divinity–because such images can easily lead us astray. This is the danger of trying to fit divine mystery within our all too human categories.

Yet even knowing this metaphysical danger, idols often occur in religion. Whether in the idols Abraham brought with him out of Haran, a golden calf created by the Jews in the desert, or the ancestral idols originally stored in the Ka'ba in Mecca, human beings too easily resort to idols in place of this unknowable divine mystery. Any person, symbol, or metaphor for divine mystery can become an idol. People seem to prefer a false certainty to no certainty at all.

It is very common in Buddhism to make a statue of the Buddha into a religious idol. But I have also seen Jews, Protestants, and Muslims do the same with their Torah, Bible, and Koran, where they acquire religious significance far beyond the spiritual teachings within them. Humans have a tendency to do this with great leaders. Whether Mahatma Gandhi, the Dalai Lama, or the Roman Catholic Pope, we assign to men a sense of divinity, which obscures their humanity. The Pope cannot be both human and infallible. These are forms of idolatry that block us from direct experience of the divine mystery and impede our spiritual understanding.

In the end, as one of my Christian mystic teachers would say, we need to let go and let God. We are not in control, and we cannot ever fully understand the nature of divine reality. Divine mystery is real and yet ultimately unknowable. We can love God with all our hearts, bring ourselves and our actions into seeking the will of God, and yet in the end, must simply trust what we will never fully understand. In times of trouble, in the words of the Carrie Underwood song, we let *Jesus take the wheel*, as we come to know the comfort of living in divine mystery.

Frankly, it is all a mystery. Everyone knows experiencing the ecstatic feeling of divine mystery can be a source of great joy. But it can also be scary awesome, like dancing wildly with the Divine when you don't know the steps or have two left feet. Virtually all living faiths have practices to access such joy for their adherents. Yet when that feeling is gone for individuals and institutions, and only liturgical traditions remain, it can be like dancing with a mannequin!

It can be horrifying to discover yourself dancing with—and depending upon—the husk of a formerly living religion. This doesn't just apply to Christian or Baptist or United Church of Christ (UCC) congregations. Many Unitarian Universalist congregations suffer from this same dynamic. We concretize that which cannot save us, blocking us from realizing that which can. So as I prepared for ordination, I vowed that my ministry would be to help revive a living faith.

This is why resilience and surrender are the foundation of every individual and collective spiritual journey. These disciplines create an environment for human flourishing, for transcending and learning to live with our obstacles and failings, so we can live mindfully and become the person or institution we are capable of being. Gratitude and generosity allow us individually and collectively to acknowledge what has been, even while audaciously seeking what can be. To live in divine mystery, it helps to have these four spiritual disciplines.

Intentionality and spirited enthusiasm can overcome mere form and lead us to inner peace and human flourishing. We can participate in the mystery by living fully, mindfully, and in the eternal now, and by accepting the divine mystery that we can never fully understand transcendent reality. We are not sole creators but can be co-creators of our destiny.

Andover Newton

I vowed to myself that if asked to participate in reviving Andover Newton I would work to discern what God was really doing in the world and find my part in making it a living reality. Leaders in turbulent and uncertain times require spiritual discipline. I would bring all I knew and had learned about spiritual disciplines to saving ANTS and its mission in the world. Over the next fifteen years ANTS would shape me as I helped to shape the future of ANTS.

The priest, minister, rabbi, or imam is expected to live comfortably within divine mystery. We cannot know with any certainty what God wants for us, or anyone else, so we live by faith alone. We cannot allow our ego-selves or overly developed self-identities to drive our behavior. A clergy person is a leader set apart, living within a faith community, but never entirely delimited by that particular community. Our first allegiance is to God, our calling, and what divine mystery is doing in the world today.

As I had once progressed from being an independent entrepreneur to being a venture catalyst, from doing for myself to being a facilitator of what needs to be done, now with my training at ANTS, I would progress from being an independent spiritual seeker to being a spiritual catalyst, helping to facilitate a particular faith community's spiritual growth. This is a scary awesome responsibility to which one can only reply, "I am ready, LORD, send me."

At its nineteenth-century founding, Andover Seminary was the first graduate-level theological seminary in America for training congregational ministers. Newton was the first Baptist seminary in America. Yet by the time they merged in the early twentieth century as ANTS, Newton was land-poor and Andover was a financially endowed shadow of its former self.

I came to love ANTS and its mission, and I devoted fifteen years of my life to its resurrection, but to do so, I first needed to recognize its peril. The middle decades of the twentieth century had been perhaps too kind to ANTS. There was strong growth among the New England congregational churches ANTS served, leading to long-term sustainable growth in terms of students, professors, and buildings on campus. My father trained at ANTS in the 1940s, surrounded by optimistic young men and exciting building projects. This was a place for growing a minister's faith to serve growing faith communities.

But when that growth ended in the 1970s, the golden age of American theological education ended with it. ANTS began a many decades long period of decline. With its large campus, many buildings, and excessive infrastructure, ANTS became a victim of its twentieth-century success. The school did an awesome job of training parish ministers but was no longer a self-sustaining institution.

Walking onto campus in 1999, it felt as if this institution was spending significant time and resources defending a dying religious tradition, a form of idolatry, rather than a living faith. ANTS was moribund. It had lived through many rounds of cost cutting and layoffs, had gradually sold off many of its physical assets to fund its operations, and had tried mightily to defend the Protestant Reformation tradition as it had been handed down from Luther and Calvin. It was obvious these were good people, sincere theologians and ministers, trying to do God's work but desperately in need of a sustainable mission and a clear vision of the future.

Their sense of self and identity was perhaps too anchored in their glorious past. Soon after I arrived on campus, ANTS elected a new president following a national search. Nick was an entrepreneurial Baptist preacher, and he immediately began the hard work of renewal to make ANTS spiritually robust and sustainable again. He built a senior management team centered on the strategic leadership of a new academic dean, the financial insights of a talented CFO, and the negotiation savvy of an experienced vice president of operations.

ANTS implemented a new revenue model, undertook further cost cutting, and brought more rigorous strategic planning to the table. ANTS greened its campus, lowered its carbon footprint by switching from oil to gas, and became a school that more nearly lived our expressed values. All of it helped, but none of it ultimately made enough difference. The decline continued, and the losses grew. Our mission would need to change to keep up with the times.

In hopes of becoming financially sustainable, Nick initiated merger discussions with at least three different seminaries, some of which would require us to radically redefine who we were as a school and the purpose of our existence. But combining two already shaky institutions turned out to be impossible. ANTS was a rapidly declining husk of its former self.

Reviving a dying institution is nearly as difficult and unlikely as reviving a corpse, but if you love the institution, you must try mightily to fulfill its existing mission or discern a new expression of its vision. Jesus Christ taught a faith that could revive the dead and dying. However, empty rituals do not connect people with the divine mystery. Simply honoring and preserving the past is like living with the corpse. But mindful intention can breathe new life into ancient rituals. Ministers who are themselves living in divine mystery can help transform their congregations.

Taking Vows

On May 16, 2004, following my five years of training and ministerial formation, I was ordained into the Unitarian Universalist ministry by the congregations of First Parish in Concord and First Parish in Watertown. Thirteen clergy participated in this service, as did representatives from the Massachusetts Council of Churches, the Unitarian Universalist Association (UUA), and our local Massachusetts Bay District of the UUA. There was also a laying on of hands by all present.

The heart of the service was the ordination vows I undertook: "To speak the truth with love and a courageous heart . . . to bring integrity into all the spheres of our life, whether ministering from the church pulpit, through pastoral care, through teaching, or in boardrooms and meetings of corporations public and private. We encourage you to bring your whole self to your work of ministry by living a balanced life, remembering always your commitments to our faith community, the wider world, and especially to your family." This was my aspiration.

My vows continued: "It is our hope you will lead in the ways of love, hope, and justice—ministering alike to human joy and sorrow, celebrating and sharing our Unitarian Universalist faith, taking time for study and prayer, and living with an open heart." It is to these vows I said, "I do." I would strive to be an instrument of God's work in the world.

Many religious traditions ask their ordained clergy to take vows. It is how we live in divine mystery. These religious vows have shaped my calling and helped me recognize my multifaceted ministry in the world. They are as important to me as my wedding vows. Committing to these vows set ablaze a further awakening of my spirit. They are how I serve the living God in all my human imperfections.

I have been set aside to be a friend of divine mystery, which I choose to call God, and to speak my truth with love and a courageous heart. Not just in the pulpit, not just in the parish, but in the boardroom, in private, and in the public sphere. I was ordained not only to bring comfort in times of sorrow but to look for signs of the Holy Spirit that represent opportunities for spiritual growth and transformation. I am to live with an open heart and a spirit of radical inclusiveness, love, and compassion. These vows brought me to parish ministry.

That same May, I received my master's in divinity with highest honors from Andover Newton, was welcomed into the Jonathan Edwards Honor Society, and was invited to join the ANTS board of trustees. I had taken the plunge to live fully in divine mystery.

A month later, United for a Fair Economy published its book *I Didn't Do It Alone*, which included profiles of highly successful people talking about society's contribution to our individual wealth and success. It featured Warren Buffett, Amy Domini, Ben Cohen, Katrina Browne, and me. In the chapter devoted to my perspectives as both pastor and venture catalyst, I affirmed: "We're all in the community together, so we have a moral obligation to look out for those who are least able to look out for themselves. We are all standing on the shoulders of all who came before us, and creating a society for our children and those who come after us. We have obligations as part of that."

Now I would earnestly take up those obligations myself by leading a faith community while not being delimited by it. Having attained financial security, Loretta and I both looked for ways in which our gifts best met the world's needs. I chose ordained ministry; she made an incredible difference in young people's lives by creating and running Funderburg Scholars.

We live in an interdependent web of being. It is important to trust our intuition. I would be shaped by my congregations but not solely by them. I was learning to speak with the moral authority that comes from being ordained as a person of God, one who has undertaken certain vows and is committed to working for the good of all. I began to find my own voice.

That August, I would go on one final vision quest to Vermont with my First Parish in Concord men's group. I decided to practice another perpetual prayer. My perpetual prayer for this retreat, repeated over one thousand times, was: "Holy Spirit, fill me with compassion, burning bright within all my intentions, filling me with hope, wisdom, and love. Amen."

I have experienced many visions in my life, but none as profound as the one that summer. I encountered a vision of the shape of eight potential decades of my life: childhood, youth, young adult, parenting adult, mature adult, senior adult, elder adult, and old age. It helped put my entire life into perspective and gave me comfort in my forty-ninth year.

I felt joyous about my childhood and youth. I was extraordinarily grateful for my progress as a young adult with a wife and family, an MBA, a nice house, and an interesting career that included being a CFO of a promising startup before the age of thirty. I also felt good about my fourth decade. I experienced career progression while also supporting Loretta's business, and I had a growing focus on parenting and family, church and community, and my own spiritual life. The first half of my life had its great rewards.

My fifth decade saw my children off to college, Loretta's and my financial independence, five phenomenal vision quests, and my seminary experience and ministerial ordination. Now I was looking forward to my sixth decade, about to begin, and the changing relationships it would bring to my life.

I also experienced a vision of my seventh decade in becoming an elder adult able to redefine my role in the world, with fewer day-to-day responsibilities and more ability to just be. By the seventh decade of life, there would be little left to accomplish, except growing deeper into the relationship with I AM. Divine mystery assured me I was living my life as I was intended to be.

But the shape of my old age, if I would be lucky enough to experience it, was still hidden in the mists of time. Who knows what my eighth decade might hold if I make it there.

These were more concrete and comforting visions than I had previously experienced on any vision quest. At one point, a dove—a traditional symbol of the Holy Spirit—actually descended upon my site and dwelt with me awhile.

I felt increasingly comfortable living into the mystery. This ministry would be the center of my spiritual practice and my life for the coming decade.

First Parish in Brookline

That fall, I teamed with Martha—a more experienced and somewhat older UU minister ordained eight years before me—to search for the right congregational fit for our co-ministry. Martha brought strengths in terms of liturgical arts, empathy, and conflict resolution. I brought my own unique combination of entrepreneurial management, finance, and spiritual seeking to complement Martha's experience. We felt like a strong co-ministry team for the right congregation.

We focused on finding a congregation that was a good fit for our combined ministerial gifts and that was within a reasonable commute from our homes in Concord and Waltham. It was like threading a camel through the eye of a needle—not possible except for creative serendipity, which is possible only through divine mystery. God finds a way.

While I was in search of a permanent calling, one of my mentors, the former president of the UUA, offered me a temporary affiliate minister position at First Parish in Needham, where he was now senior minister. Then in December 2004, I began a brief three-month interim ministry at North Parish in North Andover, filling in while their solo minister was on maternity leave with her first child. In this setting, my Budai nature began to shine. Returning from maternity leave, the minister asked me to stay on part-time another three months in co-ministry with her.

That spring of 2005, months before my fiftieth birthday, Martha and I accepted a call to become the co-ministers at First Parish in Brookline, a community that needed us. They had recently experienced several traumas and conflicts involving the wife of their senior minister, an ailing beloved music minister, a catastrophic fall with head injuries for their longtime director of religious education, and fights about deferred maintenance and the sale of their beloved parsonage. This congregation had lost its way and was in deep conflict.

So it seemed they would benefit from Martha's calm presence, empathy, and conflict-resolution skills. Their six decades of gradual decline in membership and giving had also led to their current financial problems, so it seemed they would greatly benefit from my historical perspective, deep financial knowledge, and organizational skills. We embraced this new role with high expectations but also with humility and hope. We felt we could help this ancient and beloved congregation find a new sense of its calling and rebuild itself once again.

In some ways, this co-ministry and this congregation was a marriage made in heaven. Its lay leadership included judges, partners at prominent law firms, business executives, entrepreneurs, strategy consultants, and financial investors. I had a background to understand and relate to such people with an ability to help them that many other ministers might not have. I could speak to them candidly about their lives and spiritual journeys from experience.

This congregation also included many lay leaders who had grown up in poverty or who were working class, or from a mixed racial background, or some other form of societal oppression that shamed and marginalized their lives. I could speak directly to them as well from life experience. We are riding this bus together. We were living together at the very edge of the city of Boston in a great vortex of societal change and transformation.

Yet many individual UU congregants, including some in this congregation, want a minister who is less audacious, humbler, and who uses less God language. I would have to adapt my sense of self and my gifts once again to meet their needs and better serve them as a minister while also asking the congregation to adapt itself to Martha and me. This complex parish ministry would become a growing spiritual practice of divine mystery for me.

I grew to love this congregation, in all its peculiarities. But I have an even greater love of divine mystery. My personal relationship with God, my devotion to the divine mystery, brought me to Unitarian Universalist ordained ministry. We are travelers on a journey, knowing not how long or how far we will travel or our ultimate destinations. Yet we boarded this bus together.

Dating back to 1717, the history of First Parish in Brookline deeply fascinated me. It was located in the formerly marshy area just beyond the narrow neck of land that connects Boston to the mainland. In seventeenth-century Massachusetts, this area was called Muddy River, after its local stream. As Boston filled in its Back Bay, this land became pastures and farms, initially for families spilling out from Boston's congestion but also as a pastoral setting for families repelled by urban stench. Where else would a lover of American history want to serve God?

One of the founders of this very liberal and inclusive congregation was former Massachusetts chief justice Samuel Sewall, the so-called hanging judge of the Salem witch trials. Seeking redemption, he sought a faith based upon reason and also wrote some of America's first antislavery tracts. This congregation was founded as a voice of reason in religion.

Another founder was Dr. Zabdiel Boylston, who invented the small-pox vaccine. His daughter Susanna grew up in this congregation before moving to Quincy to marry a farmer named John Adams and eventually become mother and grandmother of two American presidents.

Brookline's congregants played an important, even pivotal, role in winning the American Revolution, from organizing munitions for the battle at the North Bridge, to being the closest rebel center to Boston, to driving the British out of Boston in the battle of Dorchester Heights.

Its ministers were prominently involved in the 1805 Unitarian controversy at Harvard, which led to the formation of the American Unitarian Association and the founding of Harvard Divinity School. Rev. Dr. Frederic Henry Hedge, the minister during and following the American Civil War, was a founder of American transcendentalism with Ralph Waldo Emerson. Hedge wrote two internationally recognized books on American religion: *Reason in Religion* and *Ways of the Spirit.* I would become a great fan and follower of the transcendentalist Hedge.

Theodore Roosevelt married his first wife, a local Chestnut Hill girl, in the church's sanctuary. Some of America's greatest landscape designers, most prominently Frederick Law Olmsted, chose Brookline to live and work in, implementing their designs. Olmsted himself land-scaped the church grounds.

By the early twentieth century, when the congregation celebrated its two hundredth anniversary, Brookline claimed to be the richest town in America, based upon property values. As part of the American Arts and Crafts movement, the congregation had built itself a neo-Gothic cathedral complete with twenty-three stained-glass windows (nine by Tiffany) and a seating capacity of over five hundred people in worship.

However, that was the congregation's financial peak. For six decades, it had been in decline in terms of Sunday attendance and finances. Many Sundays in recent years, no more than fifty to sixty people would attend worship—a small remnant of the robust former congregation. The congregation's deferred maintenance exceeded its remaining endowment.

The four major conflicts this congregation had experienced in the previous twelve years caused many families to worship elsewhere. Secret-keeping and misinformation hobbled the lay leadership's ability to respond to current needs. Total congregational giving covered less than 50 percent of the annual operating costs. The congregation was drawing upon its endowment at a pace that suggested it had less than ten years left to live. Yet we had hope.

This congregation had deep roots and a prominent history. Yet in every generation, everything must be renewed, or else it will begin to fade. Martha and I grew to love this congregation, even as we wept over its intractable problems. We knew there must be a way to revive this congregation if only we gave our hearts and souls to doing so.

In leading Spiritual Autobiography classes, I would come to learn much about the congregation members' individual spiritual journeys and discover why they belonged here. A gay business professional who had been shamed out of his Methodist church, but was welcomed here, married here, and raised his children here as well. The working-class girl who had grown up here, only to have her life fall apart in young adulthood, returning here as a single mother able to count upon this community for its love and support. The senior partner at a downtown law firm, approaching retirement, seeking more meaning than he could find in playing golf in retirement. These were people on lifelong spiritual journeys for whom this community was a lifeline.

This congregation seemed to need what Martha and I had to give, so we accepted their call, rolled up our sleeves, and went to God's work. We focused on providing exciting and compelling worship to attract new families, on righting relationships to heal the breaches among existing members, and small-group ministries to deepen everyone's spiritual journeys.

In confidential small-group ministry circles, we explored the dimensions of our lives together. We introduced non-violent communication techniques to create safe spaces in these small-group ministries to allow people to share their joys, traumas, worries, and hopes in the community. I would later learn to call this meaning making through telling our stories "soul sharing." It had a dramatic and life-giving impact upon all those who participated in it. The congregation came alive!

We were almost immediately growing in numbers and also in diversity. We became a congregation more openly welcoming to gays, lesbians, and bisexual and transgender people, mounting large rainbow flags around our building to signify ours as a safe place for gender diversity. We were becoming more socioeconomically diverse as well. We began to rebuild this new congregation from the ashes of the previous conflicts.

In our second year, I introduced money workshops, which provided an environment to explore how gratitude and generosity could transform our lives. It helped greatly that in addition to the majority of members who were middle or upper-middle class, with household incomes between $60,000 and $120,000 per year, we had participants happily living on under $30,000, and a few with household incomes approaching a million dollars a year. In these small groups, we learned to appreciate, care for, and enter into beloved community with one another across vast socio-economic divides.

We renewed the congregation's work and study for social justice. And we began to acknowledge and address our historical racism and white privilege in order to become welcoming to a greater racial and cultural diversity. This was the beginning of building a more robust spiritual home for those who came to join us, dwelling in the divine mystery, what some call heaven, but which we simply called beloved community.

By the end of our sixth year as co-ministers, we could report that active membership had nearly doubled, making us one of the fastest-growing UU congregations in New England. Sunday morning worship had grown even faster, with a vibrant spirit expressed in our services. Our congregation's annual giving had tripled, representing much stronger commitments from existing members as well as the largest influx of new members in the congregation's history. The congregation was on the cusp of becoming financially sustainable once again.

We began to envision a brighter future. Everything we hoped for this congregation was at least begun.

Mountains beyond Mountains

Martha went on sabbatical and returned with new plans to retire the following year. Then it was my turn to go on sabbatical. I was determined to make the most of it, to begin writing my doctoral dissertation and to spend some much needed time replenishing my own spirit.

A good friend who was a UU seminary president suggested I travel with some of her students and their Sufi teacher to celebrate the anniversary of Rumi's ascendance into the divine mystery. So I traveled with Sufi mystics to Konya in the mountains of Turkey.

I learned whirling meditation and new ways of reading Rumi's writings. I experienced things beyond belief–dancing with the divine and having an ancient teacher plant the Ka'ba of love, the celestial presence of the divine, in my heart. The Sufis cracked me open with the power of love. We sang, we danced, we talked, we meditated. But most of all, we invoked divine presence through all these things. I was transformed. I would never be the same again.

Like that Grinch who stole Christmas, my heart grew three sizes. Now I would feel each person's pain along with them. My wife commented how much easier tears came to my eyes, sometimes over silly sentimental things or memories of childhood traumas. I became one of those bleeding heart people who carry the pain of the world in their hearts. This was another stage of my awakening to being more fully human and humane.

Then I explored Taoism for a month at a monastery in the Chinese New Territories, a mountainous part of southern China just above Hong Kong, learning how to better focus and control my intent. I read, pondered, thought, and practiced spiritual concentration. Among the fruits of this spiritual journey, I learned to control my thoughts, focus my attention, and do what seems physically impossible. I was content.

The Taoists taught me to transcend mountains with my mind, both spiritually and physically. They taught me to discern mountains beyond mountains and to discipline my mind to transcend them. I was mindful that Jesus too taught that we could move mountains with even the faith of a mustard seed. Everything good was possible with faith. These ancient mystical spiritual techniques gave me far greater control over my own spiritual journey, reminding me of the Jedi mind games in *Star Wars*. Focused intent can move mountains.

This practice completely changed my understanding of these ancient Taoist texts within the context of Chinese Confucian rules, my emerging understanding from late twentieth-century process theologians, and what we were learning from quantum physics. It was breathtakingly wonderful to combine these ancient and postmodern teachings with actual Taoist meditation and spiritual practice, especially while learning how my mind helps me to ascend any mountain. My head felt ready to explode. I returned home openhearted, with increased vitality, ready to live in the spiritual realm of being while grounding my spiritual practice in the everyday.

In the remaining three months of my sabbatical, I was living between two worlds. I used Taoist wu wei mental concentration to complete the first draft of my doctoral dissertation on emergent sustaining ministry. Yet I was still committed to my parish ministry. My mystical understandings and my practice of radical efficiency were at last one. The following year, ANTS granted me a doctorate in ministry (DMIN) with highest honors.

I had much to reflect upon as I prepared to return from my sabbatical to First Parish in Brookline. I had changed perhaps more than they had or could. I had previously surrendered my various and emerging gifts to service in this particular congregation. In return, the congregation had thrived beyond our wildest hopes. Yet what would now be its salvific vision?

Martha retired from our co-ministry in December 2012. The congregation underwent a discernment process to decide whether to call me their solo senior minister. My doctoral studies in emergent church leadership gave me some idea of what the congregation still needed in order to become financially sustainable, even while continuing to embrace our rapidly expanding racial, ethnic, socioeconomic, and gender diversity. I had such hopes for the congregation, with or without me, to discover the community they were capable of being.

In my new spiritual state, I was increasingly drawn to walking with those suffering and those facing death. Several members of the congregation had unresolved pain around their parents' death and found soul sharing could help ease that pain. We did a healing service for one of our most prominent members who was dying of brain cancer, with little expectation that, without God's help, we could reverse the cancer, but in order to provide community support in her pain. We all encounter suffering, and death, but we can help one another.

There were, however, some longtime congregants who yearned for the quietude of the 1990s church and blamed our worship changes for the loss of their concept of church. Others grieved Martha's retirement and the end of our successful co-ministry. Some wanted to see me leave as well so the congregation could make a fresh start. Still others had never liked having a minister who was a powerful, white, middle-aged, heterosexual male with a Harvard MBA and a prior business career. There were many strong and conflicting views within the community.

Some longed for a close-knit secular community instead of a "church." And if they did envision a role for a minister, he or she was most likely more pastoral, expressing more empathy for the powerlessness of the human condition, and perhaps without all my excess energy, vitality, and joy disrupting their quiet contemplation. I was not that minister.

There were so many diverse expectations and voices in the congregation. No one minister could fulfill them all. However, because I was beloved by most of the congregation, a supermajority voted to continue my ministry. So I continued as senior minister and reached out to everyone, simply doing God's work as best this flawed human being could do.

Leading through Turbulence

As soon as I graduated from ANTS in 2004, the president, Nick, had asked me to draw upon my skills and experience to help him transform ANTS's focus to what God was doing in the world today. Nick had invited me to join the board of trustees and eventually the trustees' investment committee, which oversaw our shrinking endowment. The school's operating results and endowment were in a rapid decline. If we did not radically reform the school, it would go out of existence within the next decade.

Through the investment committee, we changed managers to lower costs, lessen volatility, and ensure our investments were consistent with our values. More importantly, we installed constraints on the draw rate so the school could not spend down the endowment below $14 million, preserving the restricted portion of our endowment for our mission to future generations.

Nick then invited me to join the executive committee of the board as vice chair and to help the school prepare for his retirement. We looked to a very uncertain future. Despite ten years of extraordinary efforts, ANTS was still not financially sustainable. Our endowment and enrollment had fallen by half over the previous decade. It seemed we might have very little time left to survive as an institution. Our next president would be our last, unless we did something radical.

I was invited to chair the presidential search committee with an expectation that I would become board chair after we selected our next president. We created the most diverse search committee in the history of the school, by role (trustees, faculty, staff, students, and alumni), race, age, gender identity, sexual orientation, and denomination. We wanted to ensure that all stakeholders had a voice in our process. We wanted to discern what God was doing in the world today and seek to become a part of that work. This was another opportunity to bring my gifts in service of divine mystery.

After a national search, we narrowed our choices to three candidates: a young black male president of a successful small Southern Methodist seminary, a very experienced female seminary administrator who was Unitarian Universalist and lesbian, and a widely published, internationally respected white male minister successfully leading the largest United Church of Christ (UCC) congregation in New England.

Each of these candidates would have taken the school in different directions. Our strongest denominational affiliation was UCC, as was the largest group of students, the majority of our board, and most of our major contributors. We needed to choose someone who could enhance our standing among UCCs nationally. After much deliberation and given the dire nature of the challenges facing the school, we went with the prominent UCC minister as the best candidate to lead our various stakeholders in doing this new thing.

The incoming president, along with our UCC academic dean, led our visioning process, which resulted in a radically new and inclusive mission statement: "Deeply rooted in Christian faith, radically open to what God is doing now, we educate inspiring leaders for the twenty-first century." With a new sense of self, new hope began to emerge.

With this new self-perception—one that transcended traditional Reform Protestantism but was still deeply rooted in Christianity—we began to envision a sustainable future again. But there was no clear and obvious path to get there. We would need to be different, probably radically so, but still grounded in God and open to training ministers in the context of the emergent church environment. As our key discernment guide, we would focus on training ministers for congregationally based ministries.

During this time, my mother was in the final stages of her long life. Her energy and ability to engage with the world began to markedly decline following her eighty-fifth birthday. I took over the upkeep of all her financial records and paid all her bills. The many hours and days we spent together deeply influenced my life priorities and worldview.

I became her primary contact with the outside world, so I visited her each week, often bringing Loretta with me for Sunday afternoons playing Scrabble or eating supper at her assisted-living facility. We would frequently have long, involved conversations as she reexamined her life and expressed joys and regrets about choices she had made or her relationships with her grown children, grandchildren, and great-grandchildren.

After hip surgery in her eighty-ninth year, she never regained her old self. But she still enjoyed going outside, especially looking at the river, whenever the weather permitted.

She was increasingly confused and unable to remember things. In the spring of 2012, she finally lost the ability to find her way back to her own room or even coherently ask for help. Several of my siblings and I gathered to help her move into the nursing wing of her facility.

We now visited even more often to ensure she was safe, well fed, and had enough mental stimulation. It was time for more frequent visits. She was in the midst of an inexorable decline.

Between excruciating pains, a bad reaction to opioid drugs, and memory loss, my mom's last week of life was brutal. Rae died in her ninetieth year.

Her friends and three dozen offspring gathered to celebrate her life. She had asked to be cremated and her ashes divided, placing some alongside my dad's tombstone in Tiverton and distributing the rest in the Sakonnet River with David's ashes. Mom had a full and meaningful life and left behind so many of us who loved her so dearly.

Now compared to living and dying, it didn't seem like a particularly overwhelming commitment when I agreed to become ANTS' board chair. After all, by this stage in my career I had already served as board chair for seven for-profit companies and four nonprofit boards or committees. How hard could it be? I was soon to discover.

I became ANTS board chair in June 2014, with renewed aspirations for our school. Six weeks later, all hell broke loose. A rumor was brought to our attention that our newly elected president had been unfaithful to his wife and so could not be deemed a person of integrity. With his formal installation ninety days hence, we needed to initiate a formal investigation and report the results to our executive committee and then our board. We decided to trust in God.

With much of our work requiring sensitivity and confidentiality, ANTS became the subject of nasty or disappointed emails, blogs, and even a reprimand in the *Christian Century*. This was a legal employment matter as well as a question of moral standing. And because we were a covenanted UCC seminary and he a UCC minister, this also became a UCC denominational issue as well. Many horrified observers said if we did not fire him to set an example, this would instead be an example of white male privilege prevailing once again.

It's hard to overstate the amount of pain and agony this caused around the future of our school. It shook us to our Christian core. Yet as a Christian seminary, we also taught, and deeply believed in, the power of forgiveness and reconciliation. The board of trustees would address his lapse with Christian charity, faith, forgiveness, and heartbreak. Yet the impact on the school severely limited our options going forward.

I liked our new president, had a large role in selecting him, and wanted to see if we could still make this work. He had done incredible work as a UCC parish minister for over twenty years, was a well-regarded religious author, and a person of deep faith. I didn't think God would abandon him, and neither should the school, no matter what the pressures were.

During the earliest stages of our investigation, the president privately confessed to his sin but asked that it be treated as a private matter. Of course, that quickly became impossible to do. Our alternatives were few. We needed to maintain our integrity, our mission, and our relationship to our various stakeholders. We once again grounded ourselves in God.

In the end, our board censured his infidelity and required him to publicly confess and ask forgiveness from all the parties he had harmed by his infidelity, beginning with his own family, the board of trustees, our faculty, our students, our alumni, his former congregation, and his denomination.

We went ahead with his installation. The school had so much at stake, even though the wounds were still fresh and the pain deep. My charge to the new president focused on fidelity and promise-keeping as much as the traditional language of installation.

Through it all, we tried to behave consistently with our highest values. The school may not have survived if we chose any other path, but it was a painful path to travel. It alienated some of our friends and stakeholders. Ultimately, this path won the respect of our trustees, our faculty, our students, and many of our alumni. This cathartic process also perhaps prepared the way for a different future for Andover Newton.

These trials and tribulations also provided me with an opportunity to deepen my practice of Christianity. Trials and tribulations have nearly always served to deepen my faith. I found myself praying daily—actually, many times a day—as I worked to stay grounded in doing God's work in the world. Through the Brookline Clergy Association, of which I was the president, we began to explore the similarities and differences among the teachings of the Abrahamic traditions. Our group included deep friendships among priests, ministers, and rabbis in roughly equal numbers.

We were living in heaven and in hell on a day-to-day basis in the eternal now. Like all times of tribulation, this was also a time of spiritual deepening. I knew many others were praying for us as well as for the school as we navigated along these rocky shores.

Adventures with Shamans

My Christian faith had served me well, yet I again started to feel spiritually restless. There were more spiritual realities I had only read about.

My worries about climate change also led me to want to explore approaches to loving the earth and spiritual meaning-making in less developed places.

A South American group called the Pachamama Alliance presented at First Parish in Concord. They introduced me to an ancient indigenous people's approach to spirituality—another way to come face to face with the divine mystery outside the Western religious tradition. It felt like time for another transformative vision quest.So I reached out to the Pachamama Alliance. That summer, I found myself experiencing the ancient ways of indigenous peoples. We lived with a Mayan tribe on an extinct volcano high in the Andean Mountains of northern Ecuador.

We traveled into the Amazonian rainforest of southeastern Ecuador and into northern Peru with the Achuar people. They introduced me to ayahuasca, an ancient indigenous plant medicine for opening portals into alternate realities. I soared through the universe for hours after taking it, forever transformed by the experience. Several South American shamans opened new spiritual realities for me to explore with awe and wonder. And I wanted to explore further.

I returned spiritually refreshed to First Parish in Brookline and began to plan the new church year. I was in seventh heaven. I was a changed spiritual person, a changed spiritual leader, in touch with a different sense of divine mystery.

We had long had lay pastoral associates who visited the sick and those facing losses. Now I trained them in nonviolent communication and deeper listening skills—how to just be present to someone in pain.

A young first-time mother in the congregation, undergoing a difficult pregnancy, went into premature labor and delivered a baby boy who did not breathe for many minutes following birth. Her husband called me to meet them at the hospital.

When I met them in the neonatal intensive care unit, the doctor said their son might not survive the weekend, and if he did, he would be so mentally compromised that he might never walk, be able to recognize his parents, or be able to do anything ever for himself. We prayed together in our grief as I rubbed this tiny premature baby's bare back in expression of our love for him. The family gathered their closest friends and relatives in the hospital's small chapel.

We lifted up this child, his parents, and our grief to God. We wept. We prayed for a miracle, even as I gave the child last rites. He was beloved. As it turns out, his story had many more chapters, ending in this miracle baby eventually even being able to walk, talk, and communicate with his loving family. God works in mysterious ways and sometimes allows us to be a vehicle of his mercy, and for this, I praise the divine mystery. Yet I also know from reading the Gospels that Jesus would affirm it was his parents' faith and love that saved him.

Our church staff meetings now took on a more spiritual aspect as we became intimately acquainted with one another's joys, sorrows, and spiritual journeys. This was creating beloved community at work. We even created board agendas that devoted up to a quarter of our governing board meetings to enriching soul sharing among the nine members.

I was always either spiritually playing or praying—and sometimes both—as a way to deepen spiritual intimacy within this divine community. My sermons became more experiential and unreservedly mystic. Our Sunday morning worship deepened spiritually. Not all our members were fond or even tolerant of these changes. But our lay leadership seemed to be, and my deepening spiritual practice felt consistent with leading this faith community.

We sought to continue becoming a more diverse community as well. We didn't really have the budget for it, but by my taking a substantial pay cut and finding other funds, we hired a Latina candidate for UU ministry with indigenous roots in Chile, as our half-time assistant minister. She deepened our connections to immigrant groups in the Boston area, such as Centro Presente and the Chelsea Collaborative. Our people earned a reputation for showing up on behalf of the hungry, the homeless, the imprisoned, and the oppressed, whether at a prison vigil, a detention center, or the statehouse.

We became stalwarts in supporting each Mother's Day Walk for

Peace with the Louis D. Brown Peace Institute. I began to build ties with African American congregations. I walked the streets of Boston's poorest minority neighborhoods along with black activists.

Our justice work within the congregation deepened spiritually, while outside our congregation, our light never shone so bright. This, more than our congregation's financial and governance revival of the last seven years, was why I went into parish ministry. With my spiritual growth anchored in a UU faith community, I wanted to help make the world a better place and achieve spiritual maturity at the same time.

My pastoral counseling, especially one-on-one, increasingly yielded deeper spiritual insights for those with ears to hear and eyes to see. However, I began to hear complaints that people who came to church primarily for a sense of community felt I was encouraging them toward a spiritual growth they did not want. Some people professed weariness at the forced intimacy of greeting their neighbors in worship and exploring what the universe was calling them to be and to do.

I was indeed encouraging people to open their hearts to the spirit. But not everyone welcomed my growing insights or my focus on transformation. I came to parish ministry to befriend God and serve humanity. As my own mystic spirituality deepened, it appeared this might lead to my being called to leave parish ministry as well.

I was describing my experiences with ayahuasca to a friend in Concord when he told me his younger son, Robin, who had gone to high school with my daughter, trained for eight years in Peru in shamanic ways, including the use of ayahuasca. When Robin visited Concord a few weeks later, we had a long discussion about my spiritual journey. He said I had more yet to learn from ayahuasca in particular and the shamanic journey in general.

One of my Pachamama guides, Daniel, had said a very similar thing to me at the end of our trip the previous summer, except he thought I was being called to work with a shaman in the Ecuadorian high sierra.

I e-mailed Daniel and arranged to do a vision quest with his shaman in January 2015. Then I arranged to go on a pilgrimage with Robin in

Peru the following summer. If I was being called to this path, then I might as well travel it. I wanted to immerse myself in the depths of experience, sucking out the very marrow of the shamanic path, to see what new awakening this might lead me to.

So after leading the congregation through another winter solstice and Christmas Eve, I was ready for another spiritual adventure. I flew to Guayaquil, Ecuador, where Daniel met me at my hotel late that evening. After catching up over food and wine, we went to bed early in order to get up at 4:30 a.m. to fly to Cuenca.

Cuenca is the small city in the Ecuadorian southwest where Daniel grew up and where most of his extended family still lives. It is built around a Spanish colonial square and has a prominent cathedral. Cuenca is lovely and quaint, but the entire town can be experienced in a morning.

Late that afternoon, we headed south on the Pan-American Highway to the tiny village of Susudel. Deep in the high sierra desert of southwestern Ecuador, we left the paved highway to travel ten miles into the backcountry over unpaved, deeply rutted paths and muddy, washed-out roads between cliffs and sheer drops. It was a spiritual adventure. It felt as if we had traveled through space and time to a very different dimension and place.

Here I would undertake a fasting vision quest alone under an acacia tree in the high sierra desert, learning new aspects about reality and my own capabilities. My journey would begin and end with the disorienting and purifying experience of the sweat lodge. My physiological aids to enlightenment would include fasting, sweating, chanting, singing, mescaline, and peyote.

Juvenile condors watched over my journey as they soared aloft on the hot air currents. For the shaman, condors represent transcendence. I would recite twenty-nine prayers each day to speed me on my way and find myself again transformed.

The shaman was very strict and very serious. This was not fun. It was sometimes frightening, yet it spiritually opened me to a further awakening. I returned to the United States as a friend of the divine, a spiritual teacher, ready to speak from the authenticity of my own spiritual experiences and to draw forth the spiritual experiences of others.

Ending Well

As a culmination of our work over the previous ten years, the congregation was in the middle of a yearlong process to adopt a new congregational mission statement. At our May 2015 annual meeting, we were ready to vote on our selection: "Called by love, sustained by community, committed to justice, we strive to be a welcoming, diverse, and loving congregation that nurtures spiritual growth for individuals and families, celebrates multicultural community, and works together to demand social justice, dismantle racism, and care for our living earth." I have a deep passion for this mission.

Over the ten plus years of my ministry, First Parish in Brookline had gone from a struggling, failing congregation to one that was thriving once again with a clearer sense of its mission in the world. To stay longer would have been comfortable and satisfying. Yet it was beginning to feel as though my work there was done. With this new mission statement, it was time for the congregation to find its own sense of purpose. To move forward without me. It was time as well for me to be free to be me. I again felt a call to spiritual adventure. I left for the summer with the knowledge that change was coming—and it would be welcome!

August 2015 found me standing with my backpack and duffel bag in the heat outside the tiny Puerto Maldonado, Peru airport, waiting for my thirty-three-year-old blonde shaman to arrive. I spoke no Spanish. Eventually he roared up to the front of the airport on a motorcycle. With me, my backpack, and my duffle bag precariously balancing on the back of his motorcycle, we began our Peruvian adventure. We spent that evening in town getting oriented, then we took a small motorboat up the Rio Madre de Dios the next morning to his rainforest conservation farm.

I joined the team working on the farm for several days before we arranged another ayahuasca ceremony. The shaman had agreed to assist me, but he currently wasn't in a spiritual state to consume ayahuasca, so he suggested instead a friend of his would lead the ceremony. I had to let go of all my expectations of control and trust these shamans completely.

The vibe of the ceremony this time was completely different—and more comforting. It was created by and for a group of Spanish-speaking international expats rather than indigenous people. I felt at peace as a beloved child of God. I was content.

I returned to the United States to announce my retirement from parish ministry. Announcing my imminent departure freed me to do some of my best ministry in my final months with this congregation. We celebrated what we had accomplished together. We said our heartfelt and loving goodbyes.

Our diversity work took on new intensity, raising a Black Lives Matter banner before my departure and bringing the Louis D. Brown Peace Institute into a deeper relationship with our diversity activists to promote work on inner-city violence. We also brought the Brookline chief of police into our worship service to discuss institutional racism as it was being addressed by Brookline's community policing efforts.

I am very proud of how much this congregation transformed itself and grew in the spirit during the many years of my ministry. With adoption of our new mission statement in May, we focused our final months together on becoming a more mission-driven congregation, speaking openly about our losses, our sorrows, our joys, and our need for one another. In community, we found both comfort and transformation. Those with ears to hear it could truly hear heaven calling.

When I turned sixty that October, my Hindu friends told me that was the age to take more seriously the callings of the spirit. Awakening awaited. For my sixtieth birthday, the congregation gave me a big blow-out dance party at church. Everyone gathered with a signature cocktail called the Transcendentalist. We had a jolly time together dwelling in divine mystery, living in heaven on earth.

Of course, as a professional, I didn't share with the congregation the other reality that had influenced my decision to retire. As I prepared to leave First Parish in Brookline, some unexplained and long-deferred health issues were catching up with me. I had kept this fact largely to my family and myself.

The slow, progressive decline became more noticeable in the months prior to my retirement. I would sometimes feel as if I would doze off at stoplights or when stopped in traffic on Route 95. Sometimes during afternoon or evening pastoral counseling, I couldn't keep my eyes open, which led congregants to suspect I found them boring or didn't like them. This brought pain both to them and me.

I had no idea what was causing this deep fatigue, but it was deeply troubling. And increasingly, I couldn't get through a twelve-hour workday. I was unable to do my job to my standards, due to this sometimes overwhelming fatigue. Comparing each month's performance with the previous months', I could see a clear increase in my lethargy.

Growing up in poverty had left its mark on my physiology. That was compounded over the decades by a lack of sufficient exercise, extraordinary levels of stress, and obesity. Now I struggled with too much cholesterol, borderline high blood pressure, too many alcoholic drinks, and excessively loud snoring. My physical well-being was rapidly deteriorating.

In doing a thorough physical exam for my sixtieth birthday in October, my doctor diagnosed that metabolic syndrome, a fatty liver, and a previously undiagnosed sleep apnea were the root of many of my problems. He also discovered a troubling abnormality in my right kidney. Through an ultrasound kidney scan, the urologist found a large kidney stone and suggested we remove it immediately. But I wanted to finish strongly at the church first.

I wanted them to remember me as a transcendentalist. So I took small groups from the congregation on transcendentalist walks. We'd begin at First Parish in Concord, walking past Ralph Waldo Emerson's house, steeped in transcendentalism. We'd walk through the terraforming that transformed swampy woods to fields and pastures, down through the magical town forest known to the Alcott girls as Fairyland, up Brister's Hill into Walden Woods, and across Route 2 to Walden Pond.

Walking around Walden Pond, near the site of Henry David Thoreau's cabin, we'd eat lunch and look out over the azure water. I'd read aloud passages from *Walden* as we relaxed into transcendence. This setting in the woods, with nature, helps make transcendence possible for me. This was one of my many parting gifts to the congregation.

Final Sermon

I began the long process of preparing for my departure with joy and a new sense of self. For the winter solstice, when I would give my last Sunday sermon to this congregation, I preached about some of the lessons I had learned along my journey so far. My sermon was entitled "Living Joyfully!" Anna, a friend of mine, set the tone for our celebration with her song "The Days of Your Opening" and Van Morrison's "Into the Mystic." The cover of the order of service showed me wearing a backpack, blue jeans, and an outback hat, walking away into Walden Woods.

The congregation turned out that afternoon for a glorious farewell party. Many recounted joys and memories of our ministry together. Then I put on my traveling hat and walked into the mystic with spring in my step and joy in my heart. I wanted to leave them with a sense of what spiritual awakening looked like. Sometimes endings can be glorious.

My final sermon was one of my most audacious. I affirmed the five spiritual disciplines that bring more joy into anyone's spiritual life, which I now explore in this book.

> **Resilience:** The single most important spiritual practice in my life. Having lived with and through so many difficult circumstances in my life, I have needed to make resilience a core spiritual practice for myself. This is largely about transforming suffering.

One of my teachers compares transforming suffering through resilience to feeding a family from a spoiled dead fish. A dead fish stinks. You want to keep it as far away as possible from your supper. Yet if you compost it in the ground, with lots of water and sunshine, it can become a source of new life to make a meal for all.

Life grows forth from death. No matter how hard we fall or how difficult it may be to recover, even if we want to give up, resilience will always lead us to something good in the end. That dead fish can be transformed into food for the soul through the practice of resilience.

Surrender: It is in surrendering the separate ego-self to the greater good of the broader community that we grow. Each person chooses where and when he or she wishes to be involved in community. We are an intentional community. But a consumer approach to community seldom meets real spiritual needs.

You may not like teaching or greeting or singing in the choir or committee work. But when asked, your spiritual discipline could be: "Where does this community need me most?" The Sufis taught me the joyous power of surrendering our ego-self to discover the seven richer, deeper selves, which can be discovered through loving compassion, connection, and community. If we bring our gifts for greater good into the congregation, are drawn into service wherever we are most needed, and sacrifice our ego-self through our service, we will be transformed in the process.

This community can confront, defy, and heal consumerism, classism, racism, sexism, xenophobia, and other sicknesses of community if we confront them as a faith community. We are more powerful as a community than as individuals. We don't each get our own way, but we can do it together. This is the power of surrendering to community to discover how to do together what we cannot do alone.

Gratitude: This transforms us from spiritual consumers to people of faith. This sounds easy. We all know how to practice gratitude, but how often do we actually do it? We are grateful for our loved ones, our children, our friends, blessed things that happen to us. But what beyond these gifts?

How many of us can be like Rumi—grateful for the joys of life but also our depressions; grateful for random acts of kindness and also random acts of meanness; grateful for momentary awareness of the breaking dawn but also our accidental microaggressions? As Rumi would ask: Do we welcome and entertain them all? Do we recognize they may be preparing us for the people we were born to be?

The dark thought, the shame, the malice—can we meet them at the door laughing, grateful for whatever comes? For this is truly to know the practice of gratitude. Being grateful for whoever comes because each could have been sent as a guide from beyond.

Generosity: A generous spirit transforms the soul. Central to practicing generosity is the practice of tithing, to give back to those with a greater need than ours 10 percent of everything we receive. Loretta and I have been practicing generosity, often including tithing, in one form or another over our thirty-six years of married life. Giving generously makes what you keep sweeter.

Once you set your mind upon it, it is so easy to do. It changes your orientation to material things. Loretta and I have been richly blessed, partly because of our attitude toward money and material things but also because of our practice of tithing.

We accept what we do receive with gratitude, recover more quickly from any wounds and sorrows, look with joy to the common good, and practice generosity. We have a happier marriage, are more connected to community, and help bend the arc of the universe toward justice, all by giving away a mere 10 percent! This is a powerful spiritual discipline.

Why not be generous? The average American will have lifetime earnings greater than $1.4 million, so by tithing they can give away $140,000 to make the world better. The average family in this congregation will have a lifetime household income of over $4 million, so we can do three times as much. And some families will have lifetime household incomes three to four times *that* level.

However, generosity is measured not in the absolute amount we give but rather in its relative proportion and our attitude toward it. We read about people who never earn more than a middle-class income but who adjust their spending so upon their death they leave millions of dollars to what they care about. The spirit of generosity, with an open heart, matters more than the gift.

Mystery: To be aware of, and delight in, the presence of the divine. When Sufis share heart-to-heart, they are dwelling in the mystery. When Taoists taught me to climb mountains beyond my capability, we were living in the mystery. It is valuing the questions more than any certainty of answers.

It begins by being deeply intentional. By thinking, speaking, acting, and being full of loving kindness. You may sit in Buddhist meditation for an hour every morning, but if you then come and complain about all the things you *hate* or can't stand about something someone has done, you've *abandoned* living in the mystery. Living in the mystery is always transformative.

In many spiritual traditions, living in a near-continuous state of loving compassion, dwelling in the presence of the divine, is the single most powerful path to living joyfully. This is *the* practice for wise elders who can transcend obligations and judgments, meditating on loving compassion for all being. This is the stage of the spiritual journey I now aspire to live within. Young warriors often need to feel invincible and so may be unable to dwell in the humility of divine mystery. It is a spiritual discipline ideally suited for one's elder years.

In my life, I have often failed to live this practice while serving as an organizational leader, whether in a financial, entrepreneurial, or even a ministerial role. It may be my temperament. Or I was afraid to open my heart fully while under constant stress. I sacrificed divine mystery seeking certainty.

Now to experience this source of joy, I must first walk away from the joys and demands of community leadership in order to bring my soul to peace and to surrender to love for all sentient beings as a spiritual discipline.

Engaging Reality

I told the congregation there was a sixth discipline I had yet to fully explore: awakening. This was where my spiritual journey and life was leading me. My retirement from parish ministry could serve as a bridge into my own spiritual maturity.

When I arrived at First Parish in Brookline as senior minister in 2005, I had already strongly developed the spiritual disciplines of resilience, gratitude, and generosity. They served me well all my life. The decade spent at Brookline helped me learn how to spiritually surrender first one and then another aspect of my selfish ego-being. For that I was truly grateful. This was a lesson that could be learned only in community. We did together what we could not do alone.

Every ending holds a new beginning. These six spiritual disciplines all lead toward a more abundant and joyful life. One not focused upon individual gratification or consumption but on a common life and a common good grounded in a connection with and beyond ourselves. We become together what we could not become alone.

Now I felt called to a different relationship with divine mystery—answerable only to God, my spouse, and myself (not necessarily in that order) in order to better experience the joys of life. I was aspiring to be what my Zen teachers call an authentic person with no fixed position. Only then could I live more fully into divine mystery.

This sixth spiritual discipline requires awakening to ultimate reality. Turning sixty and entering retirement from parish ministry, I wished to spend as much of the coming decade as possible fully awake and awestruck. I wanted to openly befriend God. To live with an open heart and be unafraid of injury. To live in peace, in harmony, in joy, and in loving kindness.

In that final sermon, I had told the congregation, "I love you all dearly, not just because you deserve it, though you do, but also as an aspect of my own growing spiritual practice. Yet for me the road leads on!"

The parish committee graciously agreed for me to lead my final worship service with carols and candles on Christmas Eve 2015. After that, I planned to travel with a Harvard professor of comparative religion up the Ganges River in India on a pilgrimage to where the Buddha awoke to the fullness of his humanity. My next step was calling. I was seeking greater spiritual awakening.

But first I had to deal with my kidney stone. In a pre-Christmas operation under general anesthesia, the urologist inserted a kidney stent, but before she could blast away my kidney stone, my heart went into atrial fibrillation. My heart stopped. This was completely unexpected and rather disturbing. She quickly abandoned the operation.

Recovering from this failed operation, I knew my life was in jeopardy. Yet I desperately wanted to keep my plans to travel up the Ganges. I was scheduled to depart ten days later. So I discussed my options with the urologist. She arranged for me to visit an expert cardiologist to explore my options for treating the atrial fibrillation.

Fortunately, it turned out this cardiologist had also traveled in India—and it had been one of the high points of his life so far. With his cautious approval, I decided once again to live audaciously. I flew to India with a kidney stent to prevent my kidney stone from causing greater pain, a beta-blocker to help control my heart arrhythmia, and baby aspirin to prevent blood clots. We agreed to deal with these medical issues upon my return.

First and foremost, though, I felt a strong call to complete the pilgrimage my lifelong spiritual journey had been pointing me toward. I was heading into the mystic and perhaps awakening to the nature of reality as it truly is. By embracing the divine mystery, I could more fully discover the person I was born to be. I was willing to trust in the divine mystery my intuition assured me had prepared my way. Indeed, awakening awaited.

Perhaps I had been set upon this path into mystery over forty-five years before, when I experienced my second baptism into divine reality that morning at the Baptist youth retreat. Or when I chose the spiritual path of knowledge as Mr. Robinson introduced me to Nietzsche, Camus, and Kant. Or when Alan Watts, that mystic and rogue Zen Episcopal priest, became one of my earliest teachers. Or when exploring the writings of Christian mystics such as Meister Eckhart, Hildegard von Bingen, Teresa of Avila, John of the Cross, and Brother Lawrence taught me the Christian mystical path in my idyllic fifth year at Yale. This was my path.

Matthew Fox taught me Thomas Merton's way to God through creation spirituality. Thich Nhat Hanh taught me how to properly meditate. Huston Smith was perhaps my most important teacher, introducing me to the writings of the Confucians, Chinese Taoists, Islamic Sufis, and the whole concept of comparative religious paths into divine mystery. I found deep joy in mystery. Then through Joseph Campbell's writings on myth and magic, I discovered my way into Jungian archetypes and the collective unconscious, and eventually Budai.

I had many teachers along the path, yet the path was truly created only in my walking it. Parish ministry had provided an important incubator for my developing spiritual self. But now it was time to walk unafraid into the mystery, to stare into the cloud of unknowing, and to take the final leap.

There is an old UU joke about this experience. It seems a devout Unitarian Universalist died and found himself at heaven's gate. There was a sign that said: "To encounter God, go right. To discuss what it is like to encounter God, go left." The devout UU of course goes left.

At this stage of my life, I was too close to divine mystery and spiritual awakening to settle for mere conversation. I was prepared to encounter whatever called me forward with fear, trembling, and incredible awe. I would travel deep into mystery.

TEMPLATE FOR SMALL-GROUP MINISTRY

AUDACIOUS DIVINE MYSTERY

Chalice-Lighting Words

The first mystery is simply that there is a mystery. A mystery that can never be explained or understood. Only encountered from time to time. Nothing is obvious. Everything conceals something else. The Hebrew word for universe, Olam, *comes from the word for hidden. Something of the Holy One is hidden within.*

—"Honey From the Rock" by Lawrence Kushner

Check-in: What role does the presence of God or divine mystery play in your life?

Additional Reading from *The Dhammapada* (Eknath Easwaran translation)

Why is there laughter, why merriment, when the world is on fire? When you are living in darkness, why don't you look for light? This body is a painted image, subject to disease, decay and death, activated by thoughts that come and go. What joy can there be for him who sees that his white bones will be cast away like gourds in the autumn? Around the bones is built a house, plastered over with flesh and blood, in which dwell pride and pretense, old age and death. Even the chariot of a king loses its glitter in the course of time; so too the body loses its health and strength. But the goodness does not grow old with the passage of time. A man who does not learn from life grows old like an ox: his body grows, but not his wisdom.

Questions to Ponder

1. Why do people belong to congregations?

2. To what does life call you?

3. What vows, spoken or unspoken, have you undertaken?

4. Have you ever experienced a vision quest or spiritual pilgrimage?

5. What is the message of your life's journey?

Closing Words

Now I felt called to a different relationship with divine mystery—answerable only to God, myself, and my spouse (not necessarily in that order) in order to better experience the joys of life. I was aspiring to be what my Zen teachers call an authentic person with no fixed position.

AUDACIOUS DIVINE MYSTERY

Author's Comment

The mystical experience often takes us beyond objective reality. To aid fellow travelers on the journey, I have recounted these experiences as I remember them and as recorded in my spiritual journals. Based upon your own experiences, you can judge their validity for your reality.

Questions to Encourage Discussion

1. Have you ever experienced a dying or dead religious faith?
2. What does the author promise in his ordination vows?
3. How does his call to ministry fit with his kids going away to college?
4. Would you want to belong to a congregation such as First Parish in Brookline?
5. How attractive to you is the Sufi path into divine mystery?
6. Does the Taoist transcending mind path fit you better?
7. Have you experienced any universalizing trend among the world religions?
8. How does the author balance spiritual seeking with worldly power?
9. Would you be interested in joining a Pachamama Alliance trip with indigenous people?
10. Would you like to belong to a community of divine mystery?

Reflection

As a group, reflect upon the greatest risks you are willing to undertake in pursuit of your spiritual journey.

DISCIPLINE SIX:
AWAKENING

---

*Enlightenment: to experience the texture of life
fully. Sip of tea, hot, dazzles the tongue . . .
Rain streaking the glass on a gray-black morning. To wake from the daze.*

—"Two Poems from the Abbey"
by Miranda Arocha Smith

Enlightenment

Seeking direct experience, but mindful of my physical limitations, I found myself on a long flight to India on New Year's Eve. I was in search of enlightenment, knowledge, gnosis, wisdom, insight, oneness, ecstasy, and awakening—all terms used to point toward igniting that spark of the divine, which feels like salvation in one religious tradition or another.

Plato offered one of the most cited metaphors of this spiritual state of clarity in his allegory of the cave. He describes a group of people imprisoned in a cave since childhood, chained in such a way that a fire burns brightly behind them and casting shadows on the wall before them. Talking among themselves, they come to understand what is happening out of their range of sight simply by paying attention to the shadows on the wall. This is the only reality they have ever known.

Then one prisoner breaks free, and his reality is changed forever. As this former prisoner's eyes adjust to the sunlight beyond the cave, allowing him to see all the beauty of the real world, he is struck with awe and delight.

This is the experience of momentarily glimpsing enlightenment, to suddenly see directly what has only ever been surmised before. We live most of our lives in the shadows of reality. Many cannot see beyond the cave of our constructed reality. Others simply refuse to believe any other reality exists, even if we catch a glimpse in our peripheral vision. It is too scary to conceive of a bigger reality than what we have always known.

So, this former prisoner returns to his mates, explains what he has seen, and encourages them to join him on the journey. Few will. In fact, many people will disbelieve, perhaps even seek to kill or dismiss the person carrying this new message.

But a few will always be willing to see. The Buddha's Middle Path brought him inner clarity and enlightenment, so he declared himself awake. Then he taught his wisdom about the co-arising interdependence of all realities to all who would listen.

Sufis drink neither alcohol nor caffeine yet grow intoxicated with the sweetness of divine mystery and stumble forth to dance with the beloved. Their goal becomes mystical union with the divine. As the fourteenth-century Sufi poet Hafiz wrote (in a Daniel Ladinsky translation): "God and I have become like two giant fat people living in a tiny boat. We keep bumping into each other and laughing." Such can be a mystic's experience of awakening to union with the divine.

In Europe during the Middle Ages, Jewish mystics employed the wisdom of Kabbalah to achieve mystical union with God. Christian mystics frequently practiced the presence of God, giving us spiritual practices—such as perpetual praying, the dark night of the soul, and the incredible lightness of being—that can lead us into union with divine mystery. Sufis celebrate love's surprising joy. All three Abrahamic mystical traditions seem to point to this state of being, which is described as beyond understanding.

This is also the awakening sought by the Hindu sadhu and the Zen Buddhist monk. It is what Taoists describe as the perfect yin-yang balance in harmony with life's core vitality and spirit. Vitality has to do with our life force and spirit with our primordial essence. For many people, myself included, vitality was in ascendency during the first half of my life. It was only after midlife that spirit came into ascendency. Both vitality and spirit seek to remain harmoniously in balance, creating a sense of heaven, even as the balance shifts over a lifetime.

The Buddha taught that each person receives insight according to his or her nature. Some rely on philosophical reasoning. Others draw upon ancient sayings and traditions. And yet others rely upon their direct intuition of the divine mystery. All three function according to our nature.

I discovered for me to truly experience spiritual awakening, I must draw, according to my own nature, from reason, traditions, and direct experience. Until this stage of my life, I had not yet been ready. Given my particular life story, finally by the age of sixty, I felt I had lived enough to draw upon my reason, tradition, and experiences to discover the nature of deeper spiritual maturity. On my own pathless path, with many teachers, I traveled forth to awaken to divine bliss, to dance with the beloved.

But could I truly awaken without a sangha or spiritual community? Test my thoughts and experiences without an enlightened teacher? For decades, I had followed the path of the independent scholar and practitioner, never actually meeting most of my teachers in person. I possessed many good and valuable books with important insights and encountered mystics who taught me along the way. But I had never submitted myself to the discipline of a single master teacher. Would this be enough? Was I finally ready?

The Japanese Zen Buddhist monks had decades earlier shown me the way, set forth in their Rhinoceros Sutra, one of the oldest Buddhist texts, perhaps reflecting the Buddha's own teaching. In this sutra, early

Buddhism describes three different kinds of buddha, or awakened or enlightened beings.

The most famous, the *sammasambuddha*, usually called Gautama Buddha, achieved awakening so he could teach the path to all who followed him. A second kind, a *savakabuddha*, includes most Buddhists I have ever met. They train in one of the lineages of Gautama Buddha's followers, relying upon the Three Jewels: the teacher, the traditional teachings, and the spiritual community. A third kind, called a *paccekabuddha*, arrives at awakening through a spiritual journey of his or her own. To attempt to live into awakening on one's own requires a certain spiritual audacity, but the pathless path is there. I was following this path.

So I flew to India, arriving in Kolkata on New Year's Eve to begin 2016 by traveling up the Ganges River with a small group led by a Harvard comparative religion professor. We would journey in the footsteps of the Buddha. This would be the occasion of my enlightenment, my awakening, my coming into spiritual maturity, my bliss.

My Ganges Pilgrimage

We traveled through Bihar province, one of the poorest parts of India. This was where the Buddha taught. In the company of thousands of Buddhist monks from Tibet, Mongolia, China, Korea, Japan, Thailand, and Sri Lanka, we circumambulated the Mahabodhi Temple, the very spot where the Buddha reported becoming enlightened. We started at the highest and outermost level, and with each turning, arrived closer to our goal.

I brought my gift of blue lotus flowers to celebrate Gautama's enlightenment and gave ten rupees to every monk I encountered. At their invitation, I sat on a stone bench under the Bodhi Tree's outstretched branches and accepted blessings from dozens of Buddhist monks.

I merely dipped my toes into the vast ocean of experience in which the Buddha swam, but I dipped my toes nonetheless. The experience helped move me toward spiritual maturity. I found acceptance and affirmation from Buddhist monks and comfort and direction in the teachings. I transcended to spiritual awakening by my own feelings of peace. I was presented with Thich Nhat Hanh's *Old Path, White Clouds: Walking in the Footsteps of the Buddha,* a book I had never heard of. It is a step-by-step guide for the journey of awakening. I embraced ultimate reality with fear and trembling.

The American Buddhist nun Pema Chödrön says, "the journey of awakening takes discipline and courage." She describes her enlightened state as, "I'm in the process of becoming, in the process of evolving. I'm neither doomed nor completely free, but I'm creating my future with every word, every action, every thought. I find myself in a very dynamic situation with unimaginable potential. I have all the support I need to simply relax and be with the transitional, in-process quality of my life. I have all I need to engage in the process of awakening." I too had lived life well and was now free simply to dwell in mystery.

Spiritual awakening is both of this world and unworldly but always a dynamic situation with unimaginable potential. In *How Enlightenment Changes Your Brain,* neuroscientist Andrew Newberg says, "What is important is to realize that we can be on the path toward Enlightenment, with evidence that every step along the way improves the functioning of your brain." He found certain universal effects of enlightenment, regardless of religious belief, including feeling more open-minded; not dwelling on past mistakes; experiencing less anxiety in facing problems; and being generally happier, more peaceful, and more contented with our lives.

For those who follow shamanistic ways of knowing, Newberg's research suggests that potent hallucinogens such as ayahuasca, when properly administered in terms of dose, setting, and spirituality, "can also dramatically alter consciousness and trigger intense mystical experiences leading to positive changes in personality."

I had experienced spiritual awakening as a teenager and again on rare occasions on my vision quests. I had learned to increasingly invoke this way of being in my deep meditation practices. The Sufis had taught me how to achieve it through love's confusing joy and the Taoists through mental concentration. And the shamanic path enhanced my experiences through psychotropic medicines. All were spiritual paths into enlightenment that had prepared me for this final step.

When gathering data for his book on enlightenment, Newberg conducted a spiritual experience survey that included men and women, young and old, rich and poor, Roman Catholics, Protestants, Jews, Muslims, Hindus, Buddhists, agnostics, spiritualists, and many atheists. Based on their responses, Newberg concluded that the enlightenment experience is generally the same, regardless of prior religious beliefs. It often includes a sense of unity, interconnectedness to all beings, intensity of perception, a sense of clarity, surrender, or loss of self-control, and the feeling of being suddenly and permanently changed.

Religious beliefs and spiritual preparation do factor in how we make meaning of the experience, whether we refer to God or grace, nature, ultimate reality, or universal collective consciousness. But all these different symbol systems are trying to convey essentially the same human experience. Awakening to reality is an essential part of spiritual maturity for those with the audacity to pursue it.

Human Flourishing

Upon spiritually awakening, everything is changed, yet it all remains the same. Instead of everything obstructing human flourishing, now everything empowers such flourishing. This is a mystical teaching in most world religions.

We are transient beings with eternal life, extroverts who thrive on inner contemplation and discover pathless paths through walking in the footsteps of enlightened teachers. And it changes us. Our brains are transformed. Notions of heaven and hell are relinquished. Seeing beyond good and evil brings forth audacious vitality of spirit, conquering the illusions of self. This is the nature of human spiritual maturity.

Depending on where our life begins, it can be a long, hard journey to anything resembling human flourishing. Yet it is a journey well worth the effort. Even a modest level of enlightenment brings a sense of well-being, peace, and transcendence to those who experience it. The orthodox faithfully pass on such received wisdom from generation to generation, while the mystics seek to experience human flourishing directly.

Systematic approaches to human flourishing seem to have developed roughly 2,600 years ago. That was when Zarathustra, Pythagoras, Gautama, Confucius, and others like them in various parts of the world began to describe organized philosophical systems. Ancient Greeks taught that human flourishing, eudemonia, was the highest human good.

Of the four enlightened human beings mentioned, Zarathustra, also known as Zoroaster, seems to have placed the greatest reliance upon communal worship, living in divine mystery, to become one with God. Zoroaster's influence on Judaism, Christianity, and Islam is perhaps partly why these Abrahamic traditions place greater emphasis on community worship than do other religious traditions.

Religions came into existence to create the experience of such flourishing for their participants via systematic approaches bound together within mystery. But with each generation, wisdom dies and must be resurrected. So religious traditions facilitate the passing of these systematic approaches from generation to generation. Every religious tradition uses somewhat different terms and contexts, and each describes the spiritual path differently and also the ultimate goal. Yet each path is seeking human flourishing and each must be revived and renewed in every generation.

Zarathustra's near contemporary, Pythagoras of Samos, appeared far more interested in reason, music, and mathematics as a path into oneness with the divine. His students lifted up beauty as the highest good. While Pythagoras's and Zarathustra's approaches are often presented as in conflict, these are just two different paths, two means to human flourishing. Humanity's attempt to make sense of our lived experiences through reason and teachings.

During this same period, Master Kong, known in the West as Confucius, was leading the process to systematize the Chinese search for human flourishing. He based his path almost entirely upon relationships: ancestor worship, respect for elders, and duty to parents, spouses, and children. For Confucius, right behavior counts for far more than worshipping or reasoning about the divine mystery. Within his world view, what one thinks matters far less than how one behaves toward other people.

About the same time, Siddhartha Gautama was teaching a Middle Path between austerity and sensual indulgence for individuals to achieve spiritual awakening or enlightenment. His students experienced him as the ultimate buddha, a manifestation of enlightenment, possible to be relied upon directly.

These four nearly contemporaneous teachers set forth systematic understandings of reality that transformed the path to human well-being. The human spiritual journey was forever changed.

Because humans are transient beings, and demonstrably often do not reach spiritual maturity or flourishing in this lifetime, some religious teachers premise life's primary goal as achieving heaven or nirvana, some pure and perfect state, only in an afterlife. As a Baptist minister, my father encouraged his congregation with hopes of heaven while threatening them with fears of hell.

But mystics experience heaven in this lifetime through dwelling in divine mystery and attaining spiritual maturity. They teach that any sincere follower diligently pursuing a spiritual journey can experience awakening or enlightenment in the eternal now, and need have no fear of hell and retribution in the hereafter.

Not everyone—or even most people—needs to travel to achieve spiritual maturity or transformation. For me, however, a pilgrimage to India to walk in the footsteps of the Buddha seemed to facilitate my awakening. It helped me move beyond intellectual concepts into lived experience, to move deeper into living in the sublime mystery.

I chose to set aside my various philosophical and scientific discourses on awakening in order to experience it for myself. Like that old UU joke about going left or right, being too fond of discussing the nature of the divine gets in the way of the direct experience. This had been a challenge on my spiritual journey. As an overly educated extrovert who loves to talk and tell stories, I have a certain amount of experience with using readings and discussion as a substitute for lived experience.

Most of my Buddhist teachers were savakabuddhas and introverts, thanks to their endless hours of sitting meditation. Following in their various Buddhist lineages, most had also been taught by introverts, so they interpreted the path to and the fruits of awakening as introverts would. This focus on introversion made the meditative path more difficult for me.

So imagine my surprise to discover Gautama Buddha himself was an extrovert! How do I know? Read his life story. It had been right before my eyes all the time. This can be found most clearly in the Satipatthana Sutra, Buddha's primary discourse on the direct path to awakening. He makes sense of things through engagement with the world.

Upon rereading the Buddha's teachings in the summer of 2015, after several years' experience of traveling and living with extroverted mystics, suddenly these teachings resonated with my own mystical experiences. The extrovert's path to enlightenment led through openness and direct experiences of mystery.

Heaven and Hell

So what about heaven and hell after death? What role do they play in human flourishing? When my kids were little, my parents would sometimes come up to spend the weekend with us in Concord. On Sunday mornings, we would attend First Parish in Concord, and of course, my parents would come with us. One particularly beautiful Sunday morning, I remember standing on the church's front steps with my father following worship.

"How many people attended worship this morning?" Dad asked.

"About four hundred or so," I replied.

"And none of them believe in hell or eternal damnation?"

"We are universalists," I said, "so none believe in hell or damnation."

"So why don't they stay home on Sunday and read the *New York Times*?" he questioned.

"UUs come for spiritual community," I answered, "neither for fear of hell nor lusting after heaven."

The religious metaphors of heaven and hell are, I think, usually intended as aids to devotion. These concepts are borrowed from the mystics who describe heaven and hell as a human psychological state in the eternal now. These metaphors are often then used to encourage moral behavior and, perhaps appropriately, provide comfort during the grieving process. They can serve a very useful purpose in that regard. But they are metaphors for states of being.

If heaven and hell are to be sought after, and I think they are, it is in the here and now. To conceptualize heaven and hell as only to be expected in some hereafter does more harm than good. I believe in eternal life, but an eternity spent in a static heaven never held much appeal for me. And I am certain our loving God doesn't send anyone to hell in eternal damnation.

So why do so many people chase after these illusions? The Sunni Muslim promise of twenty-one virgins for religious martyrs seems to my ears preposterous. Even the Koran declares heaven is open to everyone, though it seems to allow for the possibility of time in a post-life correctional sphere for those who die feeling unworthy of heaven.

The Hindu notion of returning in another life as a plant or an animal seems no more than a misplaced metaphor. Even if there are more lives after death, or some form of reincarnation, this is the only life we know of from our own direct experience. So lay Buddhists working and praying to improve their lot only in their future lives seems to misrepresent the fundamental experience of the spiritual journey.

Time is an illusion. Spiritual transcendence, if achieved at all, is achieved in the eternal now. Spiritual mystics from every religious tradition affirm eternal life is accessible in the here and now, not only hereafter, not only after death. These teachings all point at a deeper mystery of human existence—how we live our lives matters very much as we seek deep, transcendent living in the eternal now rather than in some postulated hereafter.

As much as possible, one ought to always be respectful of long-established religious beliefs. But there is a limit to how far faith can exceed reason and experience. Beyond that limit, tradition becomes a dead corpse. Mystics seek the spark of the divine.

Religious traditions are subject to changing cultures, mistranslations, and corruptions over the decades, centuries, and millennia. Introverted spiritual teachers, such as perhaps Jesus of Nazareth, appear to be particularly at risk of misinterpretation over the generations. He spoke in parables and mysteries. Yet can anyone read the Gospels and not see Jesus as an introverted wisdom teacher?

To give just one more simple example of a metaphysical corruption: look at the distinction between the worldly and the spiritual. All great religious teachers appear to make a distinction between the worldly benefits for their believers and the spiritual benefits—with a clear preference for accumulating spiritual benefits.

In all their teachings, the spiritual state of being, which Jesus calls the kingdom of heaven or kingdom of God, is contemporaneous with a worldly state of being. Yet these teachings have often been corrupted to suggest worldly suffering and worldly benefits are limited to the here and now, while retributive spiritual suffering and spiritual benefits happen only in the hereafter. The underlying nature of reality is often lost.

Well-meaning religious teachers explain religious traditions in the form they came to understand them. Literal readings of ancient texts, without being tied to actual spiritual experience, can often fail us in our hour of need or lead us astray. This is why I left the Baptists.

Living faiths, however, rely upon traditions and ancient texts, but only when passed through the fire of reason and tested against our own spiritual experience. In contrast, a faith that teaches its followers to trust only in their own experience is also no guarantee of salvation. Mystics teach that all religious truths are important, yet transitory, and all paths must be rediscovered in every generation. We each must experience the spark of the divine in our lives for ourselves, interpreted with the guidance of religious tradition and texts.

My favorite metaphor for what we can know about life after death is captured by a Christian mystic tale about European water bugs. These are beings whose entire existence, from birth to death, is played out on a small pond. Three water bugs—let's call them Albert, Benny, and Charlie—are friends of roughly similar ages.

Charlie points out one day the gradual disappearance of older water bugs, one after another. Albert says that is the nature of things; all beings die and are gone. Benny wants to know where they go. So the three make a pact: whoever dies first and ceases being a water bug will return to tell the others what is on the other side of death.

One day, Charlie discovers he has sprouted wings. He feels this enormous urge to soar into the sky, breaking forever his connection with the water surface. He soars widely and wildly, giddy in his freedom, until he remembers his pact and returns to tell the others.

Unfortunately, in his post–water bug state, he can't come too close to the water surface without destroying his new wings. And Albert and Benny are still trapped on the water's surface. So all he can do is shout across the distance to them. At times, it seems they may even hear and recognize his presence, but never so much that he can explain his changes and wings. In the end, Charlie must enjoy the existence he has now, confident in the knowledge Albert and Benny will come to understand in due time.

In this sense, we may all be like water bugs. Or to use a more common analogy, the crawling caterpillar can never imagine the joys and perils of its future state as a butterfly. Thus, if a Buddhist focuses on some imagined nirvana only in a future life, or a Christian focuses overly much on heaven and hell following death, or a Muslim chases after paradise in the hereafter, these are all corruptions of the wisdom teachings about human flourishing.

Behaving well only for nirvana, heaven, or paradise in the hereafter misses important opportunities for experiencing higher states of spiritual being in the here and now. We must be transformed. Mystical teachers—including, of course, Jesus—speak of living in the present, today, not worrying about tomorrow, seeking enlightenment in lived experiences in the here and now.

The Buddha gave differing instructions, depending on the inclinations and temperaments of his listeners. We are told in the Satipatthana Sutra that prior to his awakening, the Buddha had already tried every means of achieving enlightenment without enduring success. Then he remembered the joy and pleasure he experienced as a child when deeply concentrating upon an unlikely or impossible goal.

Remembering this childhood experience, he awoke to the Four Noble Truths: 1) how our complex world of joy and suffering, and its unworldly or spiritual counterpart, arises; 2) how craving or desires of the ego-self are the cause; 3) how such conditioned existence can be released; and 4) what spiritual disciplines bring about such release.

Other Buddhist teachings had distracted me with their focus on worldly suffering. But as a mystic, the Buddha had focused upon unworldly feelings and had offered a Middle Path between worldly lust and bodily renunciation. This turns our focus toward accumulating spiritual merit in nirvana here and now. The purpose of the Four Noble Truths is to set us free in the perpetual now.

With great concentration, I traveled in the footsteps of the Buddha. My great joy upon learning deep concentration as a child made this path possible for me. The direct path he sets forth in *Satipatthana* helps us make peace with and fully inhabit our bodies. This is spiritual audacity.

If we enjoy a good meal or an intimate touch, these are to be appreciated as gifts of this world. This practice of remembering or being mindful of the good things in life is an important part of becoming fully aware. Buddha's nondelusional mindfulness leads us to cultivate a clear comprehension of what we are doing in every moment and why. Sometimes when walking in the woods or by the sea, or when sitting in mindfulness, meditation brings me to that state of ecstasy.

During the times of our life when we are students or householders, these mindful moments of ecstasy may be as close to awakening as we can come. At certain stages, we are more grounded in worldly matters than spiritual matters. We must be fully engaged with the world and the responsibilities, pleasures, difficulties, joys, and sorrows that come with it.

Spiritual maturity requires a shift in perspective. Tradition tells us that following his enlightenment, Siddhartha, the Buddha, spent forty-two days contemplating his transition from worldly to spiritual concerns. This foreshadows Jesus's forty days spent in the wilderness, being tempted by Satan with worldly pleasures and power. Afterwards, he was able to take up his career, focused as it was upon spiritual concerns, and he lived faithfully between two worlds. These traditions show it takes time to consolidate a change of perspective from worldly to spiritual concerns.

This is the purpose of deep meditation—to transform our feelings, our thoughts, and our hearts. Having made peace with our embodied state, the Buddha teaches us to make peace with our feelings. The Buddha distinguishes six types of feelings: pleasant worldly feelings and pleasant spiritual feelings, unpleasant worldly feelings and unpleasant spiritual feelings, and neutral worldly feelings and neutral spiritual feelings.

Beyond regulating our body and feelings, the Buddha taught us how to regulate our mind. From the Zen Buddhists, I learned this spiritual practice of achieving equanimity through deep meditation; from the Taoists, concentration through focusing my mind. I learned to become like Budai, the impish so-called Laughing Buddha archetype, to achieve enlightenment through my natural inclinations.

My mystical teachers built upon the inherent, intense focus and tenacity that I first experienced growing up—playing marbles, surviving Yale, and becoming a successful entrepreneur, investor, and parish minister. Like Mr. Miyagi having Daniel wax his car in *The Karate Kid*, my teachers helped prepare my own nature for enlightenment through the discipline of fifty years of seemingly unrelated activities.

My enhanced concentration allowed me to overcome inevitable obstacles in my path, including sensual desires, aversion, boredom, anxiety, and doubt. Through spiritual practices conducive to my own nature and temperament, I learned how to remain awakened. When these obstacles burn away, peace and vitality remain, leaving a greater sense of purpose for your life. Reality is seen finally for what it is. And it is a thing of beauty.

Beyond Good and Evil

For three hundred years, much of American Christian culture has been deeply Augustinian and Calvinist, often including an emphasis on guilt and shame. It need not have been so. This world view assumes people do what they do because they desire heaven when they die—or at least want to avoid hell at all costs.

But there is another view—that of an all-loving God who does not condemn us. So when God-loving Baptists such as Roger Williams and the growing numbers of no-hell universalists began teaching in Massachusetts in the seventeenth century, they were often banished to the outer darkness (Rhode Island), which still today retains some of that wonderful heritage of a loving God. Rev. John Murray, one of Massachusetts's first Universalist ministers, used to famously advise new ministers to "give the people hope, not hell."

When Massachusetts disestablished religion in 1833, you could now meet hell deniers on the streets of Boston. The Unitarians and Universalists saw explosive growth in the following decades. However, the orthodox clergy warned their congregations that speaking to such people could result in doubts about "original sin" leading to eternal damnation, and so advised them to cross the street and avoid engaging in theological debate.

Today, many American Christians who describe their faith as Bible based still fear hell, even though there is little in Jesus's teachings from which to develop a theology of damnation. These Christians are often guided more by the laws of Leviticus or the Ten Commandments. Theirs is a "thou shalt, thou shalt not" form of morality. It isn't oriented to Jesus's teachings about the kingdom of heaven or God's love. I find their faith much too narrow to encompass my experience of awakening and divine mystery.

Most Christian mystics, however, generally go beyond simple notions of good and evil. Mystics experience a world that is too big and too nuanced to fit within such law-based moral codes. Love is their law and service their liturgy. The whole notion of good and bad, right and wrong, can often be overly simplistic. It can lead to a rigid doctrinal faith without life-affirming power to save.

There is an old Taoist tale about a father and his teenage son. The son falls while riding his horse, breaking his leg. The neighbors all gather to say how dreadful this is because now he cannot work properly. The father responds, "Who's to say?" Then a war breaks out, and all the teenage sons are drafted to fight—except the one with a broken leg. The neighbors gather to say, "How wonderful." The father responds, "Who's to say?" And so the story goes on and on, with every "good" thing leading to further problems and every "bad" thing bringing forth something advantageous. Who's to say?

Many UUs quote the fourteenth-century Sufi mystic Rumi when articulating what it's like to experience the transcendent nature of reality: "Out beyond ideas of wrongdoing and rightdoing there is a field. I'll meet you there. When the soul lies down in that grass the world is too full to talk about." Mystics meditate and work to awaken and find that fullness of being.

This can seem like a threat to civic religion or any tradition where morality is employed to keep people in line. This may be why Christian-dominant cultures are so fearful of hell deniers in their midst. It's also why Sufis are persecuted or banned in many Sunni Islamic–dominated cultures. And why Chinese secular culture allows Taoist temples but not philosophical Taoist teachings to be taught within them.

Because gnosis is very individual and personal, direct experience of divine mystery has always threatened religion's role as an integral part of civic society. But personal experience is simply the nature of divine mystery. By awakening, we each can come to realize the person we were born to be.

When I was baptized as a Rhode Island American Baptist, the spiritual gifts promised me were faith, hope, love, and joy, and the greatest of these was love. Then I had a unitive experience of transcendence in the woods, and my whole sense of reality was transformed. Pursuing mystical spiritual paths gradually led to my embodying loving kindness, compassion, empathy, clarity, equanimity, mindfulness, and more joy.

In teaching me their Way, the Taoists were by far the most focused upon mindfulness, while the Sufis focused more upon heartfelt joy, and the Buddhists taught me loving compassion. Each followed their own path, but each had spiritual lessons for me.

Yet, like the Buddha, I have found my spirit of focused concentration and audacious vitality an incredible starting point—my greatest gift of all. Perhaps some of it was learned from my Baptist parents and cultivated throughout childhood. I am a unique human being with particular flaws and gifts. I brought my own nature and temperament to my spiritual search, reflecting both my inherent nature and my lessons from experience. The Buddha lifted up these gifts as helpful and necessary on any path to enlightenment.

Becoming completely absorbed, whether in worldly or spiritual matters, can bring a temporary state of rapture. The Buddha used the Pali term *piti* to describe this state of being. This word has been translated many times in many different ways including rapture, joy, delight, happiness, and even just as pleasure. But it has an intense quality of arousal and excitement. Modern positive psychology might call it being in the flow. This often leads to a peak transcendent experience, which can transform us.

The Buddha warned that worldly rapture or joy could distract us from the spiritual journey, whereas spiritual rapture or joy leads directly to awakening. Of course, the Buddha spoke of five kinds of awakening: minor awakening, momentary awakening, thrilling waves of awakening, spiritually uplifting awakening, and pervasive awakening.

Having myself experienced minor, momentary, and waves of thrilling awakening, I can only imagine the higher levels implied by uplifting and pervasive enlightenment. But they are unfortunately still beyond my personal experiences so far. There are yet more levels to this journey still to be perceived, and hence, more joy yet to be found. I continue on.

Illusions of Self

But who is this "I" who was asleep and who awakened from mundane reality? This is no easy question. We cocreate the reality we occupy, coauthor the play in which we perform, yet we have forgotten our role in the process. We cocreate and coauthor, even though there are ten thousand things beyond our control—but not *everything*.

Echoing back to my metaphor in the introduction, we are all riders on the bus. Yes, our experiences are different. No, we don't have complete control. But it is our life. With each act we perform, we play our part in the creation of our reality and enhance or detract from human flourishing.

So when we choose to identify with a particular role or sense of ourselves, we engage in a game of illusions—one we can play long and well. I have been son, student, spouse, father, consultant, businessman, entrepreneur, investor, and parish minister. Our sense of self becomes a mold that helps shape and define us. It also limits us in important ways, many of which benefit us, and some of which do not. Concepts such as gender, race, culture, age, aptitude, and abilities shape and form our experience of our lives.

This is not to say these descriptors don't point to real differences in our experiences of reality. Differences such as gender are real, and we do perceive them. But it is to say that through reimagining our sense of self, we can change our lives, edit the play. We can help define our place in this world and within this reality. Through spiritual disciplines, we help shape our own experience on the bus.

I first came to understand the illusion of self while meditating on what my Sufi teacher calls the seven selves. In orthodox Sufi theology, they are often described as stages or levels on the path to God. From lowest to highest, they are sometimes called the tyrannical self, regretful self, inspired self, serene self, pleased self, pleasing self, and the pure self. There are well-developed Sufi meditation practices to help us learn how to let go of each of these selves in their turn.

An inner teaching of Sufism is that all hierarchical thought systems create dualities, and dualities separate us from our divine inheritance. This means these seven selves should not be viewed as stages of accomplishment, but rather as aspects of being. And each aspect must be mastered through spiritual discipline—the seven heads of the hydra to be slain. No living being, no matter how disciplined, has fully transcended all seven selves. It is an illusion to claim to do so, but in attempting to conquer as many of them as we can, we bring ourselves more fully into unity with God.

Before we can pursue a spiritual path unimpeded, we must do spiritual work to transcend the tyrannical and regretful selves. The tyrannical, or selfish, self wants what it wants. It can ultimately do us great harm, and it is the self we must learn to surrender to the greater good.

Also called the moral self, the regretful self is a natural state of childhood, when we are habitually self-centered. But when childhood ends, we should put away childish things and thoughts. As part of overcoming this self, it can be a healthy step if we have the audacious resilience to seek and receive forgiveness from those we have injured.

Depending on our childhood, culture, and family's faith tradition, we each begin in a different place with different gifts and challenges for the journey. I call my journey spiritual audacity because it has grown forth most prominently from the third aspect of self, the inspired self—that is, from my genuine pleasure in prayer, meditation, and spiritual activities.

This is the source of my compassion, social justice work, and moral values. It made me restless to begin this long and difficult journey, and it still inspires passion for my path. This is what it means to me to be a spiritual mystic. For others, this self may be developed and mastered only later in life. We all start in different places, but the way leads us on.

One must achieve a degree of mastery of the tyrannical, regretful, and inspired selves in order to pursue spiritual maturity. The next three selves encountered on the spiritual journey are the serene self, pleased self, and pleasing self. These are way stations along the path to spiritual awakening, not the final destination of enlightenment itself. Yet many who set out on a spiritual journey find themselves resting too contentedly or stuck resignedly in these next stages. Again, we need some spiritual disciplines to push ourselves forward. There are mountains beyond mountains to transcend.

The discipline for transcending the serene self is generosity—of our money, time, love, and compassion. Those trapped in a scarcity mentality cannot achieve enlightenment. The spiritual discipline to transcend the pleased self is gratitude. Gratitude goes well beyond good and evil. It encompasses all experiences of life, even trials and difficulties, until we are able to welcome them all. The pleasing self is the penultimate pre-enlightenment spiritual state, recognizing that all power emerges from mystery. Only by serving the beloved community of God—life itself—can we dwell in divine mystery.

The first six selves must be self-actualized to prepare the way for our own awakening to the pure self, the self that transcends self. Upon enlightenment, one realizes the seven selves are all illusions. There is no duality, no separate selves. Whether tyrannical, regretful, inspired, serene, pleased, or pleasing, all is one with the divine. All are aspects of the reality we call ourselves. In reality we are "alone," that is to say "all one" with the universe.

This state of divine union is named differently in different religious traditions as pure being, heaven, nirvana, unity, oneness, awakening, liberation, emptiness, or transcendence. However named, it is the goal that makes the journey worthwhile, and it can be achieved by every spiritually mature human being lucky enough to live long enough, work diligently enough, and be disciplined enough to finish the journey. This journey beyond self brings us more fully into union with the divine.

Most people, though not all, find it easier to proceed within a religious tradition, with an ancient and sacred set of teachings, and within a community of faith to accept and encourage their spiritual growth. In particular, a faith community can help keep us from wandering too far from consensus reality.

Fortunately, Unitarian Universalism has been such a community for me. It has been my setting and my support for my own eclectic spiritual journey. I have roamed widely, spiritually speaking, but have always had a home where I could find, as UU congregations affirm, "the living tradition we share draws from many sources [including] direct experience of that transcending mystery and wonder, affirmed in all cultures, which moves us to a renewal of the spirit and an openness to the forces which create and uphold life."

Over the course of a lifetime, we build the story of our lives. Yours is no less than mine. We weave all that happens to us into that story. Momentary states of consciousness help bring clarity to the lived reality of our story. There is no need to completely deconstruct our sense of reality. In many ways, this sense of reality has served us well. But we need only to hold it lightly, to recognize it is an illusion.

We must recognize we have been imprisoned by our lived reality. It locks us in. Too often, we fail to realize we hold the key to the lock. We can set ourselves free. Letting go of the attachments that imprison us can be truly freeing—not in some hereafter, but in the here and now.

Much of what we regard as self is a source of anxiety, stress, and suffering in our lives. We must free ourselves from the self to transcend our natural narcissism. The exercises the Buddha taught lead to seeing directly into the true nature of our experiences. Those with eyes to see can look with clarity through to the reality beyond.

This teaching is not that different from Plato's metaphor of the cave. The community is focused upon the reality of the shadow figures passing on the wall. They are unwilling to accept the transformed sense of reality the escaped prisoner—the one who sees directly—offers them. So wake up and experience life directly; it is awesome, beautiful, and wonderful.

Dogmatic religious traditions can bind—and blind—us to an inappropriate sense of reality. But for the mystics in many of the world's greatest religious traditions, transcending this illusion is the core of the spiritual journey. Seeing the illusion of self, if only for a moment, can set us free. This is particularly emphasized in early Christian mysticism, as when the apostle Paul wrote that now we see through a glass darkly, then we will encounter reality face to face. We can transcend viewing reality through a glass darkly and learn to embrace ultimate reality face to face.

This is why Sufis say it is a kind of spiritual paradox to say God is One, Allah, and that we must surrender ourselves to God. Every mystic knows from direct experience that our independent self is an illusion. It doesn't exist. Ultimately, enlightenment brings us to the true reality that we are one with the divine mystery. Hence the paradox. The surrender demanded by Islam is the surrender of an illusion as we come to know what is real.

Despite ten thousand descriptive names, we cannot fully know the nature of God. Despite our deep attachment to our sense of self, this too is an illusion. So to achieve our heart's desire, we are instructed to surrender our illusion to the unknowable. Our ego-self will block our transformation unless surrendered. The mystic knows this is the path to joy!

Impermanence

Life is transient and fleeting. This is the challenge of living. As a sixty-year-old, I know this more viscerally than I could as a twenty- or thirty-year-old. Wisdom arises when we learn to pay attention to our impermanence.

We are born, grow up in particular circumstances, become students and scholars, hopefully find love and companionship, engage in the world of work, and take on the responsibilities of family and household. And then when our circumstances change, for better or worse, we are prepared to leave them behind, as we are called to live beyond that stage of life's journey.

As Mary Oliver concludes in her poem, "In Blackwater Woods," we must "love what is mortal . . . and, when the time comes to let it go, to let it go." Embracing life deeply, loving what is mortal with passion and perseverance, leads to spiritual maturity. To engage deeply and dearly with life while holding it lightly. Equally important is that we must eventually let it go, and the journey goes on.

During my pilgrimage to India, I was quite aware of my own impermanence—my heart had stopped ten days prior to my departure. But thankfully, my physical condition did not greatly limit me. I may have become easily fatigued, and I may have tended to piss blood, if you will excuse my indelicate but precise phrasing, but I was in a state of bliss. Upon my return from India, my urologist blasted my kidney stone and removed the kidney stent as well.

Overall, my health has significantly improved in the year following my retirement from First Parish in Brookline. Getting to the gym or walking around Walden Pond a couple times a week has improved both my fitness and my mood. I have begun to address my three decades' long metabolic syndrome to return to a state of human fitness and human flourishing.

In addition, I have rejoined the men's spirituality group I helped found twenty years ago at First Parish in Concord, and we go spiritually deeper. I am eating better than before, and Loretta's enjoying that I am even cooking for us more often. I have joined a new group of UU ministers who are mystics. I see my son, Robert, many weekdays and sometimes swap stories over dinner.

While my overall well-being has increased, my heart condition has been a bigger problem. My cardiologist had me do a sleep study to discover how my disturbed sleep might interact with my atrial fibrillation. I was diagnosed with sleep apnea, so an oxygen-breathing mask helps me sleep at night. I sleep better now than I have in years. My stress levels have significantly declined.

My cardiologist performed a cardioversion, which temporarily restored my heart's normal rhythm. We had to do it again three months later, and still it did not work for long. So I agreed to a more invasive cardiac ablation procedure to restore my heart's rhythm. For this, I needed to see a specialist surgeon at the Lahey Clinic in Burlington.

My surgeon decided that an auspicious day for the surgery would be September 22, the autumnal equinox. I prepared myself through exercise, meditation, and prayer. I put out a request for healing thoughts on Facebook. My men's group and the UU mystic ministers all agreed to pray for me that day.

It happened that the New England ingathering of UU ministers was held the day before in Bedford, the next town over from Concord. I attended the gathering, and when it came time to lift up joys and sorrows, I lifted up my procedure. I had almost another hundred UU ministers praying for me.

It also happened that the evening of September 22 was ANTS's Fall Convocation. I had been scheduled to bring greetings as board chair, but in my absence, they all lifted me up in prayer as well. This is what it means to connect with divine mystery, not to plead or ask for favors or special privileges. It is simply to practice the presence of God in community. Prayer can make an extraordinary difference for those who pray and for those of us who are prayed over. I believe in the power of prayer and good intentions to help us cocreate our experience on the bus, which is this life.

My surgeon said my operation was surprisingly quick and straightforward and that I should heal rapidly. Unfortunately, I was back to atrial fibrillation within two weeks. My heart still beats to its own rhythm. It has the audacity to define its own path, yet it serves me well nevertheless.

With the wisdom of impermanence, I feel this new stage of life is in many ways like my idyllic fifth year at Yale. It's a chance to embrace the world on my own terms while experiencing a spiritual deepening and knowing what it is to be awake. I cannot know what the future holds, but I can live deeply in the here and now, living a transcendental existence here with nature in Concord, Massachusetts.

Ralph Waldo Emerson provides a model for this way of being transcendentalist. With sufficient financial resources, he retired to his house in Concord, spending time with his wife, Lidian; their young son; and his own thoughts. He took long walks in Walden Woods and spent many evenings in deep discussion with friends far and near. He traveled the country giving lectures and writing books that explored his ideas. He made pilgrimages around the country and to Europe, exploring the ideas and practices of others.

Perhaps this is my calling for this next stage of my life: To discover my own thoughts and share them with others through the twenty-first-century social media we have today. To have the audacity to become a minor sage of Concord, appropriate to our context and postmodern age. And to enjoy this stage of my being.

Today, my most important practice in maintaining a spirit of awakening is a transcendental walking meditation around Walden Pond. I notice the weather, the sun on the water, the breeze in the trees, my step upon the path or the sand, and the joy that fills my heart. I breathe, attempting to maintain my balance between equanimity and insight. I am just present—neither thinking nor not thinking.

Never bored, my concentration remains strong and focused, yet not too attached to any objective on this journey. I become one with the trail, with the woods, and with my transcendentalist forebears. I do a little happy dance. It takes less than forty-five minutes to circumambulate the pond. In that time, I completely restore my inner state of wakefulness.

Enlightened Faith

The emerging pattern and essence of my spiritual journey is perhaps best captured by the old Zen tale called Ox Herding. A young boy hears tales of experiences in altered reality, which he comes to name the illusive ox. Having grown up in a culture where his true nature has been distorted and even forgotten, he audaciously goes in search of it. But greed for worldly goods and fear of loss rise up like flames around him. Ideas of right and wrong lead him astray. He begins to fear the ox is just a legend.

But he perseveres. Up and down mountain paths, across turbulent rivers, through trackless woods, he travels seeking the ox. On his journey, he begins to see signs of the ox. Ancient texts and traditions attempt to show him the way—each path distinctly different, yet each a manifestation of the divine mystery. He begins to see tracks of the ox, even though he is as yet unable to separate right from wrong, good from evil, truth from falsity. He travels on.

Emerging one day into daylight, he experiences his first glimpse of the ox, though he cannot see it clearly. Even with eyes focused to truly see, and ears attuned to truly hear, the best he can manage is a glimpse. But for this he is ecstatic. After many years and much practice, he encounters the ox cavorting in open fields.

For one magical moment, he tries to take control by lassoing it, but the ox slips away. The ox is awesome and wild. It cannot be tamed by another's will. Rather, the boy must develop and practice spiritual disciplines to tame his own nature, to surrender control. He learns to balance vitality with spirit.

But when he still tries to lasso the ox, he always fails. It must be free. With time and practice, however, the two become frequent companions. Living in divine mystery, the boy discovers his true nature. Thereby, the boy comes to encounter and befriend the ox. By transforming himself, he attains true equanimity and mastery. Untethered, the ox will follow him anywhere.

His struggles now over, the boy rides the ox home. Sitting astride the ox, he gazes serenely upon all that is. He is content. Only while riding the ox is he able to return to his spiritual home. The search was worthwhile.

Yet the boy still lives in delusion. The duality that led him to seek the ox continues to cloud his vision.

By enduring many spiritual adventures together, the ox and the boy eventually become one—but of course they have always been so. There is a love between them that passes beyond understanding. The illusion of selfhood falls away. The boy at last discovers he is both the seeker and the ox. Returning to the source of all being, together they transcend categorical thinking. There is no reality and no illusion. All is one. All exists and everything is an illusion.

The transformed human being journeys on. I still work on my resilience in order to approach my medical struggles with equanimity. I continue to practice surrendering my ego-self. I try to embrace whatever the universe holds for me with deep gratitude. From my abundance comes forth generosity to others, anchoring my journey in the good of humankind. Living in mystery, my life is full of love and joy. And awakening to reality, I will help others find their way.

This is human flourishing in the eternal now. My mental context has shifted. No longer following in the footsteps of earlier teachers, I go my own way. Spiritual intuition emerges like a third eye. Overflowing with feelings, I stroll through the marketplace seeking to help others.

With joy in my heart, I teach what I have finally come to realize is true. My life has a purpose. Smiling, laughing, I am content.

Looking back, my life has been so much more than that poor small-town boy could have ever imagined or hoped for. Relationships have been core to my experience of self: my father's intellectual ambition, my mother's unconditional love, my extroversion from being the middle child otherwise lost within a very big family, and my confidence from being very successful in a small-town setting. Relationships formed as an adolescent and young adult deeply shaped the world-class opportunities offered to me.

My core spiritual understanding and teaching became the power of spiritual audacity. Have courage. Do what is good. This was already clear when I first learned to play marbles. Audacity allowed me to rise above the circumstances of my birth. It helped me not only survive but also learn how to thrive. Audacity led me to pay for my college education by selling books door to door, eighty to ninety hours a week, all summer, every summer for five years.

Audacity won me Loretta's heart and lifelong companionship. Audacity led us to living in London, learning German and moving to Munich, and taking our thirteen-month-old daughter around the world. To be young and fully engaged in life requires audacity.

The energy and vitality of my life comes from applying these six spiritual disciplines audaciously. The Taoist Chuang Tzu, one of my many teachers, says audacity is what life requires and what life itself is. This is the spirit of life.

Loretta has been my salvation and constant companion. Our children have been companions and important teachers for me in living a balanced life. Bain, Genzyme, TSI, Seaflower, the Unitarian Universalist Association, and the congregations in Concord, Watertown, Needham, North Andover, and Brookline have been community ecosystems from which my true self could develop and emerge. We become ourselves in such relationships. Confucius was the first spiritual teacher to suggest that family, community, and religious community relationships are the appropriate context within which to discover our authentic selves. I am deeply grateful for all that is my life.

Global Spiritual Audacity

The Buddhist term most closely associated with what I have been describing as spiritual audacity is the Pali word *viriya*. This word is most often translated into English as energy, effort, boldness, strength, courage, perseverance, or persistence. But none of those English words, at least in their contemporary American usage, quite capture the essence of what I intend with spiritual audacity.

To embrace a transcendent experience in the woods and make it the centerpiece of a search for greater transcendence, even though it was contrary to a 1960s Baptist church's teachings, was spiritual audacity. So was seeking ever more spiritual experiences of awakening. To return to the Blessing Wood Spiritual Center five times on fasting vision quests, each time employing different mystical meditations learned from books and teachers. To travel with Sufis in remote parts of Turkey, participating in illegal rituals. To climb Needle Mountain not just once but five times.

This cultivation of audacity has been at the heart of my journey. And now comes a time to let it go and go beyond. For the path always leads on.

Much of religious practice over the last five hundred years in the age of reason was an attempt to remove religion from the dark ages, to transcend superstition, and to subject spiritual experiences to logic and reason. Ralph Waldo Emerson famously called the result "corpse-cold Unitarianism." Beginning in the nineteenth century with English translations of powerful ancient spiritual texts, it became possible to situate our individual transcendent spiritual experiences within humanity's rich spiritual traditions. It became possible through knowledge and experience to transcend the particulars of one's birth.

Our working life, home life, and spiritual life are not three separate and distinct things but three aspects of our well-being. Spiritual audacity—practicing the six disciplines of resilience, surrender, gratitude, generosity, mystery, and awakening—allows these three aspects of well-being to interpenetrate and become interdependent. This leads to far greater joy through human flourishing. As humanity's increasingly global civilization emerges in the twenty-first century, one can imagine the incredible power of the awakening that awaits humanity. I was born at the right time, and so were you, to participate in this spiritual awakening.

The very first church the Christian apostle Paul founded on European soil was in the Macedonian city of Philippi. In a long pastoral letter to the Philippians, Paul lays out the benefits of Christian faith as grace and peace from God, being grounded in God's peace through prayer, divine audacity, the experience of heavenly states now in this life, and the transformation of humility into glory.

This is a pre-Nicene, pre-Augustinian, pre-Calvinist mystical Christian faith. Paul expresses love for his congregation and rejoices in all things—the peace of God, which surpasses all understanding; contentment with whatever life brings; and courage through divine mystery. He exemplifies spiritual audacity. Despite whatever horrors have been perpetuated in Paul's name or in the name of any other Christian mystics, this Paul appears to me to be a spiritually mature being.

First Parish in Concord ends each Sunday service with a benediction based on Paul's religious teachings: "to go out into the world in peace, have courage, hold onto what is good, return to no person evil for evil, strengthen the fainthearted, support the weak, and honor all beings." This is applied global spiritual audacity. Unitarian Universalism is a faith for the twenty-first century.

The recent rise of a global spiritual perspective among mystical seekers, some of whom invited me warmly into experiencing their particular paths, has been a great blessing. Taoists have always proclaimed that their teachings are merely a tool along the way. Lao Tzu is a vehicle for the teachings rather than a founder of religion. The Tao that can be taught is not the real Tao. The real Tao can only be learned through experience. Mystics are not overly attached to objective reality.

Jewish mystics draw deep insights from the teachings attributed to Abraham, Jacob, Isaac, Joseph, and Moses—even while admitting that recent archeological and theological scholarship suggests these wisdom teachers were not necessarily historical figures. Christian mystics decry claims of salvation coming only through the Christian church in order to engage with these other rich spiritual traditions. Islamic mystics, Sufis, often claim that all mystical traditions draw from a common underground stream of wisdom that restores the world in every generation.

Increasingly, Hindu and Buddhist mystical teachers proclaim *sarva dharma sambhava,* which means all truths or religious paths that lead to salvation are equally valid. I believe so. This is a great time to open one's heart to becoming an eclectic spiritual mystic and seeker. In most mystical traditions, spiritual maturity is accompanied by equanimity, compassion, loving kindness, and joy. These by themselves make the journey worthwhile.

My favorite story of awakening to equanimity is the Jewish mystics' story of King Solomon's ring. It is told sometimes like this: Solomon was a wise and powerful king, yet his people were discontented, wars broke out, and his equanimity was perpetually disrupted. When bad things happened, they betrayed his hopes and dreams. When good things happened, he feared they wouldn't last.

He called on his wisest counselor and asked him to cure his sense of unease. Having no answer, the king's counselor went forth to find one. He was looking for anyone renowned for compassion, loving kindness, joy, and equanimity.

One day, they heard of a poor silversmith who was just such a man. Approaching the silversmith, the counselor told of the king's despair. The silversmith thought for a moment, then inscribed a silver ring with a few words. He said, "Take this—it will cure the king."

When Solomon received the ring and read its inscription, his heart indeed broke open with joy and compassion. The inscription read simply: THIS TOO SHALL PASS.

Equanimity is a sign of spiritual awakening and traditionally is one of the seven signs of awakening in Buddhism, along with mindfulness, moving beyond the teachings, drawing energy directly from the universe, joy, tranquility, and concentration. They are the fruits of spiritual maturity. I have encountered these same signs of spiritual awakening in American parish priests, both Catholic and Protestant, as well as in Ecuadorian indigenous shamans. Awakening seems to happen independent of religious tradition but is always accompanied by these seven factors.

My path has been a difficult and circuitous journey, but many of my teachers along the way have shared many of these signs of awakening. At times, I felt as though I were walking the labyrinth described in the introduction—coming within sight of the goal, only to be carried away into the outer reaches before ascending to the next level, on some kind of Möbius strip. However, when the student was ready, the appropriate teacher appeared. I am seeking now to live my life with an open heart, prepared for what may come, ready to count it all as a blessing. For when the illusions fall away, all of life is a blessing.

The Road Leads On

My many years on the board of trustees at ANTS and the last three as chair of the board seem to be bearing fruit. Despite our best efforts over a decade, we could not find a way to adequately prepare congregational ministers (United Church of Christ, Unitarian Universalist, American Baptist, and others) for their twenty-first-century ministries without their incurring so much debt that they would struggle to survive in a parish setting. However, by staying tightly focused upon our mission of preparing ministers for congregational ministry settings, we were able to consider radically different ways to achieve our mission in light of what God is doing in the world today.

We have recently announced an historic affiliation with Yale Divinity School, in which we will embed our school on their campus in New Haven. This will dramatically lower our share of operating costs and free our endowment to provide substantial scholarships for those preparing for congregational parish ministry. We have agreed to sell our beautiful campus to a worthy buyer and to relocate in order to better continue our role in preparing inspiring religious leaders for the twenty-first century.

This should be a fitting end to my last ongoing obligation as a chairman of the board. My work done, I will now step down from this role. To everything there is a season, and a time for every purpose under heaven. In less formal ways, though, I am adapting to my growing role as an elder. I am increasingly invited to help First Parish in Concord and other UU congregations in their own journeys of transformation. I am becoming an authentic person of no fixed position. I am at last free.

Like the Hindu sadhus, I now look forward to traveling about on my own. I am beginning new pilgrimages, new opportunities for re-awakening to how amazing life is, as I continue to travel with different kinds of mystics. In 2016, the Sovereign Military Order of the Temple of Jerusalem, the modern Knights Templar, offered for me to join their pilgrimage to Palestine. Walking the rocky shore of the Sea of Galilee at Capernaum, praying alone in the Garden of Gethsemane, and being baptized by the Holy Spirit in the Jordan River, thrilled my mystic Christian soul.

Then to explore some different varieties of Buddhism, I joined a trip up the Mekong River from Ho Chi Minh City (Saigon) in Vietnam into Cambodia, ending in Siem Reap at the Buddhist Angkor Wat temple complex. Along the way, and particularly while meditating under the manifold images of a Laughing Buddha in the Bayon temple, I recognized once again my archetypal spiritual teacher. There I more fully awakened to the nature of the Budai archetype in my spiritual journey—

that laughing, impish, roguish, inappropriate, and amazing teacher. He too seems to be an Enneagram Seven, the ideal archetype for my particular spiritual journey.

Now I am planning further spiritual adventures, including with Christian mystics following a monastic tradition and with those revitalizing inner-city congregations. I will potentially make a pilgrimage in Spain on El Camino de Santiago, traveling in the footsteps of the apostle James. I am excited to spend more of my life living in divine mystery.

The journey continues, but increasingly, I find I can journey nearly as deeply reading in my home library, sitting at my home computer, or just walking around Walden Pond. But these new journeys will be for a later book. The path always leads on. There continue to be many ways to be spiritually audacious these days, even as I move beyond initial awakening and seek the higher states of being the mystics describe.

What's Your Story?

Here in this book, I have grounded my spiritual journey in the stories of my life. It is all a journey of becoming, of discovering who I was born to be. This is my story. I would love to hear yours as humanity prepares for our next stage of consciousness. It is never too late. However there is an increasing urgency, many more such spiritual transformations increasingly feel necessary for humanity's and even our planet's survival in this anthropocentric age.

May you find your own way to spiritual audacity! May it help bring you to spiritual maturity! And in any case, may it always bring you joy in the midst of suffering, generosity in the midst of tribulations, gratitude even when in pain, peace in the midst of turbulence, and a sense of resting on the chest or breast of God. For you are a child of God. This is what you were born to be.

Yet a final word of "warning" about the nature of spiritual audacity and the effect it can have in your life. I give public lectures on spiritual audacity, and afterwards, someone usually comes up to me and says, "That was very interesting!" I reply that I am pleased for them but that being interesting was not my intention. I do always try to be kind because my teachers say that is the truest sign you are dwelling in the divine mystery. The next person, overhearing perhaps, often says, "I found your talk very enlightening, encouraging me to live more boldly." I congratulate them and wish them well on their journey.

Then finally someone approaches me looking befuddled and perplexed, saying, "You make me feel like I may have been wasting much of my life pursuing something other than what I was born to be." That's when I am elated! That is my impish, trickster, Budai nature. I want to encourage you to discover the nature of your own spiritual story, to learn what makes your heart sing, and to become the being you were born to be. Blessed be.

AUDACIOUS AWAKENING

Chalice-Lighting Words

Enlightenment: to experience the texture of life fully. Sip of tea, hot, dazzles the tongue . . . Rain streaking the glass on a gray-black morning. To wake from the daze.

—"Two Poems from the Abbey" by Miranda Arocha Smith

Check in: What experiences of awakening have you felt in your own life?

Additional Reading

To see a World in a Grain of Sand,
And a Heaven in a Wild Flower
Hold Infinity in the palm of your hand
And Eternity in an hour . . .
Man was made for Joy and Woe
And when we rightly know
Thro the World we safely go
Joy and Woe are woven fine
A Clothing for the soul divine
Under every grief and pine
Runs a joy with silken twine . . .
God Appears, and God is Light
To those poor Souls who dwell in Night
But does a Human Form Display
To those who Dwell in Realms of day

—From "Auguries of Innocence" by William Blake

Questions to Ponder

1. Do you find your connection with divine mystery through worship?

2. Do reason, music, and mathematics better bring you into harmony with the divine?

3. Or is your sense of self grounded in human relationships and community?

4. Or perhaps do you follow the Middle Path between austerity and indulgence?

5. How do you relate to people who feel called to very different religious paths?

Closing Words

Blessings on your audacious spiritual journey, wherever it leads you.

AUDACIOUS AWAKENING

Author's Comment

This final chapter deals with major spiritual realities I have learned over the first sixty years of my life. I wrote with the hope that if you are older than sixty, you may have your own long list of life lessons, and you may find it useful to contrast and compare my life with your own. I also had the hope that if you're considerably younger than sixty, particularly if you're a youth or young adult, that my stories would fill you with the spiritual possibilities of mature adult life, beckoning you to lead a richer, fuller life than may seem possible in your current circumstances.

Questions to Encourage Conversation

1. Which of the ancient paths to human flourishing call most to you?

2. Do you lean more toward being a spiritual introvert or extrovert?

3. Looking back over your life, do you discern clear spiritual stages in your journey?

4. Have you ever experienced, even momentarily, what the author calls awakening?

5. How does the author's six spiritual disciplines factor into your spiritual journey?

6. Are you willing to be like Rumi, welcoming whatever comes as if a gift from beyond?

7. Have you experienced Buddha's fruits of enlightenment: mindfulness and understanding?

8. What role do the concepts of heaven and hell play in your spiritual life?

9. Does the metaphor of herding the ox perhaps speak better to your spiritual experience?

10. How does the Sufi teaching of the seven selves speak to your journey?

11. Can you, like Mary Oliver, hold onto what is mortal, and then when the time comes, let it go?

12. Will you pursue your spiritual calling with boldness, courage, and audacity?

Reflection

As a group, reflect upon how you experience spiritual audacity in your own life.

POTENTIAL FURTHER READING

Spiritual Audacity

Brach, Tara. *Radical Acceptance: Embracing Your Life with the Heart of a Buddha.* New York: Bantam, 2003.
Dalai Lama. *How to See Yourself as You Really Are.* New York: Simon & Schuster, 2006.
Moore, Thomas. *The Soul's Religion.* New York: Perennial, 2003.

Resilience

Duckworth, Angela. *Grit: The Power of Passion and Perseverance.* New York: Scribner, 2016.
Reivich, Karen and Andrew Shatte. *The Resilience Factor.* New York: Broadway, 2002.

Surrender

Chu, Chin-Ning. *Do Less, Achieve More: Discover the Hidden Power of Giving In.* New York: HarperCollins, 1998.
Singer, Michael. *The Surrender Experiment.* New York: Harmony, 2015.

Gratitude

Emmons, Robert. *Thanks!: How Practicing Gratitude Makes You Happier.* New York: Houghton Mifflin, 2007.
Kaplan, Janice. *The Gratitude Diaries.* New York: Penguin Random House, 2015.

Generosity

Bonner, Barbara. *Inspiring Generosity.* Somerville, MA: Wisdom Publications, 2014.

Ewert, Mark. *The Generosity Path: Finding the Richness in Giving.* Boston: Skinner, 2014.

Smith, Christian and Hilary Davidson. *The Paradox of Generosity.* New York: Oxford University, 2014.

Mystery

Martella-Whitsett, Linda. *Divine Audacity.* Charlottesville, VA: Hampton Roads, 2015.

Smith, Huston. *Tales of Wonder: Adventures Chasing the Divine.* New York: Harper One, 2009.

Whyte, David. *Crossing the Unknown Sea.* New York: Penguin Putnam, 2001.

Awakening

Chödrön, Pema. *Living Beautifully: With Uncertainty and Change.* Boston: Shambhala, 2013.

Fox, Matthew. *A Way to God: Thomas Merton's Creation Spirituality Journey.* Novato, CA: New World, 2016.

Newberg, Andrew. *How Enlightenment Changes Your Brain.* New York: Avery, 2016.

Christian Mystics

Brother Lawrence. *The Practice of the Presence of God.* New Kingston, PA: Whitaker House, 1982.

French, R. M., translator. *The Way of the Pilgrim.* New York: Quality Paperback, 1998.

Saint John of the Cross and Allison E. Peers. *Dark Night of the Soul.* Radford, VA: Image Books, 1959.

Jewish Mystics

Heschel, Abraham Joshua. *Moral Grandeur and Spiritual Audacity.* New York: Farrar, Straus and Giroux, 1996.

Kushner, Lawrence. *Honey from the Rock.* Woodstock, VT: Jewish Lights, 2000.

Shulman, Jason. *Kabbalistic Healing: A Path to an Awakened Soul.* Rochester, VT: Inner Traditions, 2004.

Sufi Mystics

Ladinsky, Daniel, translator. *The Gift: Poems by Hafiz, the Great Sufi Master.* New York: Penguin, 1999.

Nicholson, Reynold. *The Mathnawi of Jalaluddin Rumi.* Kindle edition. Amazon Digital Services, 2015.

Yagmur, Sinan. *Tears of Love: Shams-i Tabrizi.* Konya, Turkey: Karatay Akademi, 2011.

Hindu Mystics

Eck, Diana. *Encountering God, A Spiritual Journey from Bozeman to Banaras.* Boston: Beacon, 2003.

Harvey, Andrew. *Teachings of the Hindu Mystics.* Boston: Shambhala, 2001.

Maharshi, Ramana, et al. *The Seven Steps to Awakening.* Freedom Religion, 2010.

Buddhist Mystics

Analayo. *Satipatthana, The Direct Path to Realization.* Cambridge, UK: Windhorse, 2003.

Hanh, Thich Nhat. *Old Path, White Clouds.* New Delhi, India: Full Circle, 2015.

Young, Shinzen. *The Science of Enlightenment.* Boulder: Sounds True, 2016.

Taoist Mystics

Cleary, Thomas. *Vitality, Energy, Spirit: A Taoist Sourcebook.* Boston: Shambhala, 1991.

Lin, Derek. *The Tao of Joy Every Day.* New York: Penguin, 2011.

Ming-Dao, Deng. *The Wandering Taoist.* New York: Harper & Row, 1983.

Shamanic Mystics

Descola, Philippe. *The Spears of Twilight: Life and Death in the Amazon Jungle.* New York: New Press, 1996.

Eliade, Mircea. *Shamanism: Archaic Techniques of Ecstasy.* New York: Pantheon, 1964.

Lawlor, Robert. *Voices of the First Day.* Rochester, VT: Inner Traditions, 1991.

Unitarian Universalist Mystics

Andrew, Elizabeth. *Swinging on the Garden Gate: A Spiritual Memoir.* Boston: Skinner, 2000.

Trapp, Jacob. *The Light of a Thousand Suns: Mystery, Awe and Renewal in Religion.* London: Rider, 1973.

Wikstrom, Erik Walker. *Teacher, Guide, Companion: Rediscovering Jesus in a Secular World.* Boston: Skinner, 2004.

ACKNOWLEDGMENTS

I want to thank my many mystics, mentors, and teachers along this pathless path. Of particular helpfulness as I turned toward becoming an author were already published authors John Buehrens, Martin Copenhaver, Diana Eck, Scotty McLennan, and Rebecca Parker. Anna Huckabee Tull and Jim Tull brought me early encouragement that this was a story worth telling. I wrote the first draft of this book for Sheila Heen's and Doug Stone's Business Book Bootcamp, and they helped guide me toward courses on writing creative nonfiction, spiritual memoir, and the Iowa Writers' Workshop to hone my craft.

I had reached draft seven of what was a much too long and unfocused manuscript before Amy Quale of Wise Ink Creative Publishing brought me under her mentorship and into an understanding of the entire publishing process. I am enormously grateful to my bold and insightful editor, Angela Wiechmann, who worked so patiently to help me find how best to tell my story in my own voice. Creating this book is a path I could not have walked so far entirely on my own. But just like my experience on the spiritual path, when I was ready, the person I needed seemed to appear. So I walk in creative serendipity.

I am grateful to my family—especially my wife, Loretta, and our two audacious children—for their love and support as I have traveled an unusual and sometimes scary path to my spiritual awakening. And I am eternally grateful to my many friends and my nine siblings, who have been such a part of this story. I will be forever grateful to my parents, Ed and Rae, who set me on a righteous path. I have been richly blessed. All participated in my becoming, but any false recollections or mistakes in my telling are mine alone.

ABOUT THE AUTHOR

Reverend Doctor Jim Sherblom is an author, mystic, theologian, entrepreneur, investor, company creator, venture capitalist, spiritual seeker, and laughing buddha. Jim holds a BA from Yale, an MBA from Harvard, and Master of Divinity and Doctor of Ministry degrees from Andover Newton Theological School.

Jim grew up in the middle of a very large, very poor family in Tiverton, Rhode Island. His acceptance to Yale brought this small-town boy into a maelstrom. Meeting and marrying his wife, Loretta, brought him transformed into the wider world. After graduating with highest honors from Harvard Business School, he began his career as a strategy consultant with Bain & Company, working in Boston, London, and Munich.

Jim was a founder of the Massachusetts Biotechnology Council and served as its president. His industry roles include serving as senior vice president and CFO of Genzyme Corporation and as chairman and CEO of TSI Corporation. As founding managing partner of Seaflower Ventures, he has been involved in the creation of six biotechnology and health care companies and was an early investor in at least twelve more.

At midlife, he was called into divine mystery. Through a series of vision quests and theological studies, he emerged as a spiritual teacher, preacher, and friend of God. He was called to parish ministry, serving as a senior minister at First Parish in Brookline, Massachusetts, for eleven years.

Since retiring from parish ministry in late 2015, Jim devotes full time to his writing. He mostly writes about spiritual matters, especially his travels with mystics, pilgrims, and spiritual seekers. He lives a transcendental existence in Concord, Massachusetts, with Loretta. His favorite and most frequent deep spiritual practice consists of walking meditation in Walden Woods or around Walden Pond. Jim and Loretta are the proud parents of two grown children.